REAL AND IMAGINED WORLDS

REAL AND IMAGINED WORLDS

Claude McKay's Poetry and Prose

CHARLES SCRUGGS

University Press of Mississippi / Jackson

The University Press of Mississippi is the scholarly publishing agency of the Mississippi Institutions of Higher Learning: Alcorn State University, Delta State University, Jackson State University, Mississippi State University, Mississippi University for Women, Mississippi Valley State University, University of Mississippi, and University of Southern Mississippi.

www.upress.state.ms.us

The University Press of Mississippi is a member of the Association of University Presses.

Any discriminatory or derogatory language or hate speech regarding race, ethnicity, religion, sex, gender, class, national origin, age, or disability that has been retained or appears in elided form is in no way an endorsement of the use of such language outside a scholarly context.

Copyright © 2025 by University Press of Mississippi
All rights reserved
Manufactured in the United States of America
∞

Publisher: University Press of Mississippi, Jackson, USA
Authorised GPSR Safety Representative: Easy Access System Europe - Mustamäe tee 50, 10621 Tallinn, Estonia, *gpsr.requests@easproject.com*

Library of Congress Cataloging-in-Publication Data

Names: Scruggs, Charles author
Title: Real and imagined worlds : Claude McKay's poetry and prose / Charles Scruggs.
Description: Jackson : University Press of Mississippi, 2025. | Includes bibliographical references and index.
Identifiers: LCCN 2025041539 (print) | LCCN 2025041540 (ebook) | ISBN 9781496860385 hardback | ISBN 9781496860392 trade paperback | ISBN 9781496860408 epub | ISBN 9781496860415 epub | ISBN 9781496860422 pdf | ISBN 9781496860439 pdf
Subjects: LCSH: McKay, Claude, 1890–1948—Criticism and interpretation | LCGFT: Literary criticism
Classification: LCC PS3525.A24785 Z876 2025 (print) | LCC PS3525.A24785 (ebook)
LC record available at https://lccn.loc.gov/2025041539
LC ebook record available at https://lccn.loc.gov/2025041540

British Library Cataloging-in-Publication Data available

For Teresa and Elizabeth

CONTENTS

INTRODUCTION: Artistry and Reality in Claude McKay 3

CHAPTER 1: The Search for a Spiritual Center:
The Image of the City in McKay's Poetry 19

CHAPTER 2: The Scene of the Crime:
Hogarth, Hemingway, and *Home to Harlem* 45

CHAPTER 3: James Joyce, Charlie Chaplin, and *He Who Gets Slapped*:
Claude McKay's Portrait of the Artist in *Banjo* 69

CHAPTER 4: The Cinema as Romance in *Romance in Marseille* 88

CHAPTER 5: "That Strange Place":
Claude McKay's *Gingertown* as a Modernist Short Story Cycle 107

CHAPTER 6: Home in the Hidden Spaces:
W. E. B. Du Bois's *Dark Princess* and Claude McKay's *Banana Bottom* . . 127

CHAPTER 7: Gangsters in Context:
Harlem Glory and *Amiable with Big Teeth* 149

AFTERWORD/AFTERMATH: Claude McKay and Richard Wright 169

WORKS CITED 187

INDEX 195

REAL AND IMAGINED WORLDS

INTRODUCTION

ARTISTRY AND REALITY IN CLAUDE MCKAY

To me she seemed a proudly-swaying palm
Grown lovelier for passing through a storm.
—CLAUDE MCKAY, "THE HARLEM DANCER" (1922)

I: A LITERARY LANDSCAPE

In what is arguably McKay's best novel, *Banana Bottom* (1933), the British expat Squire Gensir, based on McKay's boyhood mentor Walter Jekyll, tells the protagonist that originality in art hardly "matters," that "everybody borrows or steals and recreates in art. Next to enjoying it, the exciting thing is tracking down sources and resemblances and influences" (*Banana Bottom* 124). Gensir's remarks point to McKay's own passion for the artistry of the past. One major theme in my book is to follow that passion—not simply to track down the various literary and visual "sources and resemblances and influences" upon McKay but to show how he incorporated them in his writing, how they helped shaped it, and how he reworked them to create his own distinctive literary art. Moreover, Gensir's focus on multiple sources has relevance to McKay's delight in experimenting with multiple genres: poems, essays, novels, short stories, and even a novel in the form of a screenplay. In addition, his artistic references ranged from high- to lowbrow, including allusions to Marcel Proust and to mass culture.

This theme is also related to this book's second thesis: McKay shared with George Orwell, whom he foreshadowed, a penchant for satire and a desire to express his political views within an artistic construct (Cooper 346). What Orwell said of his own impulse to write might have been said by McKay: "I write because there is some lie I want to expose, some fact to which I want to draw attention, and my initial concern is to get a hearing. But I could not do the work of writing a book, or even a long magazine article, if it were not also an aesthetic experience" (*Collected Essays* 1: 6). He said that "in a peaceful age" he would have been a contented vicar watching "his walnuts grow" in his garden, but in a troubled political age like his own, his "starting point" was always "a sense of injustice." Although he would not have written *Homage to Catalonia* if he "had not been angry," that book was also written "with a certain sense of detachment and regard for form" (Orwell, *Collected Essays* 1: 6).

Like Orwell, McKay wanted to write (and would write) pastoral poems, but he too was driven by "a fierce hatred of injustice" that would name Winston James's first monograph on the author (James, *A Fierce Hatred of Injustice*), coupled with an aesthetic desire to turn his anger into works of art. My approach then complements that taken in Winston James's recent biography, *Claude McKay: The Making of a Black Bolshevik* (2022). James explicitly states that his intention is to deal only with McKay's political evolution: "a critical deciphering, retracing, and reconstruction of the political journey traveled by McKay" (8). I argue that McKay's politics cannot be separated from his artistry because, as Orwell saw, art brings everything into focus. Orwell's beast fable in *Animal Farm*, inspired by Jonathan Swift (e.g., Book 4, *Gulliver's Travels*), sharpens his satire on Stalin; Napoleon walking on two legs, imitating his former oppressor, is a far more effective exposure of political corruption than an angry rant—Stalin is only a pig in drag. Similarly, McKay would use Jonathan Swift's beast fable in *Banana Bottom* to deflate the warped pretensions of a political ideology.

James makes a strong point when he says that he cannot "conceive of a *non* political biography," (James, *A Fierce Hatred of Injustice* 8), but I would equally claim that you cannot write a nonartistic biography about McKay, for he always saw himself as an artist first: "My motive for writing is simply … to be an artist in words" (*Letters in Exile* 262). His political ideas were important, as James perceptively sees, but McKay's choice to engage in politics through literature inextricably links the two.

In recent years, African American critical discourse has focused on exciting new approaches such as queer theory and postcolonialism, not to mention updated appreciations of primitivism and Black radical history. These approaches have greatly expanded our understanding of McKay's poetry and prose, especially his complicated artistic position within the diasporic community and that of the radical left. Two groundbreaking critical texts have been especially enlightening: Gary Edward Holcomb's *Claude McKay,*

Code Name Sasha: Queer Black Marxism and the Harlem Renaissance, published in 2007, and William J. Maxwell's *New Negro, Old Left: African-American Writing and Communism Between the Wars,* published in 1999. Maxwell's publication of McKay's poetry in 2004 (*Complete Poems: Claude McKay*) and critics of queer theory have opened the door for younger scholars to explore the subtle and secret ways in which McKay expressed his sexuality in both his poetry and fiction.

This book returns to an older critical perspective at the same time that it attempts to take into account what happened in McKay studies since Holcomb, Maxwell, and others have opened our eyes to alternative universes within McKay's works. As I will argue, McKay was a prolific reader of texts, a fact which resonates throughout his work. Just as we can no longer read him without considering his sexuality and his "transatlantic" context, so too we cannot read him without taking into account all those authors—white and Black, ancient and modern—that formed him. Like Toni Morrison in *Playing in the Dark: Whiteness and the Literary Imagination,* he could single out white authors for harsh criticism, but that was not his main concern. His attitude toward Ernest Hemingway is a case in point. McKay simply said in his autobiography that he wasn't interested in Hemingway's racial views, that his fiction was valuable to him because it "most excellently quickened and enlarged my experience of social life" (*A Long Way from Home* 252). He wasn't talking about a philosophy of society (he could have gone to Karl Marx—and countless others—for that) but rather the significance of the minutia or events of modern life, especially its ubiquitous violence.

This was the view he took to everything he read: If a text was revelatory, he embraced it—and rewrote it, sometimes with a racial perspective, sometimes not. For McKay, the issue was always whether the writer was good or useful, not whether they were Black or white, male or female. Often the writers he admired were white, dead, and belonging to what we today call the *canon.*

In his excellent edition of McKay's *Complete Poems,* William J. Maxwell notes that McKay admitted his "fondness" for "older [poetic] traditions," a point McKay would return to time and again, and not just in terms of poetry (324). In 1917, McKay would complain to Joel Spingarn that the "policy" of *The Seven Arts* (1916–1917), the avant-garde journal that had published two of his sonnets, was "intolerant of the literary traditions of the past" (*Letters in Exile* 28). In his preface to *Harlem Shadows* (1922), he said that he found those traditions invaluable and that they paradoxically enhanced the expression of his "most lawless and revolutionary passions and moods," giving him the "the highest degree of spontaneity and freedom" (qtd. in Gosciak 24). Lindsay Tuggle has perceptively discussed the sexual implications of those remarks in terms of queer theory, arguing that the older forms allowed him to hide and simultaneously reveal his same-sex desires, but I would like to explore them from another angle (Tuggle 63–81). That "freedom" would result in McKay's multidimensional literary art, akin to the Romantic irony he would often embrace in his poetry (chapter 1). My decision to examine McKay's nonracial, non-Black intertexts springs from his own insistence that these influences made him not only a better artist but a better Black artist.

These "influences" would include filmmakers and painters, major figures in the literary canon and mavericks within popular culture, and the literary giants of modernism. McKay's sources in his poetry and prose varied from his love of Jonathan Swift and William Hogarth to the British Romantic poets to modernists like D. H. Lawrence, Ernest Hemingway, James Joyce, and Marcel Proust. As he himself said, "about art, I'm a Romantic. I salute it everywhere" (qtd. in Gosciak 24). He even salutes it when it comes to cooking food. In *Home to Harlem* (1928), both the grotesque Gin-Head Susy and the despicable Chef on the Pennsy railroad are called artists (*Home* 73, 173). About Susy: "She may be fat and ugly as a turkey, thought Jake, but her eats are sure beautiful" (*Home* 78). And when it comes to literary art, as McKay told Joel Spingarn, "What appeals to me most in literature is quite independent of race and nationality—the human feeling that transcends racial boundaries. In essence, I think all great writers resemble each other" (*Letters in Exile* 26–27).

His remark about being a Romantic points to a paradox in McKay's work and in his conception of himself as an artist. As he told Langston Hughes, "I myself, although quite in sympathy with any novel trend that is worthwhile, am rather a classicist" (*Letters in Exile* 115–116). McKay greatly admired the modernist Ernest Hemingway. In fact, some of McKay's work, such as *Home to Harlem* and his brilliant short story "The Prince of Porto Rico" (1932), is indebted to the down and dirty world of Hemingway's *In Our Time* (1925) and "The Killers" (1927). W. E. B. Du Bois was not far off the mark when he noted "the dirtier parts" of *Home to Harlem* that made him feel "like taking a bath" (Du Bois, *Crisis*, June 1928, 202). But McKay's point was that "taking a bath" was not going to change what was happening in Harlem. Only a literary genre like the pulps could express what bathwater could not clean. McKay would continue to explore Black life in lowbrow forms of popular culture such as film and the gangster novel at the same time as he would write poetry that embraced the sonnet form and praised the medieval cathedral as a sublime expression of the visual arts. In other words, he could sound like T. S. Eliot in "Tradition and the Literary Talent," insisting that literature should rise to the status of high culture, and then he would lower the literary bar in "The Prince of Porto Rico."

McKay knew that the Great War had created a new kind of literature. His alter ego Ray would note in *Home to Harlem* that the war was a turning point, that "his spiritual masters" from the previous century "had not crossed with him into the new" (*Home to Harlem* 226). Ray is referring primarily to the great social reformers of the nineteenth century, not to its imaginative literature. Although McKay would identify with the modernists, the literary past always remained important to him. As a boy, he read an eclectic mixture that included the Victorian novels ranging from Dickens (*David Copperfield, Nicholas Nickleby, Oliver Twist*) to Stowe (*Uncle Tom's Cabin*) to Zola (*Nana*) to Hugo (*Les Miserables*), which made him dream of "weaving words to make romance" (*Home to Harlem* 225). Despite his admiration for the modernists, he wrote a picaresque novel, with its echo of Fielding's *Tom Jones* (*Home to Harlem*), a novel of ideas (*Banjo*), and a *bildungsroman* (*Banana Bottom*). In fact, McKay was always reinventing himself as a fiction writer and delighted in exploring new ways to tell a story. Each chapter in my text focuses on a new way.

What is notable about both his fiction and his poetry is that he could easily switch gears, one moment writing like Jonathan Swift and the next like the Victorians or the Romantic poets. According to John Trombold, he even made Jake Brown in *Home to Harlem* "a literary cousin of Congo Jake" in John Dos Passos's *Manhattan Transfer* (1925) (Trombold 17). He could praise a genteel (and white) Mary White Ovington along with James Joyce and D. H. Lawrence. She wrote *Hazel* (1913), a novel for girls, that McKay admired, but it is doubtful she would have approved of his admiration for Joyce and Lawrence for having the courage to explore the dark, often comic, world of human sexuality. McKay thought that courage was essential to the artist. If the artist lacked that, they lacked everything. But sometimes his candor got him into trouble. As Lindsay Tuggle notes, when it came to his own sexuality, McKay walked a tightrope: the poem "Courage" illustrates "a delicate balance between secrecy and recognition" (Tuggle 75).

For a time (circa 1924) McKay was Langston Hughes's "favorite black writer" (Rampersad 86). As late as 1931, Hughes "believed Claude McKay to be the greatest living Negro writer in creative literature today," and even in 1933, after he lost faith in McKay's radicalism, he admitted to "have admired him greatly and feel that, to some extent, my own work has been influenced by him" (*Collected Works* 46, 53). When Hughes wrote about the need for the Black artist to be courageous in his famous essay "The Negro Artist and the Racial Mountain" (1926), he may have been thinking of McKay, especially his poem "Courage" in *Harlem Shadows*. Hughes wrote that "an artist must be free to do what he does, certainly, but he must never be afraid to do what he might choose" (Lewis 95). McKay never hesitated to choose what subject to write about or what artist to praise.

The list of white writers (both dead and alive) that influenced McKay poses a special irony in light of how militant and angry McKay could be, especially in his best-known poem "If We Must Die" (1919). Although the poem uses the language of the Great War poets (Wilfred Owen, Siegfried Sassoon, Isaac Rosenberg, Robert Graves, et al.) to express the American racial crisis of 1919, its rhetorical plea is also for the have-nots ("kinsmen") to stand against the powers that be. And yet, the anger in that poem is encased in a sonnet form, a poetic vehicle associated with the love poetry of the English Renaissance (Maxwell, *New Negro, Old Left* 66). Furthermore, as Josh Gosciak notes, McKay's poem is also indebted to John Milton's sonnet "On the Late Massacre in Piedmont," written in 1671, which deals with the Protestant martyrs of Piedmont who were slaughtered for their faith (Gosciak 21).

But that is not all. McKay also alludes to lines from Shakespeare's *Henry V*, the patriotic historical play about England's war with France. In *Henry V*, the English army is outnumbered five to one, a situation that the king uses to his advantage when he tells Westmoreland "If we are marked to die . . . The fewer men the greater honor" (4.3.20–23). Henry's "happy few, we band of brothers" (4.3.60) become McKay's "far outnumbered" African Americans who are hunted down "by mad and hungry dogs" as though they were "hogs penned in an inglorious spot" (*CP* 177, lines 10, 3, 1–2) Earlier, before the Battle of Agincourt, Henry gives a rousing speech to close the "breach . . . / Or close the wall up with our English dead" (3.1.1–2), the elevated tone and language are captured by McKay as he urges his "kinsmen" to meet "the common foe!": "If we must die, let us nobly die," so that even our enemies "shall be constrained to honor us though dead! (*CP* 177, lines 9, 5, 8).

McKay wrote this poem at the end of the Great War, and its last line, "Pressed to the wall, dying, but fighting back!" (*CP* 178, line 14), echoes a desperate speech made by Field Marshal Douglas Haig. When the Germans made their final push to win the war in 1918, Haig, the allied commander, issued his "'Backs to the Wall' Order of the Day": "With our backs to the wall and believing in the justice of our cause, each one must fight on to the end" (qtd. in Fussell 17). Even within the narrow scope of the sonnet form, McKay could shift from high to low and back again. Although the poem expresses rage against injustice, it is finally a love poem in the great sonnet tradition of the English Renaissance. Those "kinsmen" McKay calls upon are his "band of brothers."

In another light, some literary "brothers" are seemingly more important than others for McKay. According to his biographer Wayne F. Cooper, McKay preferred D. H. Lawrence to James Joyce: "McKay had no fundamental sense that Joyce spoke directly to him, to his problems, his hopes, or his future" (208). On the other hand, "McKay felt a psychic kinship" with Lawrence (208). As McKay himself wrote in *A Long Way from Home*, "I thought *Ulysses* a bigger book than any one of Lawrence's books, but I preferred Lawrence as a whole. I thought that D. H. Lawrence was more modern than James Joyce. In D. H. Lawrence I found confusion—all of the ferment and torment and turmoil, the hesitation and hate and alarm, the sexual inquietude and the incertitude of this age, and the psychic and romantic groping for a way out" (247). Yet Lawrence himself should be quoted here: "Never trust the artist. Trust the tale" (Lawrence, *Studies in Classic American Literature* 13). The relevant "tale," here, would be McKay's novel *Banjo* (1929), in which he addressed the issue of what kind of artist he would choose to be, a theme addressed in similar terms by Joyce in "The Dead" (*Dubliners*, 1914), *Portrait of the Artist as a Young Man* (1916), and *Ulysses* (1922).

There was another reason to suspect that Joyce was possibly the greater influence on McKay. In his fiction, especially his epic novel *Ulysses* (1922), Joyce possessed a strong sense of urban space. He once boasted to his friend Frank Budgen that, in *Ulysses*, he intended to "give a picture of Dublin so complete that if the city suddenly disappeared from the earth, it could be reconstructed from my book" (qtd. in Heggland 164). McKay's *Home to Harlem* would also deliver a distinct sense of urban place, and like in Joyce's work, the past would dictate what kind of place that place would be. In 1924, McKay wrote Arturo (Arthur) Schomburg to send him a "map" of Harlem "to fill in the blanks during the corrections of" a now-lost manuscript called "Color Scheme," a test run for *Home to Harlem* (*Letters in Exile* 89). Joyce would set *Ulysses* in Dublin in 1904, close to Charles Stewart Parnell's disgrace and death, and McKay would set his Harlem novel in 1917–18 at the end of the Great War and before the onset of Prohibition. His request reflects his passion for accuracy. Similarly, *Banana Bottom* would be set in "the Jamaican period of the early nineteen hundreds" when British colonialism was very much alive, pre–Marcus Garvey (McKay, *Banana Bottom*).

Although Lawrence spoke to McKay "directly," there is a difference between "psychic kinship" and authors who are useful. No doubt Lawrence's theme of "sexual inquietude" resonated on many levels with McKay, especially given his bisexual orientation, as did Lawrence's theme that marriage is often a trap, but Lawrence's conception of the novel was more psychological than political. In *Lady Chatterley's Lover* (1929), Lawrence said that "the novel, properly handled, can reveal the most secret places of life: for it is in the *passional* secret places of life, above all, that the tide of sensitive awareness needs to ebb and flow, cleansing and freshening" (105). McKay would certainly explore those "secret places" in his poetry and prose, but as a Black writer in both the New World and the Old, the social fabric of his personal experience and that of his characters would be foremost.

Lawrence, of course, could be quite insightful about "social life," especially about the impact of the Industrial Revolution and modernity on the English class system. A sense of place also impacted his characters. According to Mark Schorer, "Lawrence's people discover their identities through their response to place" (qtd. in Fussell 143). And there is one phrase in Lawrence's brilliant *Studies in Classic American Literature* that must have caught McKay's eye: "The Spirit of Place." McKay was very much aware of its meaning for him in the context of Lawrence's book; Lawrence had insisted that "Americans" had never come to terms with "place" in the New World. They have always remained exiles from the Old and hostile to the New. This has created, Lawrence argues, "the essential American soul . . . hard, isolate, stoic, and a killer" (*Studies* 11–18, 73), a line that may have inspired Hemingway in "The Killers."

However, the titles of some of Lawrence's best-known novels tell us where his true interest lies: *Aaron's Rod* (1922), *Sons and Lovers* (1913), *Women in Love* (1920), and *Lady Chatterley's Lover*. The titles suggest his focus on love and sexual relationships. McKay, in fact, calls *Lady Chatterley's Lover* "a beautiful love poem" and compares it to "Shakespeare's Venus and Adonis" (*Letters in Exile* 339). But as his allusion to Shakespeare suggests, McKay didn't specifically see Lawrence as a modernist the way he did Joyce and Hemingway. He refers to Joyce's *Ulysses* and Hemingway's *In Our Time* as essential modernist texts. Ultimately, no matter what white writers influenced McKay, he viewed them through the lens of his own racial experience and the condition of Africans and people of African descent in the modern world.

As with Joyce and Hemingway, there is always a tension in McKay's work between the creative self and community. At the end of "Truant" in McKay's short story collection *Gingertown* (1932), the character Barclay Oram shuts the door behind him, leaving home and family, not knowing where he is going but reflecting that "maybe his true life lay in eternal inquietude" (162). Here the portrait of the artist is the lonely rebel, whereas in the story that follows, "The Agricultural Show," Matthew Bright is a stand in for the artist as he creates an event, the Agricultural Show, that serves the community of which he is very much a part. At the end of his novel *Banjo*, McKay plays with the word "conjunction," suggesting that some linkages are better than others for the artist.

That theme—what is art? what does it mean to be an artist (Black or white)? and what is their subject matter?—is germane to the thesis of my book. In a bitter exchange of views with W. E. B. Du Bois, McKay would claim that the older scholar (and artist) knew nothing of artists like himself who make "art of life" (Cooper 244). And by "life," he meant life at the lower depths and at the jagged edges of human sexuality, but even McKay, through Ray in *Home to Harlem*, wasn't always so sure this was possible: "what was art anyway? . . . Could he create out of the fertile reality around him? Of Jake nosing through life, a handsome hound, quick to snap up any tempting morsel of poisoned meat thrown carelessly on the pavement? Of a work pal he had visited in the venereal ward of Bellevue, where youths lolled sadly about? And the misery that *overwhelmed* him there, until life appeared like one big disease and the world a vast hospital" (my emphasis) (228).

Still, McKay (through Ray) remained fascinated by "the utter blinding nakedness and violent coloring of life," for it was "something new" and better than the "dead stuff" left to Black Americans by the white ruling class: "we get our education like—like our houses. When the whites move out, we move in . . . (243). (Here is another allusion to a modernist, Jean Toomer's "Rhobert" in *Cane*.) Nevertheless, the education he got from Walter Jekyll's library and from white writers like Lawrence, Joyce, and Hemingway was not "dead stuff." His reworking of what he absorbed from those white houses would become the basis of his art.

Almost all his fiction would address questions about art and the artist, especially those that concerned him as a gay Black artist and were left unresolved in *Home to Harlem*. *Banjo* (1929), his sequel to *Home to Harlem*, would be his most explicit treatment of the artist, his dual nature, and *Banana Bottom*, would depict a female protagonist who would become the artist of her own life. His later fiction, like *Harlem Glory* (circa 1936–37, pub. 1990) and *Amiable with Big Teeth* (1941, pub. 2017), would highlight the bogus artist, the artist as confidence man. His brilliant (and recently published) *Romance in Marseille* (circa 1930–31, pub. 2020) presented the prostitute Aslima, who was an artist without a roadmap, without a script to define her, her failure anticipating Bita in *Banana Bottom*, who would find a way to connect the different cultures and places that formed her.

II: "A RIVER RUNS THROUGH IT": MCKAY'S GARDEN CITY

One connection or "conjunction" that haunted McKay was his desire to find and embrace a spiritual center in whatever place he found himself. Five years before his death in 1948, McKay found a safe haven in the Catholic Church in Chicago. He was destitute, ill, and lonely. There he began a second autobiography, *My Green Hills of Jamaica*, in which he nostalgically remembered his childhood and adolescent years under the protection of the Catholic Church. The title, of course, echoes Hemingway's *Green Hills of Africa* (1936), but it is McKay's "my" that forcefully claims his "green hills" as his own. They contain a childhood home, bathed in the blessed light of memory. According to his biographer Wayne F. Cooper, McKay told Max Eastman in 1944 "that he had always had, at bottom, a religious impulse," that the Catholic Church, which he associated with his childhood, embodied that need (360). In *Green Hills of Africa*, Hemingway said that he "felt at home" in Africa, "and where a man feels at home ... is where he's meant to go" (*Green Hills of Africa* 194). In *My Green Hills of Jamaica*, McKay sought that home in the memory of his childhood, but for much of his life, he sought a spiritual home in his poetry and prose. Like his Harlem Dancer, he remained for much of his life an outsider "passing through a storm," a pilgrim searching for moments of grace in the earthly city (*CP* 172, line 8).

In his early years, McKay claimed to be a "pagan," and not a Christian, as he told James Weldon Johnson in 1929: "I don't think there is anything of Christian morality in my writings" (*Letters in Exile* 288). He also saw himself as a "vagabond," as he said in *A Long Way from Home*, whose random movements from place to place were the source of his art (4). He told his friend Harold Jackman in 1928 that his was "a vagabond soul," even "an outlaw soul," that refused to be circumscribed by the laws of white civilization, especially those of American civilization after the Great War. However, the restrictions, as he told Jackson, "help make an artist of a vagabond" (*Letters in Exile* 232). They forced him to realize what matters. And yet the title of his autobiography, *A Long Way from Home*, refers to two lines from an African American spiritual: "Sometimes I feel like a motherless child / A long ways from home." Vagabond or wayfaring pilgrim—McKay was always looking for a place of grace.

McKay would use the image of the dance as that place of grace. Dancing is the definition of what an artist does, as he told Harold Jackman: "good dancing always gets me into an ecstasy that I would call religious, because I never have a sex feeling when I am dancing. . . . What I feel when I am dancing is the desire for a perfect union of movement with my partner" (*Letters in Exile* 249–50). That union, no matter how temporary, is the artist's "ecstasy" and the artist's religion (from the Latin "religare": "to bind"). It is an attempt to find a "perfect union" between thought (or emotion) and self-expression and between artist and audience. This of course is a utopian moment, but it is also a strategy for what Kenneth Burke calls "the encompassing of situations," or as Burke puts it elsewhere, in terms relevant to McKay, "the *dancing of an attitude*" (Burke, *Philosophy of Literary Form* 1, 9). For Burke (and McKay), literary art is a verbal dance that confronts and transforms, but does not erase, the real "situations" of everyday life. Its beauty arises from the presence of those situations, in McKay's case the hostile racism that permeates every aspect of American society. Consider the last two lines of "The Harlem Dancer": "But looking at her falsely-smiling face, / I knew her self was not in that strange place" (*CP* 172, lines 13–14). And yet her dance transforms that "strange place" into a space of beauty.

Langston Hughes's poem, "Harlem Dance Hall," as published in Arnold Rampersad and David Roessel's collection of his poems, does something similar. Its first line tells us that the dance hall without the dance and music is empty space: "It had no dignity before." It is only some dingy warehouse, but when "the band began to play" and Black people began to dance

> Suddenly the earth was there,
> And flowers,
> Trees,
> And air,
> And like a wave the floor—That had no dignity before! (339)

The pastoral blooms in the city space of the dance hall, making it, for an evening, a garden city. The connection Hughes makes between the pastoral and the city parallels what Josh Gosciak calls the "exciting new garden-city integration" in McKay's poetry (88). The dance is the garden in the city; for a transient moment it redeems Augustine's earthly city. That moment reveals a potential "perfect union" between self and other.

In McKay's *Banana Bottom*, the Jamaican natives transform Mozart's "minuet" into something new, the "mintoe." Stolen from another culture, Mozart's dance is remade into a hybrid in a setting that, in turn, is transformed by the dance. And Bita herself is transformed when she dances with Hopping Dick, someone socially quite beneath her.

The moment of her transformation mirrors the dance itself. Bita becomes the mintoe, not the minuet. When she dances, she does not shed her Anglo upbringing, but incorporates it into a second self, the one that marries two cultures: England's high, Jamaica's low. Moreover, "the waxed mahogany floor" on which she dances with Hopping Dick becomes a new space, no longer only a venue reserved for high culture (196). The moment of her dance foreshadows the novel's final image: Bita at home in the world. All this mirrors McKay's attempt to resolve the contradictory impulses within himself. He is both a vagabond and a pilgrim, a pagan and a Christian, a Jamaican and a man of many cultures. His poetry and his fiction dance those attitudes.

In *My Green Hills of Jamaica*, McKay describes his journey at six years old from his home in Sunny Ville to his brother's house in Montego Bay and then, at age sixteen, to the big city of Kingston to learn a trade. There he meets the British expat, the fifty-something Walter Jekyll who would become a formative influence upon his life. What he learned from Jekyll and his library is that culture and cultivation can exist anywhere. Books gave him his first taste of wanderlust, and he began to see Kingston as a port of embarkation, fantasizing about places from which the great ships came. At the end of his memoirs, he leaves Kingston for New York, beginning a long pilgrimage to cities which he would write about with great eloquence and insight in his poetry.

My Green Hills of Jamaica is not a simple pastoral. His memory of home is that of a garden city, a theme that he had developed with greater sophistication in *Banana Bottom*. When he remembered his early years in Sunny Ville, Jamaica, he linked an urban symbol to a pastoral setting: "My village was beautiful, sunshiny, sparsely populated, It was set upon a hill. Except when it rained or was foggy, it was bathed by the sun. The hills came like chains from the other villages—James Hill, Taremont, Croft's Hill, Frankfield and from Ballad's River. They came to form a center in Sunny Ville.... The Mount Zion church rested on the highest point in the village" (*Green Hills* 4). McKay combines the two motifs here: garden and city. In spatial terms, the eye of memory locates Sunny Ville as the focal point of the perspective, "set upon a hill," echoing Eden which also rested upon a mountain. Sunny Ville's church, appropriately named Mount Zion, also stands at the village's highest point. As a student of the Bible, McKay would know that, in the Book of Psalms and Ezekiel, a redeemed city stood on a mountain and at the center of the city was a temple, not needed in Revelation, as John of Patmos tells us, because God and his son replace the physical temple: "And I saw no temple in the city, for its temple is the Lord God and the Lamb" (Rev. 21.22). That Sunny Ville has a "ville" in its name hints of the two worlds, garden and city, that McKay brings together in his memory. In French, "ville" means city.

I want to suggest that McKay's "religious impulse" is connected to the cities he admired—they all had a spiritual center. The sense of wonder he associated with certain cities attracted him to cathedrals even in those early rebellious years when he called himself a "pagan." In *A Long Way from Home*, McKay describes a long conversation he had with George Bernard Shaw who urged him to visit England's famous cathedral towns—"Salisbury, Lincoln, Canterbury, York, and Winchester." McKay recalls being "enchanted" by Shaw's "monologue on cathedrals," who spoke of "their architectural grandeur, the poetry of their spires and grand arches, and the prismatic beauty of their great windows" (62). He called "Shaw's discourse on cathedrals . . . an exceptional thing," noting that he has not "discovered anything like it in any of his writings" (65).

He then singles out his own love of the cathedral, its vertical outside, "the vast spaciousness of the inside when it is empty." His final remarks on cathedrals tell us what attracted him throughout his own life to cities: "During the many years I spent on the continent of Europe, I never stopped in a cathedral town without visiting the cathedral. I have spent hours upon hours meditating upon the modern movements of life in the sublime grandeur of cathedral silence. And as I stood in the nave of those concrete miracles of the medieval movement of belief and faith, transported by the triumphant arches of Gothic *glory*, often I felt again the musical vibrations of Shaw's cathedral sermon" (my emphasis) (65). In the Middle Ages, a town had to have a cathedral to be called a city, the building's spiritual, vertical presence reminding humankind that the city of God lies above, not here. New York City at first sight seemed to McKay to be that city, dazzling his "sight like a miracle of might," especially after traveling across the ocean in steerage, as he took in "the immense wonder of clean, vertical, heaven-challenging lines, a *glory* to the grandeur of space" (my emphasis) (*A Long Way* 95). The "heaven-challenging," of course, calls forth Babel, and soon he descends into the city's "precipitous gorges," and the "wonder," "illumination," and "radiance" that "dazzled" his "sight" disappear, and he realizes he is only "one" of a million "insignificant" human beings in this most modern of modern cities. He "wished that it were possible to know New York in that way only—as a masterpiece wrought for the illumination of the sight, a splendor lifting aloft and shedding its radiance like a searchlight" (*A Long Way* 95).

He would never forget that view of New York, the city on a hill as St. Matthew's "candle" (and John Winthrop's) that should be a "searchlight" to the rest of the world (Matt. 5.14–15). That view helps to explain the ambivalence he felt toward New York, and the "city" within it (Harlem), expressed in both his poetry and his fiction. His writings reveal the tension between the outcast and the soul that longs for a spiritual community.

What makes Sunny Ville holy for McKay is the invisible presence of the city in the garden. Again, the Christian Bible is his source, for it begins with a garden and ends with a city. Expelled from Eden, Adam and Eve entered history, and their descendants journey toward the heavenly city, described in Revelation as a garden city: a river runs through it. "Then he [Christ] showed me the river of life, bright as crystal flowing from the throne of God . . . through the middle of the street of the city; also, on either side of the river, the tree of life with its twelve kinds of fruit" (Rev. 22.1–2). The heavenly city incorporates the lost garden, but, as Augustine reminds us, before we find that city we wander as pilgrims in the corrupt, earthly city, the city founded by Cain, the man who commits fratricide. Narrative begins with that crime, even Augustine's, so that what most of humankind knows is the grim reality of the consequences of that crime. We wander, alone and afraid, in "this wicked world as though in a flood" (644). The real city, the heavenly city, exists only as a *figura* in the earthly city, appearing momentarily as a place of grace or the grail or some other sign (like dancing). McKay was always trying to find or imagine that place of grace, a major theme in much of his writing.

Yet all this doesn't quite explain McKay's sense of place, which (again) is best expressed in his sonnet "The Harlem Dancer." The dancer projects herself beyond "strange" street in Harlem, but the street will still be there when her dance and song end. "Strange" can mean alien or hostile, but it can also mean unfamiliar, and in his poetry and elsewhere McKay was attracted to strange places. He was not Paul Fussell's "tourist" but an explorer of new worlds, new places (Fussell, *Abroad* 37–50).

Like Countee Cullen, McKay was a great admirer of the British Romantic poets, especially John Keats. The famous lines from "Adonais," Percy

Shelley's poetic elegy for Keats, are relevant to McKay's love of strange places:

> The One remains, the many change and pass;
> Heaven's light forever shines, Earth's shadows fly;
> Life, like a dome of many-coloured glass,
> Stains the white radiance of Eternity,
> Until Death tramples it to fragments. (lines 460–64)

For McKay, it would be the white world that "stains" the "radiance," not the many-colored glass, and especially not the color black. Yet he was fascinated by "earth's shadows," by the "stains," by the many colors of the earthly city, even as he sought the "One," the spiritual center of each city. He was a time "traveler" like Keats, traveling "much . . . in the realms of gold," to both imagined and real places (John Keats, "On First Looking into Chapman's Homer," line 1).

III: THE BOOK'S OUTLINE

Chapter 1 focuses on McKay's search for the spiritual center of cities, the "religious impulse" that is present or missing in cities. Chapter 2 uses both Hogarth and Hemingway to describe Harlem as a fallen city, Cain's city, in *Home to Harlem*, but, as Eric H. Newman argues in a provocative essay on "Queer Cruising," there exists "fleeting" redemptive moments and "encounters" in that novel and *Banjo* that make "imaginable a community that could appear and disappear virtually anywhere" (167).

Chapter 3 focuses on the artist as Dionysus and Apollo, two figures from Greek mythology (via Nietzsche's *Birth of Tragedy* and James Joyce's monumental fiction) that helped McKay resolve an argument in *Home to Harlem* he was having with himself over what kind of artist he wished to be. Chapter 4 describes McKay's interest in film as the basis of a novel, *Romance in Marseille*, that reads as a film script in which McKay emerges as an *auteur*. In that novel, the city of Marseille is depicted in terms of both the romance of cinema and Hawthorne and Melville's conception of "Romance." Marseille is both a dark place and illumined city—that is the double meaning of McKay's title.

Chapter 5 begins with the image of the dance in *Gingertown* as a modernist trope and the dancer as artist and ends with the last story in that collection, "The Little Sheik," in which the dancers fail to connect. Chapter

6 explores McKay's *Banana Bottom* as a response to W. E. B. Du Bois's novel *Dark Princess* (1928), published in the same year as *Home to Harlem*, a novel that Du Bois said was obscene and whose depiction of Black life was "nonsense." McKay's female protagonist, Bita Plant, combines both the pragmatism of Du Bois's Sara Andrews and the idealism of his princess from India, as McKay has her use both to make an artistry of her own life. Chapter 7 describes McKay's return to popular culture with two gangster novels, *Harlem Glory* and *Amiable with Big Teeth*, both of which have strong dystopian themes, serving as a corrective to the optimism expressed in *Banana Bottom*. When he wrote his two gangster novels, he also considered the gangster films of the late 1920s and early 1930s.

Chapter 7 highlights the influence of Jonathan Swift upon McKay, as McKay becomes the artist as satirist (as he often was in his poetry). Swift's *saeva indignatio* reminded McKay that his own savage indignation (or what he called his "fierce hatred of injustice") had a model from the past, reflected also in Old Testament.

Tying the threads of the book's outline together is the theme of McKay, the "artist in words" who struggled to determine what kind of artist he wanted to be. He began as a poet, and then writers like Sherwood Anderson and Sinclair Lewis suggested that he try his hand at prose (*Letters in Exile* 87). McKay said that he "didn't want to publish a novel by 'a Negro poet'. I wanted to publish a novel" (*Letters in Exile* 110). He was always willing to try something new. He went on to create the only best-selling novel by a Black writer in the Harlem Renaissance, *Home to Harlem*. Later he tired of what he called "the picaresque" approach. He told both his agent and a good friend that he "had about written myself dry on the picaresque stuff" (*Letters in Exile* 370, 381), and ended up writing his best novel, *Banana Bottom*. McKay had always aspired to be a satirist, even in his poetry, and hence his indebtedness to Jonathan Swift. McKay's political satire foreshadowed the dystopian world of George Orwell. Swift and Orwell described and exposed totalitarian political "systems" in the modern world, just as McKay in his poems "If We Must Die" and "The White House" attempted to expose racism in America. In fact, as he said to his fellow satirist Langston Hughes, "I believe in [the] naked exposure of everything…it can never hurt us as a race—rather help" (*Letters in Exile* 295).

CHAPTER 1

THE SEARCH FOR A SPIRITUAL CENTER

The Image of the City in McKay's Poetry

I

If I could git more into the center of things.
—BUD KORPENNING IN JOHN DOS PASSOS, *MANHATTAN TRANSFER* (1925)

In his poem entitled "Cities," McKay claimed to "love all cities," to "love their changing moods . . . their foreign ways," but he was always looking for "the center of things" beneath their "changing moods" (*CP* 223, lines 6–7). Hence, in the same poem, he alludes to Alexander Pope's *An Essay on Man* which he had read in Walter Jekyll's library (*A Long Way from Home* 13): "A mighty maze! but not without a plan" (Epistle I, line 6). McKay changes the "maze" to "movements," and Pope's God created universe to man-made cities: he loves "their mighty movements seeming without plan." The word "seeming" in McKay's line is significant. The spiritual center of individual cities is not always obvious. Sometimes it is hidden by its flux (its movement) and its "foreign ways." Sometimes it is nonexistent.

McKay was an explorer of all cities, Christian, Muslim, and cities newly defined by the Russian Revolution. The lines in his poem on "Petrograd: May Day, 1923" express both the human desires that cities embody and a warning that those desires can take a bad turn:

> Cities are symbols of man's upward reach,
> Man drawing near to man in close commune,
> And mighty cities mighty lessons teach
> Of man's decay or progress, late or soon. (*A Long Way* 225, *CP* 230, lines 21–24)

Although McKay claimed he loved "all cities," some he loved better than others, and what he disliked about some cities can tell us a great deal about those he loved. In Berlin and London, rationality rules. Berlin's architecture is masculine, "massive," "aggressive," "a stony will in ruthless Nordic style," dwarfing the human; at its center is a "dynamo" that "throbbed with sinister intent," and yet its art is sickly sweet, "rococo," as though the absence of the feminine produces grotesque extremes (*CP* 229, lines 1–4).

London is all cold granite, "a city without light and without heat," a reflection of its austere culture, made warm only by its "ancestral" authors and its fog which wraps the "tropical" McKay in a blanket. London is the human will petrified into stillness, all Apollo and no Dionysus, chilling the soul of a pagan African. "Beauty" never blooms in this "chilling atmosphere" (*CP* 232, lines 6, 11). This is not Samuel Johnson's London. There is no life in this city to get tired of.

McKay contrasts the poetic portraits of these two Northern European cities with the cities of a tropical clime that he admired: Tangier, Fez, Marrakesh, Xauen in Morocco; Cadiz in Spain. David B. Hobbs has argued that McKay saw these five poems as "a suite" under the rubric "Cities." He says further, in a nice insight, that they are unique in "their lack of attention to the specific, individual experiences that populate his novels" (Hobbs 184). However, the self does appear in these poems but always tied to a larger symbolic purpose beyond the self. In his sonnet on Xauen, for example, a "fountain" is at the city's center, "bubbling in my breast." This image in the poem's first line, echoing Revelation 21.6, becomes a metaphor for the renewal of this pilgrim's spirit, "cleansing" him of bad memories. He becomes the city itself in which the fountain's waters "flow tenderly along the avenue/Of my bruised body." In the sestet, the "fountain" is "flowing like the dawn," making this city of different shades of blue a holy city, a "gem," not of America ("the Gem of the Ocean") but of Africa (*CP* 228, lines 1–4).

Cadiz is a city of light: "In sceptered light she glows eternally." The octave of this sonnet focuses on the city's beauty, the sestet on the question of "what beauty is." The city shows forth that beauty, but McKay can only guess at its source or purpose: part of a "universal plan," or "a luxury or need," or something that can only be explained through its manifestation as the "magic, merely, of Cadiz" (*CP* 228, lines 8, 10–14)? What cannot be defined is its "magic," the visible presence of a spiritual, invisible city. McKay's poems of African cities and Spain's Cadiz are both pagan and Christian celebrations of man's attempt to express the joy of existence through urban space. They are Italo Calvino's imagined cities.

What McKay says in prose about Marrakesh appears in his poems about the exotic cities of Africa: "the city is like an immense cradle of experiment in the marriage of civilized life and primitive life" (*A Long Way* 305). All of McKay's Moroccan city poems reflect a union of opposites, and not just between "civilized" and "primitive" but between different civilizations.

Take his sonnet on "Tetuan," for example. McKay plays on the name of both the city in Northern Morocco and the name of a district within Madrid. The Moors conquered Spain in the eighth century and left their legacy, and Spain in the nineteenth century (1859–60) defeated Morocco and left its legacy. The Alhambra in Spain has Moroccan "towers" (octave), and the city of Tetuan in Morocco (sestet) has a "fountain bubbling with new life" (*CP* 227, line 12). Again, McKay links his two favorite images of a healthy city: the cathedral (towers) and the sacred river (fountain). They reflect a marriage between East and West. In his sonnet on "Marrakesh," the renewed city of peasants' "myriad huts" is set against the former twelfth-century empire of the Almohad Caliphate whose conquerors now exist as "ghosts," but in the sestet the "ruins of austere monuments" is a setting for new life reflected in contemporary music and dance. The past renews the present.

McKay knows that marriage between opposites is often at odds with the historical record. Tangier, for instance, is "the broken span / Of two opposing continents," referring to the second Moroccan crisis of 1911, when the French occupied Morocco, a prelude to World War I (*CP* 225, I, lines 1–2). In the early twentieth century, Europe and Africa were at loggerheads, and the cities of Morocco were used by the European powers as political footballs, especially Tangier, and yet, argues McKay, the poet can see a true city beneath the apparent strife, "a beauty pregnant of life's pristine womb," a symbol itself of Africa rising from the ashes of colonialism (*CP* 226, III, line 3).

It is the poet's vision that imagines a new city, a platonic archetype of the city's future. It is this invisible city that informs his vision in his sonnet on Fez.

> My eyes saw Fez, my heart exclaimed Baghdad
> In Africa! And smitten took her whole.

Imaginative sight replaces literal sight. The poet sees the magical city (Baghdad) beneath the bewildering, tangible Fez: "I am haunted by the aspect of her soul, / Obscure like her dim passages and nooks—" (*CP* 226, lines 1–2, 6–7). The poet attempts to pierce the obscurity, to reveal the "soul" of the city. He sees things "whole" because his sight is both visionary (the poet as "vates") and word-making (the poet as "poeta": craftsman). He is dancing an attitude through language, creating a city through words.

Influenced by the Romantics, McKay embraces Coleridge's definition of the poet's imagination as a faculty that can make new "wholes" from "fixed" parts. For Coleridge, the imagination "is essentially *vital*, even as all objects (*as* objects) are essentially fixed and dead"—or, to use McKay's word, "Obscure" (Perkins 452). As a city lover, he finds a plan in Fez's "labyrinthine lanes and crooked souks [markets]" where it is easy to get lost (*CP* 226, line 3). The process he describes in his poem on "Fez" foreshadows Bita's experience in Jamaica in *Banana Bottom*. Before she finds her way, she gets lost in the labyrinthian maze of a "home" she thought she knew.

For McKay, the city is an organism with a soul. Sometimes that soul is expressed by a person (Moscow) or a person and a cathedral (Petrograd), or a fountain (Xauen) or "the dance of life" (Barcelona) (*CP* 224, III, line 14). That a city must have an authentic centering principle causes McKay to reflect in *A Long Way from Home* upon the name change from Petrograd to Leningrad after the Russian Revolution.

> When I think of that great city like a mighty tree shaken to its roots by a hurricane, yet still standing erect, and when I think of the proud equestrian statue of Peter the Great, proclaiming that dictator's mighty achievement, I feel the world has lost the poetry and the color rising like a rainbow out of a beautiful name since Petrograd was changed to Leningrad.
>
> Lenin is mightier than Peter the Great. But there is no *magic* in the name Leningrad. (my emphasis) (*A Long Way* 157)

McKay for the moment forgets his politics, his sympathy for the proletariat. The magic that resides in the name Petrograd is the "achievement" that outshines the dictator. The city is "a mighty tree" that not even the Russian Revolution can uproot. Great cities have their origin in the soil.

The city as the good place is a combination of artifice and nature, a state of mind and a living reality. Created by man, the city mirrors the timeless eternal city, but as a city in this world it is an ever-evolving organism, with a specific founding, with a specific history. It exists both inside and outside of time. The name Petrograd reflects both its finite founding and its spiritual origins, its "poetry," its "magic." In his poem "Russian Cathedral," in which he celebrates St. Isaac's church in Petrograd, he attempts to express his sense of wonder for the city through his favorite image, the cathedral, "the sacred sight / Of man's divinity *alive* in stone" (my emphasis) (*CP* 210, line 14). Although the cathedral is stone fixed in a defined space, that stone is *alive*, capable of renewing each person who sees it, just as the poet who perceives the Harlem dancer has a new conception of reality.

McKay is not against having a separate city named after Lenin:

> There is magic in the name of Lenin, as there is splendor in the word Moscow. And Perhaps Lenin himself, whose life was devoted to the idea of creating a glorious new world, might have, in appreciation of the will of Peter the Great to remake the nation, preferred Petrograd to remain Petrograd. Perhaps the spirit of Lenin might have been more adequately expressed in the erection of a brand new city, rising out of that system to which he dedicated his life. Lenin without any suffix—like a perfect ball of pure gold—a city called Lenin. (*A Long Way* 157)

Later, McKay would reject Lenin's "system" under Stalin as predatory and inhumane (e.g., *Amiable with Big Teeth*), but as an ideal embodied in a city it attempts to mirror John of Patmos's heavenly city. McKay dances with the idea that Peter the Great is a John the Baptist to Lenin's Christ, or he is a Moses or David in the Old Testament, a type of Christ. Peter the Great attempted to reshape Russia by imitating the West, by bringing the West to the East, but Lenin intended to remake his nation anew and thus is deserving of a new city with a new name, one indicating the presence of a new spiritual essence.

In a figurative sense, Lenin has his own city—it's Moscow. In his sonnet called "Moscow," McKay sets a past of "Czarist instruments of mindless law" against the present in which McKay heard "the simple voice and presence of Lenin" (*CP* 229, lines 3, 11). Lenin is a spiritual presence that replaces the cathedral, serving the same function in this poem as the literal cathedral does in Petrograd. He brings to life "all the colors" of the city "laughing richly their delight/And reigning over all the color Red" (*CP* 229, lines 7–8). McKay can't resist using the Book of Revelation to celebrate a nation whose birth is secular.

Paris for McKay poses a problem, so much so that he writes two sonnets on "The City of Light" in which he ponders what kind of "wisdom" this famous city has to offer him. The problem with Paris is that the "light" in this "City of Light" is obscured by the "image" the world has of it. That image is "of brazen lust and wild licentiousness." To the myopic eye, carnality and sensual pleasure define Paris's "wonder." The city is "wonderful like all things seen through a mirage," just as its paganism is the "pagan paradise of courtesans" (*CP* 231, lines 2, 6, 8).

McKay's sestet reshapes his focus upon Paris. The city hides its wisdom beneath a mesmerizing surface. Like a snake, the city extends "her body to its sinuous length," charming the visitor but blinding him. The "fascinating glow" of her "gleaming eyes" reveals a "wisdom" only to those who probe "the depths profound upon which rests her strength" (*CP* 231, I, lines 9–14).

In his second sonnet on the city, McKay tells us what that "strength" is. It's the "resistance" to its charms that calls forth the poet: Paris "has never stormed my stubborn heart," nor whirled him around like a "drunkard." Rather, he has taken the city's "bread" as nourishment and rejected its "wine," arguing in the sestet that the true Paris is not the hedonistic paradise of the ex-pats but a "school" in which "lessons" are taught and learned if one is not to be a "fool." What "lessons" are these? Saying no to the serpent (*CP* 232, II, lines 1–14).

Paris for McKay is not Hemingway's "moveable feast," but food for survival, "nourishment" as practical wisdom: what not to succumb to. The "light" in this city is not the light of "wonder" of the Moroccan cities, nor is it the "light" of Langston Hughes's "enchantress-city," the Paris that attracts and produces artists (*Collected Works* 41). For the city that creates the artist, we need to look at his sonnet on New York, "The White City," in *Harlem Shadows*, published in the same year as *The Waste Land* (1922).

"The White City" contains a paradox. New York expresses the Dionysian energy or "chaotic surging" that McKay loves about cities, but that energy takes a negative turn when he confronts its racism. It is, after all, the *white* city. He responds to the city with equal passion:

> I will not toy with it nor bend an inch.
> Deep in the secret chambers of my heart
> I muse my life-long hate, and without flinch
> I bear it nobly as I live my part.
> My being would be a skeleton, a shell,
> If this dark Passion that fills my every mood,
> And makes my heaven in the white world's hell,
> Did not feed me vital blood. (*CP* 162, lines 1–8)

He may "toy" with Paris, but not with New York, because he can easily resist Paris's siren charms by denying their power over him. New York is a more formidable opponent because it does have power over him. He's impressed by its "might," by its "spires and towers."

The key to the paradox of his love/hate relationship to the city lies in the allusion to *Paradise Lost*, one shaped by the reinterpretation of Satan in Milton's epic by the Romantic poets—specifically, by William Blake and Percy Bysshe Shelley. The line in *Paradise Lost* that McKay rewrites is Satan's boast that "the mind is its own place and in itself / Can make a Heaven of Hell, a Hell of Heaven" (1.254–55, qtd. in *CP* 322). Given the brilliance of Satan's rhetoric in hell and elsewhere, Blake would say in *The Marriage of Heaven and Hell* that Milton was "of the devil's party without knowing it" (Perkins 70). But the more relevant line to McKay's poem is Blake's aphorism in the same text that "the tygers of wrath are wiser than the horses of instruction" (Perkins 71). Although Blake is no doubt satirizing Swift's Houyhnhnms in *Gulliver's Travels*, the Dean of St. Patrick's famous epigraph is also relevant to McKay's poem: Swift lies "where fierce indignation no longer rends his heart." As William J. Maxwell nicely puts it, McKay accepts "anger's formative power" as the source of his art (Maxwell, *New Negro, Old Left* 66–67). Winston James puts it precisely when he notes McKay's "fierce hatred of injustice," McKay's phrase for what he sees as the bitter connection between police work and prostitution (James 106). The prostitutes sell their bodies to survive; the police sell their power for profit. Like Langston Hughes, McKay had an enormous sympathy for "prostitutes, 'good-hearted bums,' vagabonds and the motley outcasts of polite society" (James 56).

Swift's *saeva indignatio* and Blake's "tygers of wrath" help to put McKay's "hate" in a larger context than something subjective—as in "Do you have a problem with anger management, McKay?" For Swift and Blake (and McKay would express his admiration for both in *Banana Bottom*), indignation and wrath are unambiguous responses to crimes against humanity. McKay's "hatred" also has a biblical precedent in the Old Testament:

Do not I hate those who hate you, O LORD?
   And do not I loathe those who rise up against you?
I hate them with perfect hatred;
   I count them my enemies. (Ps. 139.21–22) (qtd. in Barton 132)

Shelley and Byron would both rewrite Satan as the heroic rebel in *Prometheus Unbound* and *Queen Mab* and in *Cain* and *Manfred*, respectively. But it would be Mary Shelley's "creature" in *Frankenstein* that would be the Romantic era's most compelling metamorphosis of Milton's fallen angel. Reading *Paradise Lost* for the first time and comparing himself to Adam, he reflects that "many times I considered Satan as the fitter emblem of my condition." Wanting to be loved, wanting to be acknowledged by his creator, he turns in anger and frustration to "hatred and revenge," while all the while seeking justice and asking "who was I? What was I" (*Frankenstein* 87, 86, 93).

It is worth turning for a moment to Countee Cullen because Harlem Renaissance critic and novelist Wallace Thurman asserted that "the triumvirate of McKay, Cullen and Hughes" dominated the Black poetic scene of the 1920s (224). Although both Hughes and McKay as poets were fascinated by the music and dance of Black life at ground level, it is Cullen who, at least on the surface, seems to have the more striking kinship to McKay. Like McKay, he claimed to have a heart "pagan mad," to have an admiration for older literary forms, especially the sonnet, and to have a veneration for Keats (Cullen 92). Yet "pagan mad," as Gerald Early observes, would for Cullen always be in tension with Christian forgiveness, redemption, and renewal—especially seen in his poem "The Black Christ." And it would be the themes of anger, betrayal, and revenge in Cullen's *The Medea* (including prologue and epilogue) that separate him from McKay. Jason and Medea participate in a cycle of blind hatred that not only destroys the self, their children, and others but causes a complete meltdown in Grecian society.

In his only novel, *One Way to Heaven* (1932), Cullen's Herbert Newell is a thinly disguised Claude McKay who has written a novel about "a prostitute" and "a stevedore" that Harlem's upper-class members of Constancia's "Booklovers' Society" have found offensive. Cullen satirizes the snobs but doesn't let McKay off the hook: Herbert's affectation for anger is as much a facade as the feigned sophistication of many of Constancia's guests: "a very dark, belligerent young Negro, [who] was brutally frank" (469).

For Wallace Thurman, however, McKay was the best artist of the "triumvirate," not despite his passion but because of it. As he told McKay in a letter (October 4, 1928), you have "more mental depth and more emotional depth than any of your contemporaries" (165). McKay's problem in "If We Must Die," as Thurman said in an essay, is that "his message was too alive and too big for the form [the sonnet] he chose.... He could never shape the flames from the fire that blazed within him" (211). And about *Home to Harlem*, Thurman added this: "McKay is volcanic, emitting colorful streams of lava in such quantities that he smothers his story and almost suffocates his reader" (249). And yet, as Thurman notes, poetic lines like these are as hard and sharp as steel:

> Be not deceived, for every deed you do, I could match—out match;
> Am I not Africa's son, Black of that black land where black deeds are done? (212)

What McKay does with his "dark passion," his hatred, is to see it as the source of his poetic strength. That it is contained within a tightly defined form like the sonnet only brightens the flame. Instead of rejecting New York in "The White City" as a false paradise, he embraces it *because* it excludes him. New York is not only the femme fatale to whom he refuses to succumb, but she is also the Magna Mater who gives birth to a stronger McKay. She is both a vampire who sucks blood from others and, paradoxically, has the power to "forever feed him with vital blood" (*CP* 162, line 8). Her seductive nature gives birth to a stronger McKay, a stronger poet.

In "The White City," McKay defines himself both as Frankenstein's creature and the rebellious Prometheus cast out by God/Jupiter, defining who he is through the lens of seeing himself as both a city lover and an outcast. Paris teaches "lessons" to a schoolboy, but McKay wants to be a poet not a schoolboy. Paris is only light reading, but New York is the real text for him, a labyrinth of conflicting elements: the law of White Supremacy, the passion of Eros, the structures of Babel.

Perhaps the line that best expresses McKay's ambivalence toward New York is the first line of the sestet of "The White City": "I see the mighty city through a mist." In *A Long Way from Home*, he is more precise as to what he means by the word "mighty": "One loves in New York the baroque difference from the classic cities, the blind chaotic surging of bigness of expression" (*A Long Way* 133). The phrase "I see" implies that he is a witness, but he admits that he sees the city through the "mist" of his own ambivalence.

In the sestet of "The White City" the word "contemplate" in the last two lines of this Shakespearean sonnet implies that the city must be read if it is not to destroy you:

> The tides, the wharves, the dens I contemplate,
> Are sweet like wanton loves because I hate. (*CP* 162, lines 13–14)

McKay takes Whitman's catalog of the city's nouns (tides, wharves, dens, foundries) in "Crossing Brooklyn Ferry," which symbolize to Whitman the divine plenitude of New York and redefines them: the "ports" are "fortressed," the trains are "strident" (harsh, jarring), the masses "goaded" (herded like sheep), the "spires and towers" are "vapor-kissed," seen through a glass darkly. McKay reads them in terms of an oxymoron ("sweet like wanton loves because I hate,") because it is the only way he can deal with his conflicting emotions toward the city. Whitman wants to embrace everything, while McKay holds love and hate in tension by shaping the city into a manageable form, a sonnet.

The word "wanton" has its source in two *OED* words "wan" and "towen," literally meaning "difficult to discipline." In one sense, McKay sees the white city as beyond discipline or control. It tempts a person like McKay to take its prizes, but it never allows this Black man to seize them. What saves him from the city's seduction is both his indignation and the Wordsworthian distance implied by the word "contemplate." In "Composed Upon Westminster Bridge," Wordsworth can "contemplate" the city in terms of its beauty at dawn before it awakens, before it becomes a "monstrous ant-hill" (*Prelude*, bk. 7, line 149; Perkins 245). For him, the city at dawn shares the beauty of nature: "Ships, towers, domes, theatres, and temples lie / Open unto the fields, and to the sky" (lines 6–7, Perkins 288; qtd. in *CP* 322). The dawn is a moment of grace in a fallen world. London at dawn is a garden city, as Xauen is for McKay. But not so New York for McKay: all is might, noise, movement. The vapor-kissed towers are both an illusion and all too real. They shut McKay out, but they make him a poet, just as Mary Shelley's "creature" becomes the most articulate character in her great novel.

In "The White City," McKay is not only deliberately misreading Milton as Blake did, but he is also rewriting Augustine. In *The City of God*, Augustine pits the invisible heavenly city, founded by Seth and existing only briefly in this world as grace, against Rome, the earthly city as Vanity Fair. McKay's play on "wanton" as "wanderer" echoes Augustine's "pilgrim" who seeks a city outside of space and time. In *A Long Way from Home*, McKay describes his response to New York in terms of Augustine's earthly city, which often appears to humankind as a copy of the archetype: New York "dazzled my sight with the miracle of might" (*A Long Way* 95). But here the city's "miracle" is its secular "might." Its "light" can blind unless it's perceived in the right way.

In his poem "Baptism," that light as "might" takes a new turn. The poet is burned clean by the fire of the furnace, "transforming me into a shape of flame . . . / A stronger soul within a finer frame" (*CP* 177, lines 12, 14). Daniel's furnace in the Old Testament becomes another metaphor for the earthly city. In "The White City," the fires of "wanton loves" recharge his poetic batteries. In "Baptism," the city burns him clean, refining him to a purer form, like a "red ball of fire." The "pagan" McKay takes Plato's Eros in *The Symposium* and sees its "fire" as the source of his transcendence into a finer poet.

In "The City's Love," as the title of this extraordinary poem suggests, he confronts an even greater opponent than the city's antagonism.

> For one brief golden moment rare like wine,
> The gracious city swept across the line;
> Oblivious of the color of my skin,
> Forgetting that I was an alien guest,
> She bent to me, my hostile heart to win,
> Caught me in passion to her pillowy breast;
> The great, proud city, seized with a strange love,
> Bowed down for one flame hour my pride to prove. (CP 158, lines 1–8)

McKay can deal with the city's hostility, but its love is another matter. Maybe enemies should stay enemies. When an adversary reverses course, the psychological effect is unsettling. There is a temptation to let your guard down, to let your armor slip to the ground.

By ending the poem with the word "prove," he emphasizes his own ambivalent reaction to this "moment." If the word means "test," then McKay suggests that the city's momentary affection may be a harder thing to bear than the city's hatred because there is already a propensity in him to love in return (e.g., "I love all cities"). He knows that the city's "strange love" is only temporary, but the "moment" is "golden," and "rare like wine" and hard to resist, especially since "she" is "gracious," a loaded word, suggesting something more spiritual than sensual pleasure (e.g., wine). This ambivalence appears in *Home to Harlem*.

But if the word "prove" means "approve" or "verify," then another meaning comes to the fore, not a "test" but a kind of cosmic approval of McKay's "pride" in standing up to such a formidable opponent. For one brief "golden moment," the city acknowledges McKay's "warrior spirit"—the phrase is August Wilson's. He's Hector to the city's Achilles. He will lose, but the city's "strange love" is an expression of respect for a worthy adversary.

McKay's poem "The White House" should be seen as a companion piece to "The White City." City and Civitas have an etymological connection, as do home and city. For Augustine, the city is our true home, as it was for Plato and Aristotle. McKay was no exception. Jake expects Harlem to be home, to be "restorative," and though it's not, this does not negate the possibility that it could be (Fox 54). Similarly, the home in "The White House" is a metaphor for the hostile city. It is the "home" in reverse: cold, uninviting, unfamiliar, a hostile place—everything Gaston Bachelard says a "home" should not be. The house as "familiar" space "opens its doors to the world" (Bachelard 69). In McKay's poem, the "shuttered glass" shuts things in, keeps Black people out.

As students of the Harlem Renaissance know, Alain Locke had infuriated McKay by renaming the poem in both *The New Negro* ("The White Houses") and *Four Negro Poets* ("White Houses") (*CP* 309). McKay said that the original title of the poem was "symbolic" and did not refer to "the private homes of white people," but rather to "the vast modern edifice of American industry from which Negroes were effectively barred as a group." He denied that his title "meant the White House in Washington" (*A Long Way* 313, qtd. in *CP* 309). McKay was even more specific in a personal letter to Locke on April 18, 1927. Your new title, he told Locke made "me appear as a ridiculous, angry person hankering after the unattainable flesh-pots of the whites." In addition, he told Simon & Schuster, the publisher of *Four Negro Poets*, that Locke's title "places the poet in the cheap, childish, snarling position of crying out against white houses shut in his face." He was even more specific about the meaning of the title as "symbolic." The title and the poem exposed "the attitude of antagonistic white America as the Black poet sees and feels it."

William J. Maxwell is right to say that McKay "disingenuously" denied that the title referred to *the* White house (*CP* 309). It is also hard to accept his explanation in *A Long Way from Home* that the title targeted "American Industry," since nowhere in the poem is that subject mentioned. I want to suggest another possible interpretation of the poem's title, that it focuses on what McKay sees as the Ur-house. That is, it is the overarching umbrella that defines America, the rule of law that claims to ensure justice but in fact denies it. After all, the other "white house" is the Capitol Building in Washington, DC, a symbol of a new nation based on the idea of law and not on a King's whims. In the four lines before the poem's final couplet the theme of law encompasses all the images of enclosure in the sonnet:

> Oh I must search for wisdom every hour,
> Deep in my wrathful bosom sore and raw
> And find in it the superhuman power
> To hold me to the letter of your law (*CP* 148–49, lines 9–14)

The letter of the law, as the Apostle Paul observes, is at odds with "the new life of the spirit" (Rom. 7.6). Paul argues that Christians have "died to the law through the body of Christ" (Rom. 7.4); His "spirit" replaces the "letter" (law) of Augustine's earthly city.

McKay uses Paul's argument to redefine himself as a pagan in a world that is no longer Christian. The "White House" is the "white sepulcher" of the Pharisees, an enclosed world of "shuttered glass." McKay is not angry because he cannot enter the house. He's angry because he has to live in a civilization defined solely by law to the exclusion of everything else, for as Paul said, the "letter killeth." What it tries to kill or "hide," as Slavoj Žižek observes, is the "primordial prehistory of the community" (qtd. in Sue Chaplin 24) in which slavery and its aftermath are at the center of a hidden past that both defines and precedes the United States.

Law as a foundation of justice often assumes that this hidden past is unimportant or never existed since never recorded. Written law then becomes an abstraction from the age of reason, a problem in logic, and may be as fantastical as the mighty "white steel and stone" of New York. In that sense the classical architecture of the Capitol building, and New York's skyscrapers come from the same source, having their origin in a hidden will to power. McKay stands outside them both, as he says in *A Long Way from Home*: "I am a pagan. I am not a Christian. I am not white steel and stone" (134). The "White House" and "The White City" are thus cut from the same cloth, the same "steel and stone" whose foundation is the law. By shutting out the body, they attempt to imprison the spirit.

McKay treats the theme of the imprisoned spirit in terms of modern capitalism in a poem called "New York." The city's "steel and stone" recalls Egypt's grandeur as "obelisks [that] prick the eye with spires of gold!" (*CP* 239, lines 1–4). But this image of the city exists only as a capitalist fiction, a kind of urban Disneyland write large: "Its manufactures spreading piling high" can only weave "Manhattan's glorious fantasies" if there is advertising to sell the products (*CP* 339, lines 23–24, 9).

What is truly terrifying for McKay is that the language of the city used to hawk the goods has infected the language of poets. It's an Orwellian nightmare in which words that the poet once believed were "precious, rare" are now attached to stuff, turning "our thoughts, our dreams" as poets to "little prostitutes" (*CP* 240, lines 31–32). In "New York," McKay depicts the city as the locus of a Gothic landscape, a diseased civilization in which language, the metaphorical fountain of life, is contaminated.

He loved cities and he hated them, but he always found them fascinating (as did Langston Hughes), no more so than in his stunning poems about Harlem. He would explore in depth that "city within a city" in his novel *Home to Harlem* (1928) and elsewhere: his unpublished gangster novels *Harlem Glory* (1937, 1990) and *Amiable with Big Teeth* (1940, 2017), and his sociological study, *Harlem: Negro Metropolis* (1940). His poetry about Harlem would specifically focus on answering Locke's picture of Harlem in *The New Negro* (1925). Locke had argued that immigration to Harlem from all parts of the world and especially from the American South had created a "group life," a sense of community that he said was previously lacking in the African American scene. Now Black Americans shared a "common consciousness" in which the past "common condition" could be put behind them. Locke's language was pithy, aphoristic, and glib: in the past, the Negro had experienced "a problem in common rather than a life in common" (*New Negro* 7).

McKay thought Locke was too ready to find solutions where there were none. Rather than a new utopia in which history disappeared, Harlem was "a vaudeville that never stops!" (*CP*, "Lenox Avenue" 238, line 21). If vaudeville is a motley collection of unrelated acts—acrobats, jugglers, wrestling midgets, singers, comedians, and what not—then Harlem can only be defined as motley, movement, sounds (cabarets, dancing halls, crowds bursting out of subways). It is a city without a center, without Shaw's "cathedral silence," but whose center could be found in "The Harlem Dancer."

In a sequence of three poems first published in 1919, whose overall title is "Harlem," McKay's focus shifts from the unfocused medley of vaudeville in his 1938 poem "Lenox Avenue" to the image of the dance (*CP* 237). What is intriguing about the image of the dance in "Harlem" is that it takes on a different meaning in each poem, one that progressively becomes more complex. In the first poem, dance is an escape for African Americans from the world outside the cabaret: "Dancing their world of shadows to forget" (*CP* 236, I, line 14). In the second poem, the dancers become the dance, so much so that McKay as a witness becomes himself a dancer—as poet: "my heart then dances/ To the lithe bodies gliding slowly by" (*CP* II, lines 1–2). The "rapture" he experiences takes the form of an epiphany in which the dance is what defines the race within the city of Harlem: "The deathless spirit of a race revealing, /Not one false step, no note that rings not true!" The dance becomes a song, its harmony is what centers and sustains Harlem's citizens: "For them the dance is the great joy of life" (*CP* 236 II, lines 8–9, 14).

In the third poem, McKay creates a new gestalt by combining two themes from the first two poems. The dancers are "the outcasts of the earth," but now the dance becomes more than "the great joy of life." It is an expression that rivals the greatest art: "they dance with poetry in their eyes" (*CP* 237, III, line 9). Their gifts are those of the gods: "The gifts divine are theirs, music and laughter, / All other things, however great, come after" (*CP* 237, lines 13–14). The dance haunts McKay, as the song of the "highland lass" haunted Wordsworth in "The Solitary Reaper." What he sees in this poem is that America's "outcasts" are Harlem's true artists, capturing eternal truths within the quotidian flow of existence. His poem, "Black

Belt Slummers," is a send-up of those white visitors to Harlem looking for material to "mine" and who romanticize the lowly as the salt of the earth, as long as they remain in the earth and do not change. McKay says in the voice of one such "dilettante" that "they love not Beauty who desire such change" (*CP* 239, line 24).

McKay's dance is an ever-changing movement, "lithe bodies gliding slowly by," whereas these white artists want a fixed urban tableau, not all that different from the white intellectuals of *I'll Take My Stand* (1930) who desire the South to remain agrarian with everyone in their proper place. McKay later revised these three poems in 1935, as William J. Maxwell notes (*CP* 364). The line "lithe bodies gliding slowly by" bears an uncanny resemblance to Hart Crane's "Legend" (1924): "As silent as a mirror is believed/ Realities plunge in silence by." Crane, who wrote "Black Tambourine" (1921), knew that Black "Realities" glided slowly by in the invisible cellar of American life.

II

William J. Maxwell rightly sees that the focus of critics on McKay's "antipathy to cities" is not only misleading but diminishes his complexity (*CP* xxix). In publishing previously unpublished poems, Maxwell has greatly increased our understanding of McKay's urban perspective. And he is quite right to note that McKay's reflections on the pastoral world in Jamaica often occur in a city setting (*CP* xxviii). But they are not "recollected in urban tranquility," as Maxwell argues. The city, Walter Benjamin has said, leaves its "stigmata" upon memory, so that what is remembered is active, not passive—that is, the city's perspective intensifies and clarifies what we remember (Benjamin 169). Also, what McKay remembered and recreates is filtered through two literary traditions that he encountered in Walter Jekyll's library: the eighteenth-century English satirists, specifically Alexander Pope and Jonathan Swift, and the Romantic poets of the English nineteenth century: "Byron, Shelley, Keats, Blake . . . Whitman" and a host of others, including Wordsworth and Coleridge (*Rebel Sojourner* 80).

Here is an example of where the two traditions come together in McKay's poem called "Dawn in New York." The poem begins with an echo of Wordsworth's "Composed upon Westminster Bridge" and ends with an anti-pastoral motif from Swift's poem "A Description of the Morning." In McKay's poem, the beauty of New York at dawn, despite its "cheerless domes," revives his "spirit": "My spirit to its spirit thrills. / Almost the mighty city is asleep" (*CP* 172. lines 4–5) A similar sentiment is felt by Wordsworth. London at dawn wears the beauty of the morning like a "garment," and for the moment "the very houses seem asleep" (288, line 13).

While Wordsworth's poem continues to celebrate the sleeping city in terms of the pastoral, McKay turns to Swiftian satire within his poem. Swift's "Morning" poem sees the city's dawn in a grim light. As dawn awakens in London, "Betty" silently steals from "her Master's bed." Then the city slowly becomes alive in terms of a sequence of ever louder noises: men hawking coal, chimney sweeps drowning them out in "shriller notes" and "Brickdust Moll" bringing the dawn's ugly sounds to a crescendo. The poem ends with a return to an uneasy silence, as bailiffs look for criminals and as "schoolboys," who reluctantly walk to class, "lag with satchels in their hands" (*The Complete Poems* 107–8, lines 3, 17–18). In McKay's poem, as the city wakes up, Swift's reluctant "schoolboys" are replaced by McKay himself who "darkly-rebel [goes] to my work" in the hostile city (*CP* 173, line 14). Yet McKay also incorporates the grotesqueries of Swift's poem "Description of a City Shower" in which the rain brings not renewed life via a pastoral poem but swells London's "kennels" with

> Sweepings from butchers' stalls, dung, guts, and blood,
> Drowned puppies, stinking sprats, all drenched in mud,
> Dead cats and turnip tops come tumbling down the flood. (114, lines 61–63)

In McKay these become the men and women of "garish nights" whose "wine-weakened" eyes and disheveled clothes turn them into "grotesques beneath the strong electric lights." The surrealism of this moment disappears as night's "shadows" fade with the city's dawn, and we are left with a bleary-eyed poet going to a meaningless job (*CP* 173, lines 12–14).

McKay would also rewrite Swift's two antipastoral city poems in "The Tired Worker" and, even more specifically, in "On the Road." At the end of the latter poem, the white passengers step "lightly' from the train when they arrive at the city's station in the early evening, but the railroad waiters "pass out weary, listless, glum" and "spend their tips on harlots, cards and rum" (*CP* 172, lines 11–14). This is Swift's "Description of Morning" at the onset of night.

The endings of "Dawn in New York" and "On the Road" mark a nice distinction between McKay's use of Romantic irony and the satiric irony employed by McKay when he rewrites Swift's comic poems.

McKay could appropriate Swift's "savage indignation" to expose a cadaver at the core of white American culture, but he could also use

Swiftian laughter to ridicule pretense of another kind, illustrated by the proverb "the higher the ape goes the more he shows his tail." In *Banana Bottom*, Bita and Priscilla Craig visit the house of a man of wealth and refinement who owns "a beautifully bound Collection of Great British Authors," and when asked by Priscilla which author "was his favorite," he responds by saying he has no favorite: "they are all the same to me. I admire them all." Then Bita pulls down a copy of *Gulliver's Travels* and finds "the pages uncut" (*Banana Bottom* 214). This delicate Horatian satire is a gloss on what has occurred earlier to Herald Newton Day who, in pursuing a life of purity and cleanliness, "had descended from the dizzy heights of holiness to the very bottom of the beast" (175). A highly educated young man living on one plane, Mr. Day rapidly descended to another when he was discovered fornicating with a goat ("the very bottom of the beast"), or as Bita later put it a "quadruped" (219). And with that, we remember that Gulliver at the end of *Gulliver's Travels* prefers his horses to his own family, telling his "gentle readers" that anyone who has the "absurd vice" of pride should not "appear in his sight" (Swift, *Essential Writings* 502). Yet he is the one "smitten with Pride," the human ape or Yahoo who shows his anus. Modeling his behavior on his beloved, completely rational Houyhnhnms, he spends more time in the stables instead of with his wife and children, whom he can barely tolerate. McKay extends Swift's irony to include its sexual implications.

McKay's satirical interest in Swift is linked to his attraction to the grotesqueries in Goya. All three artists use irony bordering on the Gothic to expose the dark side of human nature. One device, of course, is obscenity: Swift and excrement, McKay and bestiality, humankind reduced to excrement or lust. As Matthew Hodgart puts it, "the effect of obscenity in satire is to level all men, and to level them downwards, removing the distinctions of rank and wealth. The satirist's aim is to strip men bare, and apart from physique one naked man is much like another" (30). The same is true of institutions. In *Romance in Marseille*, "The Christian Unity of Negro Tribes" offers its "spiritual assistance" to Lafala after discovering that he is now rich. McKay exposes its motive through an anagram: "C.U.N.T" (*Romance* 19). Belinda's beauty in Pope's *The Rape of the Locke* blinds her to the reality that she is mortal. She may see herself as a goddess in the mirror, and in the adoring eyes of her admirers, but Clarissa reminds her that her beauty will not charm "the Small-pox," or chase "old Age away" (canto 5, line 96). Nor will Bita's English education erase the reality that Crazy Bow "was first," something the folk community will not let her forget. Moreover, the social class bestowed upon her by the Craigs will not protect her from the vicissitudes of Jamaican society, from the courtship of the pompous Herald Newton Day to the gossip of the Grog Shop to the brutal lust of the parvenue Arthur Glengley.

But the irony most important to McKay is Romantic irony, inherited from the English Romantic poets and involving the mystery of human memory and perception. Gerald McNiece describes Romantic irony succinctly as a "multiple-levelled way of seeing in several directions," especially as this involves the question of time and place (135). It's an extension of McKay's multidimensional art.

The Romantics, including Wordsworth, Coleridge, and Keats, understood that both our present sense of time and our memory of the past could not be circumscribed within neat boxes or definitions such as past, present, and future. The past itself, for instance, could reveal itself to the human mind very much like the future. As Kenneth Burke notes: "We think of the present as 'growing out of' the past. Yet if we 'began with' the present, and next studied the documents of yesterday, then those of the day before, etc., the past would 'gradually emerge' for us 'out of' our starting point in the present. The successive disclosures of the ever-remoter past would thus be a constantly unfolding future" (*Rhetoric of Religion* 246).

Burke is also useful in explaining the Romantic poets' conception of place, especially as it explained a "multiple-levelled way of seeing." A logical positivist, Burke argues, would dismiss the possibility that "New York is in Iowa," but a poet would not, especially a Romantic poet. "Has one ever stood, for instance, in some little outlying town, on the edge of the wilderness, and watched a train go by. Has one perhaps suddenly felt that the train, and its tracks, were a kind of arm of the city, reaching out across the continent, quite as though it were simply Broadway itself extended." In this sense, continued Burke, "'New York is in Iowa' is 'poetically' true" (*The Philosophy of Literary Form* 144). Burke's argument, of course, is indebted to Keats's brilliant insight that a poetic reality is a human reality, that our conception of place and time (its "uncertainties, Mysteries, and doubts") cannot be reduced to an "irritable reaching after fact & reason" (Perkins 1209). And of course, one of McKay's favorite writers, D. H. Lawrence, would make a similar point when he said, "growing crops make the sun shine." What Lawrence was arguing against was a one-dimensional view of causation, human or otherwise, or, as Burke would say, causation reduced to a "kick in the rear," which "too patently ignores the operations of biological growth" (qtd. in Burke, *Permanence and Change* 230). Those complex "operations" also involve a human conception of time—which for the Romantics was not clock time.

Wordsworth's famous "Lines Composed a Few Miles Above Tintern Abbey" embodies a conception of time and place that has a direct bearing on some of McKay's major poems. The poem begins with Wordsworth's return to a specific place in nature above the Abbey that he visited five years ago. This visit in the *now* results in a stunning insight about the past. In the *now*, he has an epiphany. He perceives that these "beauteous forms" in nature *then* had recharged his spiritual batteries when he returned to "towns and cities" five years ago (lines 23, 27). The "tranquil restoration" that resulted from that event five years ago had an impact on his life in terms of "little nameless, unremembered, acts / Of kindness and of love" that he now attributes to that precise experience five years prior (lines 30, 34–35). It is this moment in the *now* that makes him have that epiphany, that nature had shaped his life within those five years in ways that he did not perceive *then*. It is only in the here and now, on July 23, 1798, that he understands the significance of the unfolding past.

Notice the significance of the date as time. As calendar time, it's meaningless for his life—hence the irony of the subtitle: "on Revisiting the Banks of the Wye during a Tour: July 13, 1798." In the poem neither the Abbey or the Wye appear, nor do the large events of 1798: Napoleon's Egyptian campaign, the failed Irish insurgency, and Wolf Tone's capture. What Wordsworth focuses upon is a specific spot in nature above the Abbey, a place that five years ago had a momentous impact on *his* life. His return to this place gives him a new conception of time, a foreshadowing of Henri Bergson's "duree," "lived time" as opposed to official time. In the poem, the past is never quite over, as it becomes a source of solace and strength in the future.

The present moment also promises a hopeful future, the hope that this *now* will be "life and food / For future years" (lines 63–64). Moreover, he sees his sister Dorothy, who is by his side in the *now*, as his younger self. Her "wild eyes" (l. 119) were once his. In the "after years," when she will have outlived the "wild ecstasies" of youth, she will remember this moment as seminal, the cause of her "mind" becoming "a mansion for all lovely forms" (lines 138–40).

Here then is Romantic irony. We just don't live in one time or place but rather dwell in them all at once. The past can unfold as the future, the present can unfold not only as Wordsworth's future but Dorothy's as well. Place is also fluid. Memory of the city can shine light on the present rural moment. In this regard, Wordsworth's poem illustrates Burke's "New York in Iowa." Wordsworth can have the perspective that he has at the poem's beginning because of his experience in "towns and cities" since he last visited this spot in nature. The city in his past has illuminated the present moment. He can *see* the present moment in terms of all its temporal and spatial dimensions because of what he has experienced in the city, in terms of how the city actively stimulates memory.

In "Frost at Midnight," Coleridge too plays with various levels of time and place. The poet describes a harmonious moment at midnight in a cozy cottage with his "cradled infant" in winter (line 7). The perfection of the moment is symbolized by the "secret ministry" of frost as it weaves its magic both outside and inside. Its cold beauty is at one with the poet's sense of well-being in his cottage with his child and with his memory. His perception of the soot on the grate conjures up his own childhood in the city where in school he watched a similar fluttering ribbon in a classroom fireplace. There the past becomes the present but also "unfolds as the future," as he, in the remembered classroom, "dreamt / Of my sweet birth-place, and the old church tower." Half asleep in the classroom, he imagines that the fluttering soot promises the entrance of a hoped for "stranger": "townsman, or aunt, or sister more beloved" (line 42). Thus, the past "unfolds" in multiple dimensions: as the memory of a birthplace, as the memory of a future within the past (a longed for "*stranger's* face") (line 41).

These moments within memory return him to the present in his room with his child. He claims a better future for his son than he had in his past in the city, "pent 'mid cloisters dim" (line 52). His son will be nurtured by the natural world, and thus "all seasons will be sweet to thee" (line 65). Returning to the present, the narrator makes a connection between his son's hopeful future and the "secret ministry of frost" that began the poem (line 72). The poem's last image, the "silent icicles, / Quietly shining to the quiet moon," links the present harmonious moment to the remembered past (lines 73–74). The present beauty of the frost not only presages the sweet seasons of the son's future but is itself a symbol of the unity of the poet's memory in which past, present, and future are woven into one (Perkins 422–23).

Significantly, the urban perspective in the remembered past frames the happy moment in the present. The beauty of nature, the sense of well-being in the room—these are perceived by the poet through the lens of his remembered childhood in the "great city." Even the city's negative space in the past, its confinement, shapes the way the poet perceives his son's expansive future.

McKay's poem "Winter in the Country," whose title echoes "Frost at Midnight," captures Coleridge's playful use of romantic irony in terms of time and space. McKay's poem is ostensibly about the "country" and the poet's regret that he must return to "the city's dirty basement room" (*CP*

170, line 14). Yet once in that room, the memory of the country, "this very wind, the winter birds, / The glory of the soft sunset, / Come *there* to me in words" (lines 23–25) (my emphasis). The strange place of the confined, urban room is paradoxically the place where creativity occurs, just as the beauty of the Harlem Dancer's dance is amplified because of the "strange place" of a Harlem street. In much of McKay's urban poetry, there is often a yearning for home, but ironically it is often the urban setting that gives the poet a heightened sense of home. This is not "emotion recollected in tranquility." Quite the opposite: emotion is heightened by the urban setting in which it occurs.

If we look at one of McKay's best-known poems, "The Tropics in New York," we can see its connection to Coleridge's poem in terms of Romantic irony and how the urban setting frames the poet's memory of the rural past. This wonderful poem is worth quoting in full:

> Bananas ripe and green, and ginger-root,
>   Cocoa in pods and alligator pears,
> And tangerines and mangoes and grape fruit,
>   Fit for the highest prize at parish fairs,
>
> Set in the window, bringing memories
>   Of fruit-trees laden by low-singing rills,
> And dewy dawns and mystical blue skies
>   In benediction over nun-like hills.
>
> My eyes grew dim, and I could no more gaze;
>   A wave of longing through my body swept,
> And hungry for the old, familiar ways,
>   I turned aside and bowed my head and wept. (*CP* 154)

Note that the fruit is "set in the window," an image noted by Michael North to suggest that the irony here should be directed at McKay, "a special irony in the situation of the transplanted Jamaican staring at the fruit imported from his homeland and carefully displayed behind glass. What was common at home becomes a rare delicacy, not the recipient of prizes but a prize itself. What strange process is it that can bring both product and person so far from home and then erect a wall of glass between them?" (120).

But could we not look at this image in another way, one that illustrates Romantic irony? The enclosed frame conditions perception and is a metaphor for the city itself. The fruit exists in an artificial garden, a *hortus conclusus* created by the fruit seller's window. It's the city's artifice that triggers McKay's memory of the past as something sacred, something blessed ("benediction"). His lament for the loss of the "old, familiar ways" is an example of romantic irony in that the moment in time and space in which McKay has these feelings occurs in the modern city of New York. The urban setting not only heightens McKay's awareness of the pastoral past but its preciousness. Also, the fruit in the window is Marcel Proust's madeleine cookie in *Remembrance of Things Past*—that is, a sensory experience that evokes things supposedly forgotten.

There is an additional irony here. The "old, familiar ways" are not by definition rural virtues. In his poem, "The Desolate City," he complains that "gone, gone forever [are] the familiar forms / to which the city once so dearly clung.... Forever gone, the fond familiar forms" (*CP* 205, lines 71, 79). In the poem, the fountains have dried up, the pools are stagnant, and the flowers breathe a "deadly poison" (*CP* lines 21, 29–30, 45). If the city's "familiar forms" are dead, it is necessary to cultivate one's own garden, as Bita will do in *Banana Bottom*, but what she will also do is re-create Augustine's invisible city in which the sacred garden is once more present.

McKay will use Romantic irony involving the rural/urban connection in both the poems "Home Thoughts" and "Subway Wind." In the former, his memory of what "must be happening *there*" is brought to the surface by what is happening "here / Amid the city's noises" (*CP* 156, lines 1–3). In "Subway Wind," the "captive wind" in the bowels of the city reminds him of his tropical home in which the trade winds "float" above his island "fresh and free" (*CP* 178, line 16).

But the poem that best illustrates McKay's indebtedness to both Wordsworth and Coleridge's use of romantic irony is the poem which he will use as a preface to the first story in his short story collection *Gingertown* (1932): "The Harlem Dancer."

Again, the urban setting, as the title indicates, is what frames what the poet perceives. The poem depicts a moment in time and space in which a young girl dances and sings to a group of laughing and "applauding" young men and "prostitutes" (*CP* 172, line 1). Their "passionate gaze" is simultaneously mocking, puzzled, and lustful (l. 12). The poet's gaze is different from the gaze that desires and devours; he sees the girl's dance as an aesthetic moment that reveals, through memory, a homeplace at odds with "that strange place," a street in Harlem, in which the dancer finds herself (l. 14).

The boys and girls who watch her see none of this. Their "gaze" is rooted in the finite and limited world of the now, whereas the narrator sees her dance as an act that transcends time and space. Although the poet believes the dancer's true "self" is not in that "strange place," he most certainly is—his presence as poet is what gives her presence a voice that is different from her song.

There are two conceptions of place in the poem, as there are two conceptions of time; her time and his. Moreover, the question of *nostos*, home, multiplies: her home is an imagined space, a pastoral, but the poet's home is the urban space where creativity occurs. Dionysus will always need an interpreter and a partner.

William J. Maxwell notes that McKay's poem "The Desolate City" is "indebted" to T. S. Eliot's *The Waste Land*, "published the year before McKay's poem was composed" (*CP* 344). There are two other sources: James Thomson's nineteenth-century poem *The City of Dreadful Night* (1874) and Coleridge's "Dejection: An Ode" (1817). Both belong to a Romantic literary tradition that was at odds with Eliot the "classicist" and an admirer of the Elizabethan and metaphysical poets.

In *A Long Way from Home*, McKay spends two pages talking about Thomson's "great" poem, quoting lines in which the "desert" overwhelms the city (18–19). He even quotes Frank Harris who says that "perhaps you have a *City of Dreadful Night* pent up in you," and as if fulfilling Harris's prophesy, he includes "The Desolate City" in *A Long Way from Home*. Thomson's poem influenced Eliot as well, the polluted Thames alluding to Thomson's "waste marshes" (Thomson I, line 25), but Thomson's connection to McKay's poem is the dead garden at the heart of the city: "Though the Garden of thy life be wholly waste, the sweet flowers withered, the fruit-trees barren," there is always the "Vine of Death" as a release (Thomson I, (1)).

McKay recycles Thomson's imagery. In McKay's diseased city, the garden's "flowers" are "breathing deadly poison from their lips" (l. 45), an allusion perhaps to another garden in the great American Romantic short story, Nathaniel Hawthorne's "Rappaccini's Daughter": "And every lovely moth that wanders by, / And of the blossoms fatal nectar sips, / Is doomed to drooping stupor, there to die" (*CP* 204, lines 46–48). Rappacccini protects his daughter by making her immune to what kills the intruding insects, shielding her from the outside world by condemning her to live in the deadly garden.

McKay's deadly garden no longer harbors children, but it was not always this way:

There was a time, when, happy with the birds,
The little children clapped their hands and laughed;

And midst the clouds the glad winds heard their words
And blew down all the merry ways to waft
The music through the scented fields of flowers. (*CP* 205, lines 61–65)

These "familiar ways" are gone, familiar not because they are rural virtues in a pastoral but in a living garden in a city. McKay repeats the first four words from a passage in Coleridge's "Dejection: An Ode":

There was a time when, though my path was rough,
   This joy within me dallied with distress,
And all misfortunes were but as the stuff
   Whence Fancy made me dreams of happiness. (Perkins 433, lines 76–79)

Coleridge uses a metaphor that McKay will borrow, in "The Desolate City" and elsewhere, to express his dead artistic self: the "fountains" of Coleridge's creativity have dried up (Perkins 433. line 46). His opium addiction "suspends what nature gave me at my birth, / My shaping spirit of Imagination" (lines 85–86, Perkins 433). His creative imagination is only one manifestation of the fountain. The other is the "mighty fountain" in *Kubla Khan*," the sexual energy that is the source of Kubla's ordered "gardens." For beneath the artifice of the "sunny spots of greenery" is the chaotic sexual energy that creates it: "as if this earth in fast thick pants were breathing, / A mighty fountain momently were forced" which erupts in a "swift half-intermitted burst" (Perkins 431. lines 18–20).

In McKay's poem, the sexual metaphor is the same: "the many fountains no more spurt," and "the pools lie poisonously still" (*CP* 204, lines 30–31). The first line of "The Desolate City" makes the connection to Coleridge quite clear: "My spirit is a pestilential city." The city itself is a metaphor for not only McKay's physical illness but for his creative impotency—the thesis of Coleridge's great poem. The irony of course is that while both poets complain in their poems of creative malfunction, they nevertheless manage to write two great poems.

McKay's treatment of the city in "The Desolate City," is different from Eliot's depiction of London in *The Waste Land* because each is grounded in a different literary tradition. McKay's focus on the self is at odds with Eliot's impersonal artistry: "Poetry is not a turning loose of emotion, but an escape from emotion; it is not the expression of personality, but an escape from personality" (Eliot, *Selected Prose* 43). Not so for the Romantics whose poems often focus on the self from Wordsworth's "egotistical sublime," to Byron's *Manfred*, to Whitman's "Song of Myself."

Although McKay's "pestilential city" is a metaphor for his sick "spirit," the poem's grotesque, surreal imagery ("a host of yellow flies . . . / That came down *snow-thick* from the freighted skies") has a racial tinge to it, especially the "skeleton's caress" embedded in the urban garden's "loveliness" (*CP* 204, lines 55, 57) (my emphasis). But the truly distinguishing feature of McKay's city is its deadly stillness, "as cold as death" (line 51). In *The Ancient Mariner* after the Mariner kills the albatross, all "motion" comes to a stop ("As idle as a painted ship / Upon a painted ocean") (lines 116–18, Perkins 407). In McKay's poem, the stillness has a history—everything has remained the same despite Emancipation.

A good example of the difference between Eliot and McKay is their use of James Joyce. Eliot sees the greatness of Joyce's *Ulysses* in terms of its "mythical method" which gives structure to "the immense panorama of futility and anarchy which is contemporary history" (*Selected Prose* 177). Eliot will praise Joyce for reconfiguring the past in *Ulysses* so that his text, rooted in myth but taking place in contemporary Dublin, reshapes our view of the past, reorders the monumental (white) literary tradition. After *Ulysses*, we will never read Homer's *Odyssey* quite the same way again. That tradition is what Eliot believes a writer must master before he even begins to write. This is what Eliot means by saying that a writer must have a "historical sense" (*Selected Prose* 38). It is a literary tradition we would now call the "canon," one tightly defined by a "historical sense" that does not include African American history or literature within it.

In contrast, McKay will use the tension between Dionysus and Apollo in Joyce (by way of Nietzsche) to express the tension within himself as an artist, the major theme of *Banjo*. He will express two versions of the artist through the image of the dance, the one who focuses on the artifice of the dance, the other on its ecstasy. In the letter to Harold Jackman quoted earlier (April 22, 1928), McKay had described the dance as something religious, something beyond passion, but in the same letter, he was also responding to something Jackman had said previously about music, and by implication about dance: "this business of feeling the music so deeply that we almost become intoxicated is beyond me." McKay responded: "If you have never been intoxicated by music, I feel sorry for you" (qtd. in Gosciak 15). In this letter, McKay describes himself as both Apollo and Dionysus. Thus, McKay's tradition is more fluid than Eliot's. It's whatever he finds in it that is useful, but for him the most useful is that which reflects his own "contemporary history" as a Black man in a hostile world.

That said, both *The Waste Land* and "The Desolate City" are poems, like Yeats's "The Second Coming," that are artistic responses to the Great

War. And both chart the desecration of the landscape as a symbol of some deep-seated malaise in the culture. For Eliot, the crisis comes earlier when science, the Reformation, and the Industrial Revolution break apart the unified sensibility of a culture. That sensibility was reflected by the metaphysical poets, and we see its fragmentation in *The Waste Land*. When Sweeney, Eliot's lowlife Irishman, visits a London brothel, Marvell's great poem, "To His Coy Mistress," serves as commentary: "But at my back from time to time I hear / The sounds of horns and motors, which shall bring / Sweeney to Mrs. Porter in the spring" (lines 196–98). The passion of Marvell's "carpe diem" poem, which moves suddenly and effectively from high comedy to the grim reaper, is at odds with what Mrs. Porter has to offer, diluted passion with a price tag. The gap between Marvell's poem and "contemporary history" is the waste land itself, a world in which the artistic past is seen as "withered stumps of time" (line 104). It is this world of fragments that the Fisher King has shored against his ruins. Although Eliot put his fragments together into a collage that form the poem itself, it is doubtful whether the Fisher King's "ruins" (his sexual impotency and Western Civilization's spiritual "dryness") will ever recover from ruin.

McKay too deals in fragments (the fruit "set in the window"), prostitutes, and sordid urban landscapes, but the literary past that orders these things is the Romantic tradition and Coleridge's imagination redefined through a racial and personal sensibility. Also, his urban satire will be indebted to eighteenth-century authors like Swift and Pope and reimagined to fit his "contemporary history." Swift's "savage indignation" will become "If We Must Die" and "The White House." And he will revise Hogarth's *The Harlot's Progress* (1833) to reflect a racial world that Hogarth could not have imagined.

There is no lack of subtlety or complexity in McKay's city poems, nor in his novels. He can write a comic antipastoral on the order of Thomas Hardy's "The Ruined Maid," ("A Country Girl," *CP* 77) or focus upon those qualities that distinguish a single city from its fellows. He can use the city as a trope for the self ("The Desolate City") or he can focus on the city's complexities, as he does in *Home to Harlem* (1928), *Banjo* (1929), and *Romance in Marseille* (circa 1929–1931). Although McKay's use of Romantic irony can be found primarily in his poetry, there are moments in *Banana Bottom* where the comedy goes in "multiple directions."

CHAPTER 2

THE SCENE OF THE CRIME

Hogarth, Hemingway, and *Home to Harlem*

"Home to Harlem" was the grandest thing in years.
Dancing, swift, and alive.
—LANGSTON HUGHES TO CLAUDE MCKAY, JUNE 27, 1929 (*SELECTED LETTERS* 87)

Home to Harlem is not a whodunit, nor could it be categorized as a crime novel, but crimes and violence permeate the novel. Harlem is the scene of crimes in which the scene is the crime. McKay's Billy Biasse is the detective who points this out: "Wese too thick together in Harlem. Wese all just lumped together without a chanst to choose and so we nacherally hate one another" (*Home to Harlem* 285). To illustrate his point, he tells Jake about a "spade prof" standing on a corner holding books and handing out Marxist pamphlets who is punched in the face by "a bad n----r" for no reason. Billy socks the assailant in return but has this to say to Jake: "I tell you, boh, Harlem is lousy with crazy bad n----rs, as tough as Hell's kitchen, and I always travel with my gun ready" (285–86). This is probably the source of Hughes's "Nigger Hell" and not Susy's tirade against the lust she perceives in Harlem's cabarets: "This here Harlem is a stinking sink of iniquity, N----r hell! That's what it is" (99). Either way, hell is the legacy of slavery that haunts McKay's cityscape. Jake returns "home" in 1919 to an ongoing war in Harlem, after not being allowed to fight in the war "over there" because of his color. Alan Hochschild puts duality in another context, the larger American scene in which the government targeted all dissidents during the Great War: "Just as the war in Europe was being fought on several fronts, so was the war at home" (83).

Harlem was originally Dutch (Haarlem), and the Dutch brought the first slaves to the New World in 1619. Before it became New York, New Amsterdam was a trading port, foreshadowing the World Trade Center, a tradition of capitalism whose focus was (and remains) property. Fitzgerald captures that theme nicely at the end of *The Great Gatsby* in which the Dutch, having glimpsed the New World as a second paradise, proceed to cut down the "trees that had made way for Gatsby's house" (Fitzgerald 189). Amiri Baraka would call his play *Dutchman* (1964) because property such as Gatsby's house includes human property. Jones's Clay is only one of many seduced by Lulu's promises, doomed like others to live and die in the confined space of a New York subway, a Black version of the myth of the Flying Dutchman. In *Home to Harlem*, as Billy notes, Harlem's segregated space is a repetition of the slave pen.

Near the end of *Home to Harlem*, McKay gives us a story within a story. In a separate chapter (chapter 17), he has Ray tell a story about Jerco and Rosalind, a pimp and his prostitute, whose devotion to one another left a profound impact upon his life. His upper-class friend James Grant had referred to pimps as "the last ditch" of human behavior, and Ray responds with a tale of someone in that ditch who "also loved" (*Home* 242, 245). People, in other words, are not always what they seem. But the ultimate irony of the story that Ray tells is that although Grant and his class can pretend to be above the fray because of their education and money, their smug, self-satisfied world is just as vulnerable as the one Jerco and Rosalind occupy.

The tale also works on another level, something like Kenneth Burke's "representative anecdote" (Burke, *Grammar of Motives* 323–25). Although it seems to be a story in a minor key, everything in the novel swirls around it. It symbolizes the maelstrom in which the Harlemites live and die. It underscores the irony of the novel's title—Harlem is a city of the homeless (Whalen 145). It is not only Jake who becomes homeless in Harlem—it is Ray as well. His background explains why he came to Harlem in the first place. The American marines invaded his native homeland Haiti in 1915, "an invasion," as Mark Whalen notes, "that critics such as James Weldon Johnson likened to Germany's invasion of Belgium" in World War I (144). Ray is rendered homeless before he even arrives in Harlem (*Home* 138, 154–55). Together Jake and Ray share the spotlight as McKay's protagonists, the natural man and the intellectual, two sides of McKay himself.

The transatlantic situation of Haiti calls attention to McKay's hidden theme about Harlem. It too has been invaded by America's white power structure. It can't be a home for Jake or any African Americans because of its invasion and occupation by the United States. However, McKay plays with the idea that Harlem is a possible home, suggested by the "to" in the novel's title: in the direction of. As we have seen in chapter 1, home for

McKay takes different forms: it can be a village or a city that has a spiritual center, or a room where creativity flows ("Winter in the Country") or a street that is transformed by a performance ("The Harlem Dancer"). It can be a kind of no-man's-land in a positive sense, "owned by nobody" (Whalen 81) despite being "owned." It's space that is continually being contested, redefined, and reshaped by the vibrancy of Black life, especially by its cabaret and queer culture. Eric H. Newman argues that queer "cruising" in McKay's work creates temporary, shape-shifting communities that form and reform like an amoeba:

> Rather than fixed in a domicile, city or relationship, home emerges across *Home to Harlem* and *Banjo* as that which is discovered in the perpetual movement epitomized by the novels' cruising narratives. Cruising, in other words, finds a home everywhere in a world where the traditional, closed-off home is no longer a stable object for building and maintaining a happy life. In its promiscuous openness to the other, and in its refusal to invest in any one object as a sustainable resource for pleasure or happiness, cruising in these novels offers a very contemporary mode of surviving the conditions of capitalist modernity. (176)

This is very nicely put, but I would argue that there is a downside to this perspective as it pertains to Jake. In one sense, he's a vagabond artist like McKay himself. He responds passionately to beauty, to exciting situations, and to new encounters. And he's a man who lives by a code, imposing a strict discipline upon himself in certain specific situations (he won't scab, he won't hit women, and he faces the world without whining). Yet this discipline is at odds with the dark side of his Dionysian life: he gets the clap, and he almost gets killed. The question arises: to what extent does Jake's passion for living compromise his attempt to make an artistry of his own life? His exuberance for living makes him the vital person that he is, and it is commensurate with the vitality in the Harlem he wants to call home, but it also creates the possibility of self-destruction ("quick to snap up any tempting morsel of poisoned meat thrown carelessly on the pavement"—228, 229). Langston Hughes's two views of McKay's novel ("Nigger Hell" and "dancing, swift, and alive") is an accurate assessment of McKay's twin themes.

Given his English education, McKay would know of William Hogarth, the famous eighteenth-century engraver and artist. He mentions him in *Amiable with Big Teeth* in the context of an ironic portrait of a Black artist who claims fame by association with both Hogarth and Goya (*Amiable with Big Teeth* 232). More specifically, Ray's tale of Rosalind echoes Hogarth; Jerco's death, Goya. Rosalind's tale is a rewritten version of Hogarth's famous series of engravings called *A Harlot's Progress* (1732).

Hogarth called his narrative series of engravings artistic portraits of "modern moral subjects." And, as David Bindman notes, they depict "the moral journey of the soul toward salvation or perdition," which is expressed through "the geographical progress through London" (55, 79). Ray's warning to Jake, who like Hogarth's "rake" has contracted a sexually transmitted disease ("You can't just go on like a crazy ram goat as if you were living in the Middle Ages" (206)), points to a parallel between modern Harlem and eighteenth-century London. That McKay bookends his novel with Felice, the prostitute who saves Jake from the fate of the "ram goat" and herself from Molly's fate, is not a denial of Hogarth's "progress" series but a revision. Jake and Felice find "happiness" by fleeing perdition, but the happy ending is not the novel's core. Its real core is the perdition they flee.

McKay and Hogarth seem strange bedfellows—a Black modernist whose Harlem has its source in racial conflict and an artist from another century and country whose satire focused on high and low life in contemporary London. Yet both McKay's Harlem and Hogarth's London are versions of Vanity Fair in *Pilgrim's Progress*, another book in Walter Jekyll's library. If we wonder about the English Hogarth as an influence on a Harlem Renaissance writer, we need to consider not only McKay's nomadic life (Harlem was only one of many cities he lived in and wrote about), but his education in his native Jamaica.

Looking back, McKay is grateful that Walter Jekyll had put his "excellent library at my disposal" (*A Long Way* 13). What the young McKay read in Jekyll's library are mostly English authors, the British Romantics (especially "the lyrics of Shelley and Keats") and "the late Victorian poets" but also Milton's *Paradise Lost*, Pope's *Dunciad* and *Essay on Man*, and "the Elizabethan lyrics," as well as books reflecting Jekyll's eclectic tastes, ranging from Dante to Goethe to Baudelaire (*A Long Way* 13). Only one American work makes the list, Whitman's *Leaves of Grass*. Hogarth's presence in Ray's tale should not be surprising, especially since so many literary artists like Henry Fielding admired him (Paulson 202). Jake in *Home to Harlem* is a kind of modern-day Tom Jones in need of prudence in his dealings with women (*Home* 206).

Yet prudence is not going to save Rosalind. She and Jerco both depend upon her life as a working girl to support them. Their life seems romantic to the young Ray (but immoral to the students in the boarding house where they all live), but when she contracts syphilis and dies, everything suddenly falls apart, ending with Jerco's grotesque suicide. In describing the absence left by Rosalind's death, Ray focuses on clothing that was once animated by her presence, especially the fur coat that Jerco refused to sell when she was sick.

Here is Ray's description of their wardrobe when she was still alive: "Rosalind's coat was hanging there, and it gave me a spooky feeling, for it looked so much more like the real Rosalind than the woman that was dozing there on the bed" (258). Other clothes are "hanging there too"—silk and satin gowns—and in the corner "soiled champagne-colored silk stockings," four pairs of expensive shoes. What this catalog of clothes refers to is the penultimate engraving in the *A Harlot's Progress* series. Molly is dying in a chair, her idiot child sitting on the floor beside her unaware of her impending death, and above her are her clothes hanging on a line—stockings, gloves, her undergarment—that have more life than the woman below them. The ultimate grotesquerie of this scene is not the two quacks arguing over which potion killed her, nor the servant rifling through the trunk to steal Molly's things, but the clothing as a symbol of her formless life. Her empty clothes define her life: *vanitas*, whose English translation is emptiness. An innocent who embraces urban promises, Molly ends her life in a seedy garret. Molly's end lies in her beginning; her first day in London foreshadows her last. The pitfalls that entrap her lie in a city she doesn't understand.

This theme of the lightning descent into the abyss in such narrative engravings as *A Harlot's Progress* or *The Rake's Progress* (1735) or *Marriage a la Mode* (1743) finds a home in McKay's novel. McKay gives us several mini portraits that recall Hogarth. Elijah Bowers was a "big guy" who ran a hugely successful cabaret in Brooklyn, and "knew swell white folks in politics, and had a grand automobile and a high-yaller wife that hadn't no need of painting to pass." But one night he killed someone in his cabaret. His downfall, as one character tells it, was swift, the conciseness of the storyteller's language matching the rapidity of the nosedive. Although his lawyers "got him off . . . they cleaned him out dry. Done broke him, that case did. And today he's plumb down and out" (64). Similarly, there is Billy's account of the "spade prof," as well a brief summation of what happened to the famous Black conductor James Reese Europe, gunned down "by a savage buck of his race" (286, 319).

A visual anecdote even closer to Hogarth's Molly is the story of Madame Suarez who, like Bowers, ran a thriving cabaret and who, contemptuous of "no-'count n----rs," catered solely to the Black upper-class. Her Cuban blood set her apart; "she moved like a queen among the blue-veins of the colored sporting world" (104). Her hubris blinded her. Allowing big spending whites to patronize her place, she failed to see that some of them were undercover cops. Like Bowers, her fall is quick: "Madame Suarez, besides being fined, was sent to Blackwell's Island for six months" (110). From a thriving cabaret to Blackwell's Island—a change of place defines Suarez's precarious identity.

In plate 2 of *A Harlot's Progress*, Molly was the mistress of a rich Jewish merchant, but in plate 4 we see her beating hemp in Bridewell prison. In Harlem, the high becomes low overnight, as Jake will discover when his womanizing results in a dose of the clap (a repetition of what happens to Tom Rakewell in *The Rake's Progress*).

In Hogarth's work, the comic or satiric often metamorphoses into the gothic grotesque, as when plate 2 in *A Harlot's Progress* (Molly's kicking over the table to distract her Jewish keeper from seeing her clandestine lover creeping out the door) becomes plate 5, the indifference of others to Molly's death, or plate 6 in which the comic and the gothic seem inseparable—Molly's wake in which the mourners are engaged in various worldly activities, some sexual, around the periphery of the open casket. In a layover in Philly, Ray and Jake visit a brothel run by Madame Laura, a woman Jake knows. Ray is impressed by the domesticity of the scene until he sees Madame Laura with her eleven-year-old son, who is drinking a glass of champagne. To Ray, the boy seemed out of place, "a reed fading in a morass." Quite suddenly Ray "felt a violent dislike" for the "atmosphere" of the place: "At first he had liked the general friendliness and warmth and naturalness of it," but the boy's presence, "and his being the woman's son disgusted him." Ray felt that "the boy did not belong to that environment and should not be there" (192–93). Scenes like this one are ubiquitous in Hogarth, from the syphilitic child oblivious to Molly's death and her wake in plates 5 and 6 to plate 6 in the *Marriage a la Mode* series (1743), in which the child who attempts to hug her dead mother is already carrying the syphilis that killed her.

It is the suddenness of the downfall that links Hogarth and Hemingway in McKay's mind. In Hogarth, whether it be *A Harlot's Progress* or *The Rake's Progress*, the abrupt change from engraving to engraving is deliberate. The downward spiral for the harlot and the rake is rapid. Virtue or prosperity disappear in a minute. So too in Hemingway. In "The Three-Day Blow" getting drunk with Bill doesn't disguise the fact that for Nick the long relationship with Marjorie was "all gone" in a matter of minutes (*In*

Our Time 47). In "Big Two-Hearted River: Part I" in the same text, Nick and his friends' seeming permanent friendship with Hopkins abruptly ends with a simple sentence. After Hop's promise to meet them on Lake Superior next summer, "they never saw Hopkins again" (141). In *In Our Time* (1925), seemingly permanent places like the logging town of Horton Bay ("The End of Something") or Seney ("Big Two-Hearted River: Part I") disappear, almost overnight: "The thirteen saloons that had lined the one street of Seney had not left a trace" (133). Unforeseen catastrophes can occur anywhere in a Hemingway text. What happened to Seney had happened to villages in France and Italy during the First World War in which Hemingway served as an ambulance driver in Italy. As Geoff Dyer observes, "The Great War ruined the idea of ruins. . . . Cottages and villages did not crumble and decay—they were swept away" (Dyer 120). McKay's praise of Hemingway's writing as having "most excellently quickened and enlarged my experience of social life" is connected to this theme of "swept away," (*A Long Way* 252).

The Hemingway text McKay admired most was *In Our Time* (1925), for it "contains the frame, the background, and the substance of all of Hemingway's later work" (*A Long Way* 251–52). One reason McKay set his novel in 1918–1919 is that, like Hemingway *In Our Time*, he wanted to emphasize the relationship between the war "over there" and the war at home. When Jake returns from the Great War, he returns to a war zone. He went to Europe to fight in in the war, but the segregated American army put him on the docks in Brest doing manual labor. After becoming a deserter and then living for a brief time in rough-and-tumble East London, he worked on a boat taking him to New York and Harlem. A fugitive from the war, he romanticizes Harlem as home, and, for the first six chapters of the novel, it appears to be just that. But what he discovers, in addition to the war within Harlem, is expressed best by a character in a recent novel, *The Underground Railroad* (2016), by Colson Whitehead: "The conflict in Europe was terrible and violent . . . but she took exception to the name. The Great War had always been between the white and the Black. It always would be" (288).

A key theme in Hemingway is that the violence of the war is mirrored by multiple kinds of violence and disorder in the United States and the modern world, ranging from the racial warfare in "Indian Camp" and "The Battler," to the gender conflict in "Out of Season" to police brutality in the American city (chapter 8 ("I can tell wops a mile off")), to the corrupt horse racing in "My Old Man." Indeed, the ending of "My Old Man" could serve as a coda for *In Our Time* and a major theme in *Home to Harlem*: "seems like when they get started they don't leave a guy nothing" (129). The "they" could refer to the gangsters who kill Joe's father or to the demonic forces unleashed by modernity, especially the Great War.

It is for this reason that both Albert Murray and Ralph Ellison linked Hemingway with the blues tradition (Ellison, *Collected Essays* 186; Murray 37–38). Ellison would say of Hemingway that his fiction "was imbued with a spirit beyond the tragic with which I could feel at home, for it was very close to the feeling of the blues" (*Collected Essays* 186). Albert Murray used Hemingway's famous line that "writers are forged in injustice as swords are forged" (*Green Hills of Africa* 50) to promote his thesis that "antagonistic cooperation" is the essence of the blues: "The fire in the forging process, like the dragon which the hero must always encounter, is of its very nature antagonistic, but it is also cooperative at the same time" (Murray 38). Murray is referring to Kenneth Burke's paradox that "competing principles" can create a "cooperative act": Iago and Othello are both necessary for the tragedy to unfold, just as the brutal racism within American society can produce great art (the blues) and great artists, a theme in McKay's "The White City" (Burke, *Philosophy of Literary Form* 76).

But there is also another implication involving Hemingway's connection with the blues. Muddy Waters's blues line "You can't lose what you never had" parallels Nick's sad realization that "it was all gone," a sentiment repeated three times as though Nick's relationship with Marjorie had never existed in the first place. The blues impulse is the recognition that human happiness is ephemeral, perhaps even unreal—a theme implied in Hemingway's incisive last sentence in *The Sun Also Rises*: "Isn't it pretty to think so." This is Jake's response to Brett's sentimental view of their relationship that, if Jake had not been physically impaired, they "could have had a damn good time together" (*Sun* 251). "Isn't it pretty to think so" is Jake's grim assessment of what they "never had."

If Harlem as home is also an illusion, then *Home to Harlem* is a blues novel, "imbued with a spirit beyond the tragic." McKay said that he had been accused of being a Hemingway imitator more than once but that his fiction is more "subjective" and "loose" than Hemingway's "objective and carefully stylized form" (*A Long Way* 250). Perhaps this distinction accounts for the "loose" blues mix of sentimentality, comedy and violence that runs throughout the novel. It may also account for the difference in each author's admiration for Hogarth. Hemingway's choice of the unsentimental "Gin Lane" engraving lacks the pathos of Molly's death (*Islands in the Stream* 258).

What Hemingway "quickened" and "enlarged" in McKay was something already there, the African American and Marxist views that he articulated in *The Negroes in America* (1923), a book based on an address given to the Fourth World Congress of the Comintern of 1922. William J. Maxwell has noted its relevance to what is now known as Black cultural studies, the insistence that "the approach to culture" is "a site of struggle" between those trying to "capitalize" on Black culture at all levels (high and low) and those who want the unvarnished truth about Black life (Maxwell, *New Negro, Old Left* 87). McKay believed that Hemingway had no desire to "capitalize" on anything, that his steady, unflinching gaze upon modern life had no political agenda.

The basis of his admiration for Hemingway lies in Hemingway's American "rough" perspective, something distinctly "un-European." He added that Hemingway took the "streets, barrooms, the ringsides" of common life and "lifted" them "into the realm of real literature," an echo of McKay's response to Du Bois: making an "art of life" (*A Long Way* 252). In talking of Hemingway's art, McKay might have been describing what he had accomplished in *Home to Harlem*. The "utter blinding nakedness and violent coloring of life" grounds his brilliant novel. The vitality and violence of the novel were intertwined. McKay transformed the chaos of Harlem's mean streets into a meaningful critique of this city within a city.

McKay is also responding to the essential question Hemingway poses in *In Our Time*: how does one keep afloat in a world knocked sideways by the Great War? The "social life" of Harlem appears at times to be a bloodbath, or as Felice puts it, a "blood-baff" (306). And yet this is *where* Jake meets Felice and where he lost and found her again, even though finding her nearly costs him his life when Zeddy pulls a knife on him. It's a "hard-boiled" moment, two men fighting over a woman (Jake pulls a gun on Zeddy), and yet the connections between *Home to Harlem* and *In Our Time* are not limited to this. Not only does the sense of impermanence and loss permeate both texts, but the implications of the Great War for the American scene are relevant to each work, especially for the themes of place and placelessness, home and not home.

When *Home to Harlem* (1928) was first published, McKay was accused of out Van Vechten-ing Van Vechten, writing a novel that was even more sensational than *Nigger Heaven* (1926). The cabaret scenes, the promiscuous sex, the hard drinking, jazz and blues—all were in the two novels. McKay thus became known as the "black Van Vechten" (*CP* 367). In *A Long Way*, McKay set the record straight. If you want a white influence upon my work, it's Hemingway not Van Vechten. He did not dislike *Nigger Heaven*. He saw it, as he told Van Vechten, as the "pioneering novel" about Harlem, but he wanted to claim a realism in *Home to Harlem* that he felt was lacking in *Nigger Heaven*. He knew that the connection people saw between his novel and Van Vechten's had something to do with the "romance" of Harlem, but he identified with Hemingway's attack on the "false romantic-realists," writers that Hemingway rejected as "fake" (*A Long Way* 251).

This posed a problem for McKay. He doesn't reject "romance," only its simplification. In an unpublished letter to H. L. Mencken in 1925, he noted romance's subtle connection to reality. He refers to a manuscript now lost: "['Color Scheme' is] a realistic comedy as I saw it among Negroes on the railroad and in Harlem. . . . I thought it would have a happy effect to drape the harsh reality in such a romantic skeleton" (CM to HLM, August 2, 1925).

"Color Scheme" was a precursor to *Home to Harlem*, but McKay's description applies to *Home to Harlem*. For the portrait of Harlem that McKay gives us in *Home to Harlem* (1928) is, in its own way, as grim as the "killing streets" in James Baldwin's "Sonny Blues." Although the "romantic skeleton" would consist of the comic, picaresque adventures of McKay's Jake, Harlem's "harsh reality" is the novel's actual theme. Again, Billy Biasse: "Wese all just lumped together *without a chanst to choose* and so we nacherally hate one another" (my emphasis) (*Home to Harlem* 285). This lack of choice is due to the dark truth that this "romantic" city within a city cannot escape the reality of American history. In *Banjo* (1929), Banjo puts Billy's observation in slightly different terms: "we kain't afford to choose, because we ain't born and growed up like the choosing people. All we can do is grab our chance every time it comes our way" (*Banjo* 319). In defining the ambiguous nature of Harlem, Ray would say that "the composite life in Harlem was like a comic opera," a mixture of slapstick and tragedy (173).

Harlem's "harsh reality" would become the basis of the novel's gothic substructure. As Avil Horner and Sue Zlosnik note, "the roots of the gothic lie in the comic as well as the tragic" (*Gothic* 7) and if McKay bears any resemblance to any other Black novelist it would have to be Chester Himes and his comic noir fiction, or Richard Wright's *Lawd Today* (circa 1934–37). In any event, McKay's Harlem would be different in kind from the Harlem of Alain Locke's "group life" and "common consciousness," James Weldon Johnson's "Culture Capital" and W. E. B. Du Bois's "Talented Tenth." Its "social" perspective upon Harlem would be influenced, to a great extent, by Hemingway and the Great War and, as Gary Edward Holcomb and Eric H. Newman observe, queer culture.

McKay's "romantic skeleton" is a surface that hides a darker depth, a version of Hemingway's famous iceberg thesis before Hemingway defined it in *Death in the Afternoon* (1933). On the surface, the novel could be seen as a wild roller-coaster ride, or rather as a Harlem held together by a montage of visual images. It is possible that McKay had seen Ezra Pound's remarks in *The Dial* in 1921. Pound observed that narrative in a village is "linear," but in the modern city, "the visual impressions succeed each other, overlap, overcross, they are 'cinematographic'. . . . They are often a flood of nouns without verbal relations" (110). Hemingway was Pound's friend, and in a letter to Edmund Wilson (October 18, 1924) about his forthcoming *In Our Time* (1925) he discussed his technique in that short story cycle in terms of long shots and close-ups: "Like looking with your eyes at something, say a passing coastline, and then looking at it again it again with 15X binoculars" (Burhans 89).

McKay would alternate between long shot and close-up in his depiction of places and people within Harlem, indicating that the city resists a single generalization (e.g., "Culture Capital"). The center of Harlem in McKay's novel is always shifting its focus. What he gives us are selected close-ups and isolated stories. Like Hemingway, McKay's common theme is rewriting American history in terms of its buried past which can only be revealed through a history of moments, often grotesque. What separates the two modernists is that McKay would reinvent Hemingway. His racial spin on Hemingway would be a unique form of urban Gothic. As Teresa Goddu observes, and as Leslie Fiedler had earlier observed, "History creates the Gothic, and in turn the Gothic reinvents history" (Goddu 132). This reinvented history takes race out of the basement and puts it in the center of the house, giving us a new way of looking at the house.

In McKay's novel, Harlem is full of life, but it has no center, no unified community, nothing to give structure to its "promiscuous thickness" (267). Here is one reason why McKay admired Hemingway whose characters, as his biographer Michael Reynolds notes, were "essentially homeless men, not only without family but without a town to call home" (Reynolds, *The Young Hemingway* 53). This is one aspect of the "social life" McKay responded to in Hemingway, but, paradoxically, he did so by giving us a strong sense of place in his novel. He gives us the specific details of each cabaret: Barron's depended "on its downtown white trade"; the Congo catered to "the unwashed of the Black Belt"; Tammy Hall "protected" the Baltimore until the police raided it for mysterious reasons. He also gives us details of homes and streets (Gin-head Susy's home at Myrtle Avenue in Brooklyn), eating establishments ("Aunt Hattie's chitterling joint in one Hundred and Thirty-second Street") and beauty parlors and flop houses. As he has Ray say in *Banjo*, "for a man to love a nation" is "a most unnatural thing . . . Man loved places" (137).

This sense of place is another thing he may have learned from Hemingway. As Michael Reynolds again notes of Hemingway, "no matter where he took his readers, to what foreign country or strange experience, he always gave them what he later called 'the way it was': the people, the weather, the look and feel of a place" (*Hemingway: The Paris Years* 21). Reynolds may be thinking of advice Hemingway gave a fellow writer, John Herrmann, on September 26, 1928: "Make the *place* as well as the people and action.... That action does not want to take place without taking place somewhere—You must make the place too—I dont mean just description—Make it" (*Letters* 3:445).

His advice has relevance to the famous passage in *A Farewell to Arms* in which Frederic Henry sets the patriotic rhetoric of the Great War against the reality that the soldiers knew to be true: "There were many words that you could not stand to hear and finally only the names of places had dignity" (*Farewell* 161). The "names" had "dignity," even if the "places" no longer existed; they were a reminder of a world before the war in which places mattered. They are remnants of a world that the Great War had erased. No-man's-land, a term whose origin predates World War I, was a nonplace—not an imaginary place (another meaning of "utopia"), but a real place divested of life, community, and civilization. It was a vast cemetery of rotting humans, horses, dogs, decimated farms and villages, broken machinery, and the detritus between the two trenches on the Western Front, a grotesque parody of "Man's Land." No-man's-land negates space as place—place that was once invested with a human presence. Or put another way, as Harold Pinter does in his play *No Man's Land*, it is dead space "which never moves, which never changes, which never grows older, but which remains forever, icy and silent" (50). McKay has Ray refer to the world the war created in *Home to* Harlem as "the vast international cemetery of this century" (227).

No-man's-land is Harlem's world and Hemingway's. In Hemingway's short story "A Clean, Well-Lighted Place," the older waiter understands the old man's need for refuge; Krebs in "Soldier's Home" thinks home will restore him but returns to find it a foreign land. Like Jake at the end of *Home to Harlem*, he leaves for another city, Kansas City, just as Jake leaves for Chicago with Felice. Jake, says McKay, had a "perfect contempt for place," but he flees England for Harlem, Harlem for the railroad, and later Harlem for Chicago (42). Like Hemingway's old man, he's looking for a place to land.

McKay gives us Harlem as home in all its messy contradictions. In *Home to Harlem* Ray finds hateful "its brutality, gang rowdyism," but he also found "joy" there which "glowed gloriously upon him like the high-noon sunlight of his tropic island home" (267). As McKay says in *Banjo*, "man loves places, and no one place, for the earth like a beautiful wanton, puts on a new dress to fascinate him wherever he may go" (137).

With Jake in mind, Felice in *Home to Harlem* will point to the paradox of being an African American in the United States. You were right to desert she tells Jake: "what right have n----rs got to shoot down a whole lot a Germans for? Is they worse than Americans or any other nation a white people" (331–32). And yet in her plea to Jake to not follow Ray to foreign parts, she says, why become a "swallow . . . nevah settling down no place? This heah is you' country, daddy" (332). Here, in short, is McKay's ambivalence—the desire for a "place" and the reality of a "no place." Jake will choose the former with Felice because it is his "country"; Ray believes that "no place" is his fate, like the older waiter in "A Clean, Well-Lighted Place." He will leave for Marseilles.

One of the best examples of place and placelessness in Hemingway is his great short story, "The Killers," (1927) published a year before *Home to Harlem*. When the story begins, we don't know where we are, other than observing two men enter a place called "HENRY'S LUNCH-ROOM." They discuss and argue over what they "want to eat," a conversation so banal that at first we don't see the implications of its banality (Hemingway, *Complete Stories* 215–16). That is the nature of evil in the modern world—trite, commonplace, unoriginal. Yet their innocuous entrance into this small-town diner will change the lives of the people in it forever, especially Nick Adams.

Their appearance is a radical disruption of normal life, but then again Hemingway's point is that the killers *are* normal life, a foreshadowing of Hannah Arendt's banality of evil. Once you expose the idea of the "normal" as a fiction, then official American history begins to seem that way as well. In Hemingway's story, we never see the people or institutions that send the killers to the small town. We only see the killers, the tip of the iceberg, just as the cops who send Madame Suarez to Blackwell's prison in *Home to Harlem* are the killers sent by hidden powers. "The dignity of the movement of the ice-berg," Hemingway said in *Death in the Afternoon*, "is due to only one-eighth of it being above water" (192). It is here perhaps we see a connection between Hemingway and D. H. Lawrence's "essential American soul" that is "hard, isolate, stoic, and a killer." Hemingway's and McKay's killers are not only "hard," but behind the scenes.

The opening scene in "The Killers" is a parody of a domestic moment: the killers from the big city are going to kill someone who will be sitting down to eat. The scene also mirrors an American moment: people show up unexpectedly to kill you, just as Jake's best friend Zeddy suddenly turns on him. And note what may have struck McKay as truly grotesque in Hemingway's story, the dark despair of the man the killers came to kill, the Swede. He refuses to run, believing that there is no longer a place to hide. His counterpart is Lonesome Blue in McKay's *Banjo*.

The Swede's homelessness is the modern condition. It is the "social life" that McKay's Jake returns to who believes at first that Harlem is different from all other places. Harlem is, as McKay reminds us in *Harlem: Negro Metropolis* (1940), a world in which its economy is controlled "by outsiders." For "there is not a Negro-owned dancing hall in Harlem" (89, 118). Just as the two killers in Hemingway's story have invaded the small town, the larger white city, New York, and by extension, corporate white America, has invaded Harlem. Jake finds out, as does the Swede, that in the postwar world there are no protected places, no cities of refuge. The question raised by Hemingway is this: what kind of "social life" do we have in a particular place, a question McKay will ask not only of Harlem but Marseilles. One answer for both authors is that whatever the "social life," uncertainty in all places is the norm. As Madame Suarez discovered, a nonplace suddenly replaces place.

McKay will recreate Hemingway's Swede in Aslima in *Romance in Marseille*. The Swede tells Nick that he "got in wrong" (Hemingway, *Complete Stories* 221), the only explanation he gives for why the killers are after him. With Aslima, we know what the wrong is. She betrayed Lafala by robbing him, resulting in the loss of his legs. Despite their reunion, he no longer trusts her. And even if he pays for her passage "back home," she tells him, "What home? I have no home to go back to. I have no parents, no relatives. I would be a stranger going back alone as much as I am here" (McKay, *Romance* 123). When, out of compassion, her rival La Fleur tries to warn her that her pimp Titin is going to kill her for betraying him with Lafala, she "was apathetic. She did not care about anything," including being killed by Titin (128). The Swede will be killed off screen; McKay's novel ends with Aslima's brutal death. But the "social life" for both is the same; both are caught in a web of circumstances outside of their control.

McKay and Hemingway also meet in their mutual admiration for Henri Barbusse's *Le Feu*. Hemingway said that it was "the only good war book to come out of the last war" (qtd. in William Dow 72). In *Home to Harlem*, Ray thinks of it as "a grand anti-romantic presentation of mind and behavior in that Hell-pit of life" (227). The connecting link between the two authors' praise of *Le Feu* is two-fold: domestic space and the uncanny space of No

Man's Land. One of the most powerful scenes in *Le Feu* occurs when the narrator accompanies a friend in the latter's search for his village and his home. They find the spot where the village should be, but there is nothing there: not "some semblance of locality," not even any rubble—just empty space (Barbusse 139). And here is the shocking thing: "nothing has any shape." When Peterloo, the friend, looks for his house, he suffers an existential breakdown: "It's here. . . . No it's not here. I don't know where it is . . . where it was." The impact of the void, the familiar gone, is devastating. The narrator says of Peterloo that "he was looking for the homeliness of rooms scattered in infinite space, their internal shape and half-light cast on the winds" (141).

Barbusse perfectly captures Freud's *unheimlichkeit*, the sense of being unhoused and thus without a self, a condition that McKay's Jake slowly comes to realize about himself. Barbusse extends that sense of un-housed to the larger landscape in which there are no "words" to transcribe its surreal surface: "what does it all mean, all this . . . all this that we can't even name" (305). His narrator keeps looking for metaphors to find the familiar in the unfamiliar: "a dismal place . . . looks like a section of a huge wheel stuck in the mud, or the broken sails of a windmill" (248). He resorts to language from fairy tales: the "balls of dust" from a bomb explosion "take on the shapes of fabulous dragons" (192). The failure of language to describe the indescribable is symptomatic of the death of the domestic, the sense that human beings have a place in the world, that space can be defined as place.

Hemingway does something similar in *In Our Time*. In the italicized sections separating the stories, Hemingway uses a pattern of domestic images or motifs to emphasize homelessness. In chapter 1, the fire of a makeshift "kitchen" is seen as a danger though "fifty kilometers from the front." In chapter 2, a "blanket" covers a woman giving birth during the Greek evacuation from Turkey. In chapter 3, a "garden wall" serves as a convenient place to slaughter Germans as they try to climb over it. In chapter 4, an "iron grating from the front of a house" is a both an obstacle and a shooting platform for the English soldiers, who are very upset when they have to give it up. In chapter 5, the "wall of a hospital" serves as a place for executing Greek ministers; and in chapter 6, "an iron bedstead" hangs "twisted" out of the missing wall of a house in a street where Rinaldi lies dying and where Nick, wounded in the spine, declares a "separate peace" from the war. McKay knows that African Americans don't have the luxury of a separate peace. Yet, as Hemingway's stories on the home front show, a "separate peace" is not to be found there even for white people.

Both the Great War in *Le Feu* and the war zone in *Home to Harlem* show human beings reduced to animals. The trenches in *Le Feu* have changed the men to "sinister troglodytes half emerging from their caverns of mud" (33, 41). Throughout, Barbusse describes the shocking transformation of men to bears, penguins, Neanderthals, gorillas, marmosets, chickens, ants, moles, hyenas, cattle, and insects. It's a Darwinian evolution in reverse, Paul Fussell's "Troglodyte World" (Fussell 36–74).

No doubt thinking of *Le Feu*, McKay comments with wry irony on H. G. Wells's query about whether it is possible that Black people can achieve "common citizenship in a world republic"—this "after the appallingly beastly modern white savagery of 1914–1918" (*A Long Way* 123). Yet McKay will follow Barbusse's pattern of naming human beings after animals because he sees what war does to people: Zeddy is an ape, Jake a hound, the chef a rhino, the fourth waiter a mule, Congo Rose a leopard, and Billy a wolf who "eats his own kind."

Hemingway himself will use this technique to describe the post–World War I generation in *The Sun Also Rises*. Brett is a vampire, Robert Cohen a "steer," Jake a gelding, the bull a killing machine and the bull ring the world in which it is difficult to hold a "purity of line through a maximum of exposure" (*Sun* 172). McKay was especially impressed by the bullfighting sketches in *In Our Time*. He called them "six miniature classics" (*A Long Way* 252). Only one of those sketches illustrates a "purity of line." The other five show either unpredictable chaos or human frailty—terror and exhaustion, cruelty, incompetence, cowardice, and frustration—all those things that make it into McKay's novel. At the end of *Home to Harlem*, Jake seeks both a domesticity that protects him from himself and Hemingway's "separate peace," Nick's desperate and impossible attempt to find some neutral space in which to live a life without consequences.

Hemingway's famous iceberg theory in *Death in the Afternoon* (1933) comes too late to influence *Home to Harlem*, but McKay would later call the book in which it appears Hemingway's "masterpiece" (*A Long Way* 251). Nevertheless, the double perspective (romantic skeleton, harsh reality) in *Home to Harlem* is quite similar to Hemingway's distinction between surface and depth. The "romantic skeleton" is the cabarets, the sex, and music, like the hard drinking and sexual promiscuity of the group of wastrels in *The Sun Also Rises*. The "harsh reality" of Harlem is the brutal violence and grim poverty that encompasses Jake and Ray, just as Hemingway said in a letter to Fitzgerald that "the only instruction" in his novel "is how people go to hell" (*Letters*, vol. 3. 75).

There is a moment in "Indian Camp," the opening story of *In Our Time*, that McKay must have remembered. The story is ostensibly about the young Nick who, after seeing his father successfully perform a Cesarian operation on a Native American woman, "felt quite sure that he would never die" (19). But he has also seen the woman's husband slit his own throat, a terrible moment that nevertheless recedes in his consciousness because of his father's triumph. What he doesn't know is that the husband's death is not caused by his wife's suffering but by the fact that the husband knows he is not the father of his wife's child. What lies beneath the surface is the shadowy figure of Uncle George who disappears at the end but who was passing out cigars at the beginning. On the surface, this is Nick's story, his coming of age in which death is overshadowed by life, but the nightmare beneath the surface is a history of racial conflict. Although the husband kills himself because he knows he's been cuckolded, that act is a repetition of acts of violence and subjugation in the past. The morning in which Nick rows back to their home is a false dawn, a romantic skeleton. The "camp" is the central truth of the story—a temporary shelter that is not even a shelter if a wolf can enter the fold.

The same can be said of the hidden truth in *Home to Harlem*. The novel appears to celebrate Jake's sexual escapades and Harlem's Dionysian zeitgeist, but the real story lies elsewhere. McKay's Marxist perspective is relevant here. As Terry Eagleton says in *Why Marx Was Right*, beneath the surface of what we call civilization, "lie violence, lack, desire, appetite, scarcity and aggression." Quoting Adorno, he refers to the "horror teeming under the stone of culture" (Eagleton 146). An early reviewer of McKay's novel, Burton Rascoe caught its essence: it was a book "to evoke pity and terror" (qtd. in Cooper, *Sojourner* 246).

If we look at *Home to Harlem*'s tri-partite structure, Eagleton's nouns—especially violence and aggression—make sense. The first part focuses on Jake and Harlem and begins with Jake meeting and losing Felice and ends with Jake leaving Harlem for the railroad. McKay says that Jake joined the railroad "to break the hold that Harlem had on him," especially its "atmosphere," (125), but the real reason is that living with Congo Rose means he is no longer able to shape or control his own life. Jakes lives by a code—"never lived off no womens and never will. I always works" (40)—but Rose calls it into question. She sees him as her "big, good slave" (41). For McKay, she is symptomatic of a world turned upside down by racial oppression, whose real source is economics. Congo Rose is the bread winner, insisting that her "man" beat her if he is to be a man. The sub-text here is that sexual violence becomes a substitute for a manliness that Jake doesn't have, because he doesn't have a job. Jake won't scab, but he won't join the union either because he knows the good jobs go to whites. He finds himself in the position of living "sweet" with Rose when living off women violates his self-reliance. His is an impotence that mirrors another impotence in *The Sun Also Rises*, the physical impotence of Jake Barnes.

Jake's relationship with Rose reflects the paradox of Harlem. As a dancer, Rose is perfection itself; as a woman, she is warped by a system she doesn't understand, as are the other women in the novel—with the exception of Felice whose name hints of a utopian promise beyond the finite world of Harlem. That world is defined by men out of work, by loan sharks like Nije Gridley, and by ubiquitous violence—on the dance floor, in games of crap (Zeddy/Nije), and on the streets. The ultimate paradox lies with sexual identity. The popular songs reflect a hostility to gay sexuality, "a bulldycking woman and a faggotty man," yet Billy Biasse, who will become Jake's best friend, "eats his own kind" (36, 92). The conflict between what is conventionally accepted and what actually exists is reflected in the same blues song in which the singer doesn't "understand" why some people prefer the same sex: "Oh baby how are you/Oh baby what are you?" (37). In the novel, the "how" (how well you are doing) is connected to the "what" (who you are, including your sexual identity).

The novel's second part focuses on the railroad where Jake meets Ray and ends with Ray leaving Harlem on a ship "going across the pond." The third part begins with Jake's return to Harlem, where he finds Felice before going with her to Chicago. Each section can also be connected to people: Jake and Zeddy dominate the first part, Jake and Ray the second, and Jake and Billy Biasse the third. Billy's presence in the third is significant. As the "wolf," he hints at the "savage" nature of Harlem caused by its economic subjugation to the white power structure. Zeddy's metamorphosis is a case in point. He changes from warning Jake in the first part to not trusting Black people with his secret that he's a deserter, to using it against Jake. It's not just jealousy of Jake who takes Felice away from him that causes this—it is the nature of Harlem itself that turns friend against friend, female against male, female against female, as the stories of Yaller Prince and the "hen fights" illustrate.

That Billy gives Jake a gun to counter Zeddy's knife in the third part underscores the novel's echo of the madness of the Great War. In a sense, the railroad car in the second section foreshadows the third; it is Harlem in small, the "Treeing of the Chef" (160–87) foreshadowing the theme of revenge and violence in the third, as well as underscoring the animal imagery that runs throughout the novel. McKay may have had "The Killers" in mind when he had Jake square off against Zeddy. Pressed further by George for a motive for killing the Swede, one of the killers, says: "We're killing him for a friend. Just to oblige a friend..." (*Complete Short Stories* 218). In this world, the word "friend" no longer has any meaning.

Gary Edward Holcomb has perceptively noticed the connection between McKay's Jake Brown and Hemingway's Jacob Barnes in *The Sun Also Rises* (Holcomb "Hemingway and McKay," 138–40 passim). He points out that Jake Barnes's sexual impotence stands in contrast to "Jake Brown's lusty appetite for copious sexual activity" (140). To be more specific, Hemingway's Jake has lost both penis and testicles in the Great War, probably due to a land mine, and suffers emotionally, especially at night, from his condition. Despite their physical differences, the two Jakes are alike in key ways. Both men are stoic and live by a moral code. Hemingway's Jake never trades on his wound for pity, and sees in Pedro Romero, the bullfighter, a model for virtuous behavior: "the holding of his purity of line through the maximum of exposure" (*Sun* 172).

Neither code works for each man. McKay's Jake claims he never hits women, but he strikes Congo Rose, and because he won't scab, he is forced to borrow money from a loan shark. The "social life" of Harlem is the "maximum exposure" that keeps him from "holding a purity of line." Zeddy's treachery—declaring in public that Jake is a deserter—puts Jake in danger from the authorities. The ultimate moral compromise for Jake is that he now carries a gun in a place he thought of as home. He has become a soldier in a different Great War but one related to the one "over there" where he was not allowed to carry a gun but where insane behavior was the norm.

Hemingway's Jake fails because he betrays Montoya's faith in him, their mutual understanding that some things are sacred and not to be contaminated. When Jake introduces Brett to Romero, knowing that the promiscuous, hard-drinking Brett is a threat to the young matador's integrity as a bullfighter, he has yielded to an emotion at odds with what he knows. His is the Apostle Paul's fallen will: knowledge is no match for desire. He cannot have Brett, so he gives her to Romero as his surrogate. No wonder Robert Cohn calls him a "pimp" (194).

Jake's moral failure illustrates a key theme in McKay's assessment of Hemingway: "When Hemingway wrote, *The Sun Also Rises*, he shot a fist in the face of the false romantic-realists and said: "You can't fake about life like that"" (*Long Way* 251). McKay singles out Michael Arlen's *The Green Hat* (1924) as an example of "false romantic" realism, a novel supposedly about the postwar 1920s but whose clever style is the novel's real subject, a fine gloss that hides an empty depth. It is modernism as counterfeit. McKay may be thinking of a line in *Death in the Afternoon:* "If a man writes clearly enough any one can see if he fakes." Waldo Frank's book on Spain (*Virgin Spain*, 1924) "seeks to mystify where there is no mystery but is really only the necessity to fake to cover lack of knowledge or the inability to state clearly" (*Death* 54). What McKay liked about *Death in the Afternoon* was that it was as much about the art of writing as authenticity as it was about bullfighting.

In *The Sun Also Rises*, Hemingway sees the authentic bullfighter ("the holding of his purity of line") as a model for the artist in a postwar world. Although he had experienced "violent death" in the Great War, he felt he needed to understand it in another context if he was to be a writer. Hemingway believed, after all, that death is the fundamental fact of our existence, so he went to Spain to "study" the subject within the ritually defined space of the bullring (*Death* 2). What he discovered is that "the bullfight" is not a sport but akin to a "tragedy" (*Death* 6). It is an enactment within a confined space in which the bull always dies, and the matador may. What is at stake for the matador is his behavior in his encounter with the bull, that single-minded killing machine.

The soldier in the Great War experienced death as random and unpredictable; he was without protection or knowledge. Not so the matador. He learns the rules: how and when to work within the terrain of the bull, when not to. The grace of artifice that he achieves is contingent upon his bravery and his "technique," but with this proviso: "It is one thing to know the rules in principle and another to remember them as they are needed when facing an animal that is seeking to kill you" (*Death* 17). Here is one explanation of Jake's failure with Brett. It also explains why, in *The Sun Also Rises*, so many bullfighters resort to faking it, "developing a technic that simulated this appearance of danger in order to give a fake emotional feeling, while the bullfighter was really safe" (172). McKay saw this as a description of the false "romantic realist," someone like Robert Cohn who uses technique to avoid confronting the ultimate exposure, the void within the self.

Romero is "the real thing" because "the holding of his purity of line" when exposed to "violent death" creates the necessary illusion that we are not merely cannon fodder as soldiers were in the Great War. Hemingway's qualifier, however, is that although the aesthetic act is a moral response to "maximum exposure," it exists for only a short duration: "all stories, if continued far enough, end in death, and he is no true-story teller who would keep that from you" (*Death* 122). The bull in the bullring is death itself, but looked at from another angle, the bull always dies. In that sense, he symbolizes the inescapable human fate. And he is forgotten.

This is another perspective upon Ecclesiastes, the Old Testament source of the epigraph to *The Sun Also Rises*. The epigraph itself is hopeful: one generation replaces another, and so we live in hope that the "Lost Generation" is not the last word. But there is another theme in Ecclesiastes, and another passage in *The Sun Also Rises* that illustrates this theme. It stands as a counterpoint to the nineteen-year-old Pedro Romero's talent. It's a version of the vanity of human wishes, especially our desire to be remembered: "There is no remembrance of former things, nor will there be any remembrance of later things yet to happen among those who come after" (Ecclesiastes 1:11). Place these lines alongside the seeming digression in *The Sun Also Rises*, in which we are told the breeding ancestry of the bull that Romero killed and whose ear he gave to Brett as a symbol of his love and esteem. Jake tells us, in objective, documentary prose, that the bull came from "the bull-breeding establishment of Sanchez Taberno, and was killed by Pedro Romero as the third bull of that same afternoon. His ear was cut by popular acclamation and given to Pedro Romero, who, in turn, gave it to Brett, who wrapped it in a handkerchief belonging to myself, and left both ear and handkerchief, along with a number of cigarette stubs, shoved far back in the drawer of the bed-table that stood beside her bed in the Hotel Montoya, in Pamplona" (202–3). What is disturbing about these lines is not simply their theme—the "popular acclamation" of the ceremonial act reduced to an ear among cigarette stubs that will soon become garbage—but the fact that even Pedro Romero (whose name is mentioned twice) will be forgotten and become as insignificant as the ear of the bull that he gave Brett. Remembrance is a disappearing act, erasure from a planet that is indifferent to our existence, made all the more Gothic by the objective prose as if in describing what happens to the ear Jake was describing the objects in a landfill. McKay, who read Schopenhauer, would not have been surprised by either the passage from Ecclesiastes or Hemingway. Who except McKay remembers Madame Suarez? Or Rosalind?

McKay keeps reminding us of this grim reality in *Home to Harlem*. Elijah Bowers, Madam Suarez, Yaller Prince, "Zeddy's Fall," Rosalind and Jerco—their fates, large or small, are indicative of what lies in wait, not just their precipitous departures but the memory of their presence in Harlem. Only the storyteller keeps them alive, just as Shelley's poet keeps the statue of Ozymandias from sinking into the sand. The storyteller preserves what time consumes.

Both Hemingway and McKay were interested in artists who painted realistic pictures or grim sketches of war. Hemingway claimed that he learned "as much from painters about how to write as from writers" (Bruccoli 118). His favorites (in addition to Cezanne) were Bosch, Breughel, Goya, and El Greco—all painters with dark themes (Watts 26–28, 68–70, 128–39; Bruccoli 118). Hemingway and McKay both admired the German artist George Grosz and his dark, satiric sketches of World War I in *Ecce Homo* (1922) (McKay, *A Long Way* 240–41; Knust 235), and Goya whose *Los Desastros de la Guerra* were Gothic sketches of Napoleonic invasion of Spain in the early nineteenth century. McKay linked Chaplin's film *Shoulder Arms* (1918) to "Goya's grotesqueries" (*A Long Way* 117), and Hemingway saw Goya's brutal sketches as examples of an artist who fearlessly did not shut his eyes to the terrible realities of war (*Death* 3).

One reason McKay admired Hemingway is that Hemingway, like Goya, did not shut his eyes. For that reason, "I could care less" about what his "personal attitude may be to the material that he has used (252)." It's a nice distinction: whether Hemingway is a racist is irrelevant because his fiction made McKay see the world honestly and in a new way. McKay wanted to avoid "right think," the kind of thinking that always places African Americans in a good light. Many Harlem intellectuals attacked stereotypes as unreal because degrading, and yet McKay said in his novel that "one day your theory may be upset" when you meet someone far more perfect as a stereotype than any you encounter in fiction (McKay, *Home* 63–64).

Hemingway's own treatment of African Americans could be insightful, layered, and often provocative. In *A Farewell to Arms* (1929), Frederic Henry calls Othello "a n----r," only to find out that evening that he is going to be arrested by the Italian police in the morning for desertion, thus putting him in the position of being a fugitive slave (*Farewell* 222). Is Bugs in "The Battler" (*In Our Time*) a sadist or Ad's friend? In any event, the master/slave relationship is reversed, an irony involving American history that the young Nick Adams has yet to learn. "The splendid n----r" in *The Sun Also Rises* could be an example of Hemingway's racism or possibly of a boxer who honors a code of behavior, no matter how corrupt, and he is a foil to Jake who fails to honor the very thing that gives his life meaning. In *For Whom the Bell Tolls* (1940), Pilar tells Robert Jordan the story of a loyalist mob in Ronda, Spain, who threw the local fascists over a cliff, and the tale triggers Jordan's memory of a mob who lynched a Black man in a small American town, a terrible incident that he had witnessed as a child (*For Whom* 116–17). Here Hemingway draws a parallel between two traumatic moments. In an unpublished story "The Porter," George, the "Negro" train porter, befriends a young white boy named Jim, describing for him the perfect technique of using a razor in a fight. He then provides a counter narrative. He calls the razor "a delusion" that doesn't protect Negroes: "Only n----r ever knew how to defend himself was Jack Johnson and they put him in Leavenworth" (*Complete Stories* 576). And if they don't throw you in jail, they cheat you. Take the great middle-weight boxer Tiger Flowers: "if he was white he'd have made a million dollars" (576). The only thing "you get in this life," he adds, is "a point of view," but you can't depend on that to save you. In *A Farewell to Arms*, Hemingway underscores that message in lines that Ralph Ellison would see as a blues motif: "You did not know what it was all about. You never had time to learn. They threw you in and told you the rules and the first time they caught you off base they killed you" (*Farewell* 280; Ellison 186). And when they kill you, as they do in the Great War, you undergo a metamorphosis: "The color change in Caucasian races is from white to yellow, to yellow-green, to black" (*Complete Stories* 337).

In *To Have and Have Not* (1937), "the rules" are broken when a client skips out without paying his bill, leaving Harry Morgan, who makes his living taking the wealthy fishing, in an economic bind. From this point on the odds are against him, leading to a downward spiral from which he cannot escape. Before he dies, he has this epiphany: "No matter how a man alone ain't got no bloody fucking chance" (*To Have* 225). Hemingway makes us see, through Harry, that we are all in the same soup, that we are all "alone." It's the "how" that levels us all: no matter what we do, whatever "rules" we have learned, some little thing can level us to the condition of being a "n----r." The novel has its share of racism (Morrison, *Playing* 69–91), but the blues refrain is its overarching theme: happiness as an illusion, loss as the great leveler.

Darkness exists at the edge (or the center) of both McKay and Hemingway's writings. McKay would respond to racial injustice with Jonathan Swift's "savage indignation," and Hemingway, Malcolm Cowley would argue, belonged with those "nocturnal writers" such as Poe, Hawthorne, and Melville (Cowley 317). But there are also utopian moments in both writers: Jake Barnes walking to work in the early morning Paris light, his trout fishing in Burguete, and Nick's camp and the river in "Big Two-Hearted River, Parts I and II." And yet at the end of the river is the "swamp" where fishing would be "tragic" (*In Our Time* 155). So too with Ray whose mental life was "suffering, horribly real," yet laced with moments of beauty. The river always has two hearts.

At one point in the novel, Ray remembers a line from a French poem "L'ideal," (1865–66) by René-François Armand "Sully" Prudhomme. "Et l'ame du monde est dans l'air" ("The soul of the world is in the air"—156). That soul is light that has traveled from a distant star but will only enchant a future age: "Enchanter les yeax d'un autre age" (www.poemes.co>l-ideal). Ray calls the remembered line a "moment's respite," but its implication for the Harlem in McKay's novel is significant. The "light" from this city on a hill (uptown!) is invisible, perhaps dimly seen in Harlem's Dionysian energy and in the perfection of Congo Rose's dance: "They danced, Rose and the boy. Oh, they danced! An exercise of rhythmical exactness for two. . . . They were right there together, neither going beyond the other" (93).

McKay's citation of Prudhomme's poem in the midst of his sometimes grim, sometimes comic treatment of Harlem raises the question of who McKay thought were his ideal readers. He addressed the question in an unpublished letter to James Weldon Johnson in the same year *Home to Harlem* was published. He complains to Johnson about prejudiced or condescending white people and narrow-minded Black people (hide-bound middle-class intellectuals) and ends by saying "We must leave the real appreciation of what we are doing to the emancipated intelligentsia of the future while we are sardonically aware now that only the intelligentsia of the 'superior race' is developed enough to afford artistic truth" (*Letters in Exile* 246). Although he admits that he's caught between a rock and a hard place, he expressed the hope that one day not only will African Americans respond to his art, but he will also have "kinsmen" of all colors who will be his readers. And he hopes that they will understand that his *Home to Harlem* is a "real proletarian novel,"(*Letters in Exile* 246) with "real" people who can't be reduced to the "underworld" or the "working class," but who "backbite and fuck like people the world over" (*Letters in Exile* 122). Given the recent excitement over his newly found unpublished manuscripts and the renewed interest in his poetry and prose, perhaps Prudhomme's "light" has come true.

In *Home to Harlem*, Ray's "moment's respite" foreshadows a line from Italo Calvino's *Invisible Cities* (1972). Raissa is a "city of sadness" in which "runs an invisible thread that binds one living being to another for a moment, then unravels, then is stretched again between moving points as it draws new and rapid patterns so that at every second the unhappy city contains a happy city unaware of its own existence" (Calvino 149). Perhaps Jake's nostalgia for Harlem (*nostos*: home; *algia*, a longing for) at the novel's beginning is not so much a quest to recapture the past as it is an anticipation of finding a home in the future.

Home to Harlem is a novel of lights and shadows and patterns of connections that "unravel" and then reconnect in tenuous moments of perfection, in Rose's dance, or in Harlem's "cruising" community. But as always, things fall apart, the center does not hold. Hemingway could never have written *Home to Harlem*, but he helped McKay see the nuances, especially McKay's stark perspective upon the American scene.

CHAPTER 3

JAMES JOYCE, CHARLIE CHAPLIN, AND *HE WHO GETS SLAPPED*

Claude McKay's Portrait of the Artist in *Banjo*

> I do hope Joyce's splendid heavyweight will reach you as I have sent it camoflaged [sic] under the light-weight protection of Monsieur Paul Morand whose facile cleverness may be innocuous enough to make his name acceptable to American puritan imbecility.
> —CLAUDE MCKAY TO HAROLD JACKMAN (*LETTERS IN EXILE* 231)

On June 3, 1927, Harold Jackman had asked McKay to send him a disguised copy of James Joyce's *Ulysses* (1922), the modernist novel that would have a lightning impact on twentieth-century literature. Its absence in the literary world, in Hugh Kenner's words, would be akin to "a twentieth-century physics without Relativity" (12). McKay, said Jackman, was to rip off the title page and the first two pages and send them in a separate envelope, thereby hiding the "obscene" novel from the authorities when McKay sent it.

McKay responded on June 27 that he had found "a sample copy" in a bookstore in Marseilles but it had been sold before he could purchase it. He would write "a friend" in Paris to "get your 'Ulysses'"(*Letters in Exile* 196). The novel, of course, would not be published in the United States until 1933, but who had time to wait? Jackman clearly had to because it would be almost nine months before McKay sent it. When McKay wrote Jackman on March 10, 1928, from Marseilles, he implied that he had already read Joyce's "splendid heavyweight" of a novel (*Letters in Exile* 231). In his autobiography *A Long Way from Home*, he said that "*Ulysses* was published when I arrived in Paris" in 1922, that "a good friend" had given him a copy, and "a bad friend swiped it" (246). Even before 1922, McKay's Ray in *Home* to *Harlem* remembers how he had been "startled by James Joyce in *The Little Review*" in 1918 in which the first seven episodes of *Ulysses* had first appeared (*Home* 227; Litz 142–43). The ultimate praise for Joyce was this: "I cannot imagine any modern and earnest student of literary artistry of that period who did not consider it necessary to *study* James Joyce" (*A Long Way* 247) (my emphasis). McKay did his homework. In a letter to Max Eastman, he said that James Joyce is "a Don Quijote of contemporary literature, but that is the James Joyce of *Ulysses*" (*Letters in Exile* 393). *Banjo* (1929) is a novel with two versions of the artist, both indebted to Joyce's *Ulysses* because Joyce juxtaposes Leopold Bloom and Stephen Dedalus as two different kinds of artists

A sequel to *Home to Harlem*, *Banjo* is in many ways an old-fashioned novel of ideas, via Dostoevsky. Also, McKay's subtitle, *A Story Without a Plot*, echoes Thackeray's *Vanity Fair: A Novel Without a Hero* (1848). And since McKay's novel is about an artist, or rather two artists, it belongs to the prewar genre of novels about an artist's education such as Goethe's *Wilhelm Meister's Apprenticeship* (1821, 1829) and Romain Rolland's *Jean-Christophe* (1902–1912), as does Joyce's *A Portrait of the Artist as a Young Man* (1916). What makes McKay a modernist like Joyce is his attempt to grapple with issues of art in a post Great War era, especially as they pertain to the condition of African Americans in a new diaspora.

Despite McKay's disclaimer, there is a plot in *Banjo* although it is disguised like Jackman's copy of *Ulysses*. That plot would be tied to a dualism in Joyce, seen not only in *Ulysses* but in Joyce's earlier short story cycle *Dubliners* (1914) and *A Portrait of the Artist as a Young Man*. The plot revolves around two conceptions of the artist, first outlined in Nietzsche's *The Birth of Tragedy* (1872), and then embodied in Joyce's texts, his juxtaposition of Gabriel and Michael Furey in "The Dead," the last story in *Dubliners*, of Stephen Dedalus and Lynch in *Portrait*, and of Stephen and Leopold Bloom in *Ulysses*.

Joyce's biographer Richard Ellman has observed that Joyce alternated between infatuation and parody when it came to Nietzsche (Ellman, index), but there is no doubt that he took seriously Nietzsche's distinction between Apollo and Dionysus. McKay read Nietzsche in Walter Jekyll's library (*Green Hills* 70). At the heart of Nietzsche's *Birth of Tragedy* is Arthur Schopenhauer, the gloomy German philosopher who helped Nietzsche define the presence of Dionysus in Greek culture and who McKay read "a lot of" in Jekyll's translations (*A Long Way* 14; Winston 65). In *The World as Will and Idea* (1818), Schopenhauer sets the world's blind "will" to reproduce against humankind's resistance to being reduced to cannon fodder in an endless cycle of procreation and death. For Nietzsche, that resistance took the form of the creation of a "dream" world, a representation of existence which gave meaning to human experience. Behind this "illusion" are the gods, but specifically Apollo, the god of light who expresses himself in the "plastic forces," the artifice of sculpture and painting (Nietzsche 16). The greatness of "*Attic Tragedy*" in fifth-century Greece lay in the tension between these two "hostile principles," their uneasy marriage (27).

The Apollonian and Dionysiac artists differ, the one believing in the principle of the individual who can make sense of the world through artifice, the other expressing the world's "primal Oneness," its "pain and contradiction," through "music" (Nietzsche 29). As the entry for "Nietzsche" in *The Johns Hopkins Guide to Literary Theory and Criticism* succinctly puts it, Dionysus exposes "the underlying reality concealed by the Apollonian appearance of the world" (Groden and Kreiswirth 516). However, each needs the other, the one not taking the "dream" too far in believing that its artifice is *really* reality, the other not losing oneself in the ecstasy or misery of human experience (Groden and Kreiswirth 16).

The story "A Painful Case" in Joyce's *Dubliners* illustrates this theme in terms of a painful epiphany. On Mr. Duffy's bookshelves are two works by Nietzsche, *Thus Spake Zarathustra* and *The Gay Science*. Imitating Nietzsche's aphoristic style in both, Mr. Duffy deludes himself with this false epiphany, at least in the context of the story: "Love between man and man is impossible because there must not be sexual intercourse and friendship between man and woman is impossible because there must be sexual intercourse" (Joyce, *Dubliners* 108). This utterance, as he came to discover later, prevented him from expressing the affection and sympathy that Mrs. Sinico needed from him. He "thought that in her eyes he would ascend to an angelic stature" (Apollo), but only if his affair with this married woman remained asexual (Joyce, *Dubliners* 107). When she wants something more, he breaks off the relationship and later reads in a newspaper that she was struck by a train and killed. He is stunned by the truth.

His real epiphany is that he was responsible for her suicide. In denying her passion (Dionysus), he had denied her friendship: "Why had he withheld life from her? Why had he sentenced her to death? He felt his moral nature falling to pieces" (Joyce, *Dubliners* 113). Without the life force, you get Dionysus's dark side, the nightmare of "falling to pieces."

What artifice means is shaping, craftsmanship—in a word, giving existence meaning through a figure like the Greek artificer Daedalus who makes wings that fly above a life of misery and suffering. In "The Dead," the last story in *Dubliners*, Gabriel would like to fly out of Ireland whose intellectual and cultural paralysis he finds stultifying. Near the story's end, however, he becomes Icarus, Daedalus's son, falling from a height to which he imagines he has soared. About to leave the annual party given by his aunts, he sees his wife Gretta above him on a staircase absorbed in listening to a song and he thinks that "if he were a painter, he would paint her in that attitude. . . . *Distant Music* he would call the picture if he were a painter" (Joyce, *Dubliners* 211). In this moment, he sees himself as Apollo, shaping what he sees and then, when they return to the hotel where they are to spend the night, controlling the erotic moment that he thinks will follow.

The shock comes when Gretta tells him that a boy in her past sang that song, that hearing it brought back her memory of him. He had died of heart failure at seventeen years old, although Gretta tells Gabriel that she thinks "he died for me" (Joyce, *Dubliners* 221). Gretta's raw Dionysian story of passion, loss, and death shatters Gabriel's Apollonian dream, his sentimental and picturesque portrait of her. There is nothing "distant" in what she tells him about Michael Furey, the boy she was "great" with when she was young. He has this Dionysian epiphany: "Better pass boldly into that other world, in the full glory of some passion" (224).

What is shattered as well is the illusion of himself flying above his fellow Dubliners. The snow that covers Ireland as he looks out the window of their hotel is the mortality that levels all human ambition. The ghost of Michael Furey becomes the "furies" that punish human pride. "At that hour when he had hoped to triumph, some impalpable and vindictive being was coming against him, gathering forces against him in its vague world" (221–22). Apollo's world is the visible "plastic arts"; Dionysus's world consists of "vague" invisible forces. Yet the two are woven into a single fabric.

In *Portrait*, Stephen Dedalus appears to be Joyce himself, flying above the "nets" that hold back the "soul . . . from flight" (Joyce, *Portrait* 220) Those "nets" are Ireland's history, "the nightmare," Stephen says in *Ulysses*, "from which I am trying to awake" (Joyce, *Ulysses* 42). Echoing his spiritual father, the Greek Daedalus, he wants to "forge in the smithy of my soul the uncreated conscience of my race" (Joyce, *Portrait* 276). Ireland's history is the cause of Ireland's paralysis—the history of the Roman Catholic Church, England's oppression. As an artist, as an artificer (Daedalus: "skillfully wrought") Stephen wants to be Apollo, the artist as craftsman who can escape the past by creating something new, just lying beneath the surface which only needs to be expressed.

Yet as critics of Joyce have noticed, there is an irony directed at Stephen throughout the novel. His conception of art is too cerebral: flying above the "nets" means disdaining the quotidian life, as when he refers to the Irish as a "race of clodhoppers" (Joyce, *Portrait* 272). Flying too high means the sun god, whom you want to emulate, can melt your wings.

There is a scene in the novel in which Stephen's abstract theory of art is called into question. He is talking to Lynch, his lowlife friend who serves as a comic gadfly. Stephen tells Lynch that the true "esthetic emotion" is "static," that the mind is arrested and *raised* above desire and loathing" (my emphasis). Lynch responds by saying that if "art must not excite desire," why did I write my name "in pencil on the backside of the Venus Praxiteles in the Museum" (Joyce, *Portrait* 222)? Stephen responds satirically—"I speak of normal natures"—but this doesn't answer Lynch's point: "was that not desire?" Kenneth Burke notes that Lynch's remarks are not "irrelevant heckling," but part of the novel's "motivation" ("Definitions" 441). Joyce's point is that the aesthetic response includes desire because art does not exist apart from the finite world. Venus as a nude sculpture is an artifice, but she is still nude, and still Venus, the goddess of desire.

In *Banjo*, there is a parallel moment to this comic moment with Lynch. Ray tells a funny tale about posing, "in the nude," like a piece of sculpture for a group of art students in Paris. As he is positioned in his "static" pose, the students asked him what he liked about "African Negro sculptures," and he told them that it was "the feeling of perfect self-mastery and quiet self-assurance that they gave" (McKay, *Banjo* 130). One day, as he was posing for the students, he recalled an erotic moment from a Harlem cabaret and he had an erection, only to be saved from acute embarrassment by the "clattering" of his fallen "staff." So much for art that rises above desire.

Joyce's answer to Stephen will not be Lynch but Leopold Bloom, the artist as the Wandering Jew. Stephen will need Bloom to put his feet on the ground, to confront what Joyce calls the "ineluctable modality of the visible" (*Ulysses* 45). The world doesn't go away because Stephen wishes it to, or because he arrives at a theory of art in which desire disappears. In *Ulysses*, Bloom wonders if the same goddess in the same museum has an anus and plans to find out. He's a Lynch on a higher plane, although he does masturbate on the beach, excited by Gerty McDowell's undergarments and her Venus-like buns. Despite all this, or perhaps because of it, Lenehan says of Bloom "there's a touch of the artist about old Bloom" (*Ulysses* 302). It is his love of life's minutiae that makes him an artist. Like his original Hungarian name "Virag" (flower), he springs, as Anthony Burgess notes, "out of common earth." If Stephen is Joyce, he will "need" Leopold Bloom "to write *Ulysses*" (Burgess 105–6).

And if Ray is McKay, as critics have observed, he will need Banjo to write his novels and poems. For *Banjo*, like *Ulysses*, is a tale of two kinds of artists, the Apollonian and the Dionysian. Banjo's identity is tied to his instrument: "It's moh than a gal, moh than a pal; it's mahself" (McKay, *Banjo* 6). The rhyming slang tells us that he is the hip-hop artist of his day, the Orpheus of popular culture whose banjo, like Orpheus's lyre, charms people into dancing. His favorite song is "Shake That Thing," linking his music to sexual ecstasy. Banjo makes claim to being an artist, but he is an artist of a certain kind, made clear by McKay at the end of part 1 of the novel's tri-partite structure:

> Shake That Thing! That jelly-roll Thing!
> Shake to the loud music of life playing to the primeval round of life.... Shake that thing! In the face of the shadow of Death. Treacherous hand of murderous Death, lurking in sinister alleys, where the shadows of life dance, nevertheless, to their music of life. Death over there! Life over here! Shake down Death and forget his *commerce*, his purpose, his haunting presence in a great shaking orgy. Dance down the Death of these days, the Death of these ways in shaking that thing. (my emphasis) (57)

McKay links death's "haunting presence" to life at its most intense, its most "primeval," moments. That is the kind of use value Banjo gives his audience, the primal passion that not only acknowledges its "commerce" with death but laughs at it, dances it "down." His music reveals its opposite, death, through an expression of life at its most intense as does Keats's "joy" in "Ode to Melancholy" (Perkins 1187, lines 22–23).

The Marxist side of McKay in this novel plays with the economic implication of the word "commerce." The beach bums panhandle from American ships called "The Dollar Line," indicating how much American affluence post–World War I has permeated Europe. The word also points to the question of exchange value versus use value. Banjo's music is valued in various ways by the multiple Black vagabonds who arrive in Marseilles's docks from all over the world—from Africa, West Indies, America and beyond. Some value it for its energy, some for its potential for making money, some not at all. Even Banjo gets caught up in the money frenzy with his utopian dream of creating an orchestra and becoming wildly successful, "setting pretty in this heah sweet dump without worrying ovah mah wants" (14).

Sometimes people who should value the banjo refused to honor it as a Black musical instrument. Bugsy complains to Banjo that his banjo is "the instrument of slavery." Perhaps so, says Banjo, but in his hands, it is transformed into something else: "I don't play no Black Joe hymns. I play lively tunes" (90). Like Henry Tanner's famous painting *The Banjo Lesson* (1893), McKay redeems the instrument from white interpretations. In her book *That Half-Barbaric Twang: The Banjo in American Popular Culture* (1994), Karen Linn points to this passage as an example of the "ambivalence" that African Americans still had about an instrument associated with the Plantation Tradition and the minstrel shows. Even though its cultural meaning was changing during the Jazz Age, the banjo was still linked by white popular culture to those estranged "from civilization" (75, 46).

McKay's point is that Banjo's music isn't simply "lively." It reflects the life force that puritan American civilization refuses to acknowledge. "In *Banjo*, McKay said that "the banjo is preeminently the musical instrument of the American Negro. The sharp noisy notes of the banjo belong to the American Negro's loud music of life—an affirmation of his hardy existence in the midst of the biggest, the most tumultuous civilization of modern life" (49). In "Sonny's Blues" (1957) James Baldwin takes a musical instrument from high culture, the piano, and has Sonny express Black culture at ground level, the blues, as August Wilson will do in *The Piano Lesson* (1987). McKay takes an instrument from low culture and has it express life at its essential level, that is, the Dionysian truth of human existence, especially Black existence. America's "tumultuous" culture, on the other hand, is the life force reduced to Henry Adams's sexless "dynamo."

McKay knew that this instrument from low culture was associated with the Negro as clown, and he would focus on the Negro as clown in his 1922 review for *The Liberator* of Leonid Andreyev's popular play *He Who Gets Slapped*. The play was the hit of the season; it ran on Broadway for 185 consecutive nights in 1922. McKay went to see it with a white friend, but when the manager saw McKay, they both were "shunted" upstairs to the balcony—which to McKay gave an extra poignancy to the play's title.

In his review, McKay said that Andreyev had not the slightest clue as to who gets "slapped" in American culture. But then he added a note on what Andreyev might had accomplished under different circumstances: "Ah, if the accident of birth had made Andreyev a Negro, if he had been slapped, kicked, buffeted, pounded, n----red, ridiculed, sneered at, exquisitely tortured, near lynched and trampled underfoot by the merry white horde, and if he still preserved through the terrible agony a sound body and a mind sensitive and sharp to perceive the qualities of life, he might have written a real play about Being Slapped" (*Passion of Claude McKay* 70; also see *A Long Way* 144–45). He then made a personal appeal to the playwright, one that has a relevance to Banjo, the clown as artist: "Dear Leonid Andreyev, if you had only risen out of your introspective Nihilistic despair to create the clown in the circus of Hell, the clown slapped on every side by the devil's red-hot tongs, yet growing wiser, stronger and firmer in purposeful determination, seeking no refuge in suicide, but bearing it out to the bitter end, you might have touched me" (*Passion of Claude McKay* 70). But he doesn't stop here. He compares his situation of being a Black face in the balcony to the white faces on stage and in the audience below him. It's a divided space that points to a historical reality, one not addressed by the ahistorical, sentimental play or the white people in the theater: "Poor, painful black face, intruding into the holy places of the whites. How like a specter you haunt the pale devils" (71).

Then comes the devastating satiric punch. What is shown on stage pales beside the primal crime: "How can they bear your presence, blackface, great, unappeasable *ghost* of Western Civilization" (my emphasis) (*Passion of Claude McKay* 72).

There is an additional irony. What McKay is calling for—an honest treatment of who precisely gets slapped in American culture—will be Victor Sjostrom's stunning, silent film *He Who Gets Slapped* (1924), based on the play but revised visually to express a critique of America's cruel racial system. McKay's review probably influenced Sjostrom's cinematic treatment of Andreyev's play.

Sjostrom constructs the plot around Apollo and Dionysus, theft and humiliation, agency and repetition-compulsion. The key image in the film is the white mask, the disguise that also reveals. It becomes the obverse of minstrelsy's "blackening up."

Paul Beaufort, played by Lon Chaney, is a brilliant scientist who, in the film's beginning, discovers through his enormous research the "origin of mankind." He entrusts his wealthy benefactor, the baron (Marc McDermott), to present his paper to the academy, but the treacherous baron claims the theory for his own. Then he steals not only Paul's intellectual property but Paul's wife. When Paul accuses them both, the baron slaps him, as does his wife, the latter calling him "Fool! Clown!"

In his despair, a clown is what Paul becomes, and his act, being slapped over and over again by fellow circus clowns, makes him famous. What is especially terrifying in the film is the close-ups of the laughter, both by his fellow clowns but especially by the audience who delights in Paul's humiliation and misery.

Since the circus takes place in enclosed space, the circular arena, the audience becomes the world, a point made by Sjostrum when at various moments in the film we see Paul as clown holding a spinning globe in his hand. The spinning world is a world that doesn't change—it just keeps on spinning. However, the clown holds the world. He is its axis, the fixed reference point. Lon Chaney is a white actor but in white face he becomes the clown as artist who exposes the cruel underpinnings of the spinning world.

No one recognizes Paul in his disguise, including the baron. Not only is his identity removed but even his name. He is referred to throughout as "HE" as in the pronoun of the film's title. He is the "HE" who is humiliated; his only actions are to repeat ad infinitum the Ur act of being a ghost who haunts the American Republic, the theme of McKay's review.

Sjostrom keeps reminding us that he is making an American film about race. The film's opening image is not a white face but a neon face encompassing a Black face with huge lips and a wide smile which is repeatedly slapped. Moreover, the diminutive clowns who slap HE are dressed in white robes and their face coverings look like Ku Klux Klan hoods. At one point the camera focuses on the baron playing with a noose, a counterpoint to the cloth heart which HE wears on his clown's clothing which is then ripped from him during his performance in a moment of a ritualized lynching.

But it is the process of "whitening up" that is the ultimate gothic scene, the transformation of a man to a cadaverous clown, condemned to act out a racial fantasy again and again, foreshadowing Sandy in Richard Wright's *American Hunger* (1945, 1980), whose behind is endlessly kicked, and Tod Clifton in Ralph Ellison's *Invisible Man* (1952), whose marionette doll reenacts, over and over again, roles African Americans are forced to perform in real life.

The film has a conventional Hollywood subplot in which two lovers must overcome adversity. Consuelo (Norma Shearer) is the daughter of the impoverished Count Mancini (Tully Marshall) who works in the circus because of her poverty and who partners with Bezano (John Gilbert), a celebrated bare-back performer. Together they ride a white horse. The white horse, their white skin—these are very different signifiers from whiteness as a form of death in life.

Together Consuelo and Bezano make a perfect team, both in art and in real life, but their romance is threatened by Consuelo's father, who attempts to sell her to the lecherous baron. Virtue and love finally triumph, the baron and Consuelo's father conveniently chewed up by a lion set loose by HE, but what is underlined by Sjostrum is not the lovers' victory over adversity but their blindness to HE's condition. Consuelo turns out to be no different from the white audience who mocks HE's suffering. Near the end of the film, when HE confesses his own love for her, she not only laughs at him but slaps him, refusing to take him seriously or to even see him beneath the white makeup.

This is the cruelest cut of all. It is one thing for the crowd to be insensitive to HE's condition, but it is quite another thing for Consuelo to scorn him. During the film, she has earned our sympathy because she is about to be sold by her own father into domestic slavery. But her blindness and Bezano's indifference to HE reflect a larger pattern of racism that permeates everything, even the beautiful people who remain blissfully isolated in their own world. The film has a happy ending of sorts, lovers united and bad people dead, but what remains is the audience who, although they thrill to the performances of the lovely couple, continue to laugh at human misery as embodied in the clown.

In his critique of Andreyev's play in *A Long Way from Home*, McKay implies that he has seen Sjostrum's film: "I felt that if Negroes can lift clowning to artistry, they can thumb their noses at superior people who rate them as a clowning race" (141). This is exactly what HE does, and of course it is why McKay admired Charlie Chaplin. In his despair, the crown transforms his misery into art. And this is also why McKay entitled his novel *Banjo* and not Ray, even though Ray, as a version of himself, is a larger presence in the novel than Banjo. McKay is also thinking of Banjo in terms of Charlie Chaplin, the clown as artist.

In a chapter in *Banjo* entitled "The 'Blue Cinema,'" Ray and some white friends view a pornographic film. McKay uses this as an occasion to critique popular culture, especially white American popular culture. Disgusted by what he has seen, one member of the group makes this generalization: "whether it is blue or any other color of the rainbow, the cinema is for the mob. . . . It will never be an art." Ray objects: "Pictorial pantomime can be just as fine an art as any. What about Charlie Chaplin?" which gets this response: "He's an exception. A conscientious artist with a popular appeal." Ray counters: "all real art is an exception," and "you can't condemn an art wholesale because inartistic people make a bad business of it" (McKay, *Banjo* 216). Not only is this McKay's defense of popular culture but even mass culture such as the cinema. An aspect of McKay's modernism was his fascination with cinema, despite his belief that most of the time Hollywood makes "a bad business of it." Even the cynical Bugsy in *Banjo* wants to see a "Hoot Gibson film" in Marseilles (10).

When McKay called Chaplin "the lord of the cinema" in *A Long Way from Home*, in the context of referring to Charlie Chaplin's artistry several times in his autobiography, he was paying him a genuine compliment (*Long Way* 116–19). One occasion stands out. At a dinner party at which both McKay and Chaplin were present, McKay saw Chaplin astound his audience with "comic tricks" that "were swift and sure like the sharp lines of Goya," different from, McKay added, the "clowning which he uses so lavishly on screen" (*Long Way* 117). Yet clearly, they are not that different: clowning and Goya belong to the same canvas. Together they stand in contrast to pornography as McKay defines it in "The 'Blue Cinema,'" which Ray sees as just the opposite of Banjo's music which is an affirmation of the life force.

For McKay, pornography is a kind of death wish, desire reduced to the mechanical, the "calculating," as if in creating disgust in its audience its "moral purpose" was "to terrify and frighten away all who saw it from that phrase of life" (McKay, *Banjo* 214). Pornography, for McKay, is Dionysus turning on himself, Eros as Henry Adams "dynamo," America's "tumultuous" civilization becoming Goosey's "United Snakes" (117). Pornography as pseudo-art is only one story in *Banjo: A Story Without a Plot*. A character who has seen the blue movie said he wanted "to go to the roughest and dirtiest place we can find" (216). Knowing that Banjo is a real artist, Ray sardonically suggests they all go to the Ditch to hear Banjo play, for the life force of "Shake That Thing" is the direct opposite of the death wish of "The 'Blue Cinema.'"

According to Linda Williams, pornography does have a plot. The "money shot" takes place within a "narrative," within a sequence of repetitious moments that lead to a climax (Williams 94, 95, 121) The "frenzy" of America's "tumultuous" culture, a point McKay keeps returning to, is like pornography in that its climax is cruelty for those who are victimized by it. This theme is illustrated in McKay's poem "The White House," whose law endlessly repeats itself, biting its own tail. That is its climax (*CP* 149, line 12).

McKay had another purpose in mind besides setting the blue movie against Banjo's music. Like his life, Banjo's music is open, fluid. McKay illustrates this at several points in the novel. About Banjo, Ray says, "life for him was just one different thing of a sort following another" (McKay, *Banjo* 27). And more specifically, "The grand rhythm of life rolled on everlastingly *without beginning or end in human comprehension*, but the patterns were ever changing, the figures moving on and passing, to be replaced by new ones" (235) (my emphasis).

In the "Proteus" section of *Ulysses*, change is the major theme, but Stephen makes a distinction between *nacheinander* and *nebeneinander*, time and space (45): "one thing coming after another . . . one thing coming next to another" (Burgess 101). The words "conjunction" and "commerce" suggest that *Banjo* does have a plot, a plot in which space (things next to another) replaces the traditional pattern of things coming after another.

Or rather, the patterns that are formed depend upon juxtaposition, always changing: Ray and Banjo, Banjo and Bugsy, Banjo and Latnah, Banjo and Lonesome Blue, and finally the juxtaposition of ideas, arguments over the nature of Black life in a white civilization. Although the patterns are "ever changing," behind them is the permanence of the life force of Black culture: "Commerce! Of all words the most magical . . . forever going hand in hand with the bitch bawdy" (307).

That life force is why Ray wants to remain connected to Banjo and the other bums. Banjo grounds Ray as an artist. Without him, Ray would become a kind of Stephen as Hugh Kenner describes him in the "Proteus" section of *Ulysses*: "Stephen's thoughts tend to be arcane, woven if not of wind then of insubstantialities, fine words, swift perverse associations, the mind enamoured of its own prestidigitation" (45).

One sees that difference between Bloom and Stephen in terms of the way each responds to the finite world. As Bloom walks Dublin's streets, "Grafton Street gay with housed awnings lured his senses. Muslin prints, silk, dames and dowagers, jingle of harnesses, hoofthuds lowringing in the baking causeway. Thick feet that woman has in the white stockings. Hope the rain mucks them up on her" (*Ulysses* 213). Here the tangible landscape is set against Stephen's reflections on Sandymont strand in the "Proteus" section of the novel. With Stephen, everything "visible" is filtered through "thought"; that is its "modality." Bloom is Banjo, responding to the world with his "senses."

Bloom as the Wandering Jew also exists in the same relationship to Dublin as the bums do to Marseilles's authorities. His confrontation with the patriotic "Citizen" in Barney Kiernan's tavern has its counterpart in Ray's harassment by the Marseilles police and Banjo having his instrument unjustly seized by a white restaurant owner. If Stephen needs Bloom (the father reuniting with the "son": Ulysses and Telemachus), Ray needs Banjo, his surrogate son (Burgess 107). But as Merve Emre observes in her recent insightful essay on *Ulysses* in *The New Yorker*, "if "Ulysses teaches us anything it is that nobody is ever only a father and a son" (Emre 73).

Ursula K. Le Guin describes Ray's need when she talks about her own fiction in Apollonian/Dionysian terms: "Apollo, the god of light, of reason, of proportion, harmony, number—Apollo blinds those who press too close in worship. Don't look straight at the sun. Go into a dark bar for a bit and have a beer with Dionysus, every now and then" (Le Guin xxi). Just as Banjo needs Ray to complete him, so too Ray needs Banjo to complete him. Ray is the Apollonian artist who uses print culture to express Black life but who has a "beer" with Banjo to keep himself grounded. For Nietzsche, the brilliance of fifth-century Greek art was that Apollonian reason and the Dionysian life force were held in an uneasy balance or tension, but Nietzsche would also note that Schopenhauer expressed the "yawning abyss between Apolline plastic arts and Dionysian music" (Nietzsche 76). Here is Ray's dilemma. If he is to depict Black life in his poetry and prose, he will have to bridge that gap by "bring[ing] intellect to the aid of instinct." This also involves the paradox of living in a "civilization" that attempts to deracinate Black culture, one that denies "love of color, joy, beauty, vitality and nobility," while it has publishing houses that publish his writings (McKay, *Banjo* 164).

And there is another paradox. Ray identifies with Banjo and his group of Marseilles bums because they have not had their vitality erased by "white morality." Like them, he has lived the "laboring life, and the most precious souvenirs of it were the joyful friendships he had made among his pals. There was no intellectual friendship to be compared with them" (McKay, *Banjo* 202). Yet for all that "he could not scrap his intellectual life and be entirely like them. He did not want or feel any urge to "go back" that way" (McKay, *Banjo* 322).

For that matter, Banjo has no interest in Ray the actual writer. Ray talking about his work is one thing, but when Banjo sees his slightly "soiled" manuscripts and "shabby collection of books, he quickly lost interest" (McKay, *Banjo* 69). So how to bridge the gap between print culture and popular culture, or between Apollo and Dionysus? A similar problem existed for Joyce. How do Stephen and Bloom connect in *Ulysses*, or Stephen and Lynch in *A Portrait of the Artist of a Young Man*, or Richard and Robert in *Exiles*? In one sense, for both McKay and Joyce, the artist will always remain an outsider, an exile. Stephen as the lone artificer, Bloom as outcast in his own country is mirrored by Ray who will always remain outside the world of highbrow, African American society ("movie-picture imitations") and "fake" intellectuals and the "bums" of who belong to the Ditch (116).

Although the eponymous hero of the novel, and a flawless artist who lives in the present and takes things as they come ("always" landing on "mah feet" no matter how far the "drop'), Banjo lives a precarious life (17). When he loses his banjo to debt (229), the man who says his instrument is "mahself" ends up working in coal, a kind of Orpheus in the underworld. The orchestra that he wants to put together and which he hopes will bring him worldly success always remains elusive, calling attention to his dependence upon the commercial world. Latnah, the woman he takes up with and who really does have her feet on the ground, is scornful of his cavalier attitude toward money. If you are going to play in these dives, she tells him, you need to pass the hat around.

Ray, too, is vulnerable, dependent as he is upon the publishing world. McKay found out the hard way when Alain Locke changed the title of "The White City" to "White Cities," just as he was always living on the edge of poverty, asking friends for money, never making enough money to survive from his writing despite his passion to write: "More and more the urge to write was holding him [Ray] with an enslaving grip and he was beginning to feel that any means to achieving self-expression was justifiable"(65). But "white beachcombers" steal his books and his manuscripts, just as Banjo loses the thing that is "mahself" (236). "Self-expression," no matter how important to the person who expresses the self, takes place in an indifferent world.

How is the conflict between the Apollonian and Dionysian artist resolved if it ever is? In addition to Charlie Chaplin within popular culture, the artist as clown, there is the rich tradition of Black oral culture—specifically the art of storytelling.

The chapter called "Story-Telling" begins with Goosey complaining that Ray should give a positive spin to the race and "publish" flattering stories about "how these race boys live in the Ditch" (115). Ray responds by saying that the "real story-teller" is not interested in uplift or how the race is portrayed or the color of his audience but in the truth of the story. Hence, he begins with an African folk tale in which a wicked aunt tries to feed her niece to a crocodile, but the crocodile turns out to be a handsome prince who marries her. They both return to the aunt's house and forgive her. Wishing to be punished, the aunt insists that she should be fed to the leopards, but the husband and young bride only want to restore the home, garden, and family.

Ray's tale is simple and sentimental, but he knows that this kind of story provides a link to another African fable, told by another member of the group. Bugsy then tells a tale about a monkey who dupes a leopard. The monkey happens to be a man, a slave named Sam who as a trickster (Henry Louis Gates Jr.'s "signifying monkey") claims to find things that he himself has hidden on the plantation. "From that time" on, Bugsy says, "the American darky started in playing the coon and the white man is paying him for it" (125). This story inspires Banjo to tell a personal story about a white man who did pay him, but the story "ain't no monkey-coon affair." His story involved a same-sex relationship with an affluent white American. The group who hears the story about the "bugger" expects Banjo to make fun of the white man but is disappointed: "I wouldn't want a better pal to travel around with" (127). Ray then reverses Banjo's fable by telling a story about his erection as he is posing for the art students of Paris, caused not by "a pretty Parisienne" but by his memory of gorgeous Black women at the Sheba Palace in Harlem. This story, beginning and ending with Ray, is the circular end of a round robin of stories, snakes that do not bite their tails.

Ray ends this round robin of stories with a story that is comic, humane, and communal: the restored garden of the first story morphs into the Sheba Palace of the last story. Ray doesn't control the narrative so much as he orchestrates it, fulfilling the dream Banjo has for creating an orchestra in which his instrument will be the dominate sound among many musical voices. Behind all this is McKay himself, the ultimate conductor of the disparate voices of the novel. He connects them through his interwoven narrative of multiple stories, even Jake's, who at novel's end visits Marseilles. That he is referred to as *"Home to Harlem* Jake" is McKay's reminder that his novel is an artifice that encompasses other stories (292). That is, storytelling by itself is not enough, for it leaves out the "formally challenging" and sometimes unresolved experiences within a book like *Ulysses* (Sehgal 70).

At the end of *Banjo*, McKay plays with the idea of connection when Ray suggests that they bring Latnah with them on their travels. Banjo rejects the idea by responding that "a woman is a conjunction," linking us in ways that would make life difficult for us and limit us as artists: "Gawd fixed her different from us in moh ways than one. And theah's things we can git away with all the time and she just kain't" (326). Banjo's point is self-centered but brutally true from his perspective. This is not as sexist as it sounds. McKay reminds us that there are different kinds of conjunctions. Jake "liked" being married to Felice, liked being a father, of "no longer being the wild stallion, but a draft horse in harness" (306).

What McKay is arguing through Banjo is that women connect men in different ways, as men do women (27). What Banjo does not see is that Latnah is an artist of her own life, foreshadowing Bita in *Banana Bottom*: "Whatever personal art she might use as a woman to increase her chances was her own affair" (32). Through Ray, McKay presents us with the figure of the author whose function is also one of "conjunction"—with the reader, with other storytellers in the oral tradition. In his brilliant poem, "The Harlem Dancer," McKay is not only the poet who describes the dancer but, as her creator, he is also her partner in the dance.

The choice Ray and Banjo have made means that "home" as Jake knows it will never be theirs. Their home will be the artifice of telling tales. McKay does not say that one kind of "conjunction" is better than the other. Each choice comes with its own rewards and costs. Jake and Felice choose marriage, family, and heterosexual sex. The artist "connects" stories, experiences, in a web of artifice. If there is a sexual "connection," it is a fluid sexuality of an unconventional nature.

But "choice" is perhaps not the right word. Choice presupposes a rational world in which plots are possible. It's the world the white people live in, "the choosing people." They can choose because they believe they are the chosen ones, the authors of a narrative about America from which African Americans are excluded, Toledo's "leftovers" in August Wilson's *Ma Rainey's Black Bottom*.

Jake and Felice meet accidentally, separate, and meet again accidentally. They see their "chance" and they take it. So too with Ray and Banjo, the chance they seize is a same-sex relationship, but it is also a marriage between Apollo and Dionysus. A ménage à trois with Latnah is disruptive because it creates a new "conjunction," a new narrative, one that threatens the artistic integrity of each man. It's a hard choice, but that is one plot in the novel, among plot lines. McKay will explore another kind of "conjunction" in *Romance in Marseille* and *Banana Bottom*. He's not against the "marriage plot," as *Banana Bottom* will illustrate, but if the artist is part Proteus, as well as Apollo and Dionysus, McKay is intrigued by the number of possible plots and "conjunctions" there are.

A final word on conjunctions. It is worth considering the sea change in attitude by Black intellectuals on the whole question of "influence." In recent years, there has been a reluctance to admit to white literary influences, as the nation's persistent racism has cast doubt on whether white people are capable of any authentic commentary on Black life, either as historians or imaginative writers. It is difficult to say when this change occurred but as early as the 1990s, Toni Morrison in *Playing in the Dark: Whiteness and the Literary Imagination* (1992) focused on the silencing of Black characters in Willa Cather's *Sapphira and the Slave Girl* and Hemingway's *To Have and Have Not* (*Playing in the Dark* 18–28, 69–86), noting that this silence reflected a larger refusal to see the presence of slavery and its aftermath as formative forces that shaped American history and its literary imagination.

Nevertheless, despite this recent trend, it is almost impossible to imagine a Harlem Renaissance without white influences. The obvious example is Carl Van Vechten, but he is only one of many. Jean Toomer openly told Sherwood Anderson that both *Winesburg, Ohio* and *The Triumph of the Egg* "are elements of my growing. It is hard to think of myself maturing without them" (Toomer 148). And, of course, all students of *Cane* know how much

Waldo Frank helped Toomer as editor and advocate, in addition to the impact that Frank's short story cycle *City Block* (1922) had upon Toomer.

This is only the beginning. Langston Hughes found the "*Adventures of Huckleberry Finn* so thrilling that he remained a lifelong admirer of Mark Twain," and was pleased when a reviewer compared his use of the vernacular in his Simple stories to Twain's (Rampersad 1: 19; 2: 223). According to Hughes, Wallace Thurman read everything and "wanted to be a *very* great writer, like Gorki or Thomas Mann," but in comparing himself to authors like "Proust, Melville, and Tolstoy," he made himself miserable (*The Big Sea* 235). Jessie Fauset was clearly indebted to Edith Wharton, her Angela Murray in *Plum Bun* having a source in Wharton's Ellen Olenska in *The Age of Innocence*, as the two attempt to navigate the treacherous social landscape of New York society. Fauset's "passing" theme would be repeated by Nella Larsen in her novel *Passing*, with its echoes of Fitzgerald's *The Great Gatsby*. Her Tom Bellew is modeled on Fitzgerald's Tom Buchanan, both arrogant white men who are physically strong but mentally obtuse figures who stand in the way of Clare and Gatsby who try to "pass." George Schuyler was known as "the black Mencken," but Mencken's impact did not stop there. James Weldon Johnson also admired him and took his advice in *Black Manhattan* "to single out the strong points of the race and emphasize them over and over and over; asserting, at least on these points, that they are *better* than anyone else" (*Along This Way* 305). Repeating what he had said in *The Book of American Negro Poetry*, he called on the Black poet in *God's Trombones* to find "something like Synge did for the Irish . . . to find a form that will express the racial spirit by symbols from within rather symbols from without" (Johnson, *God's Trombones* 8). In *Black Manhattan*, his Black city was "better" than the large metropolis because it had a strong sense of community, a theme in Alain Locke's *New Negro*, indebted not to Mencken but to Van Wyck Brooks's *America's Coming-Of-Age* for its thesis. The great migration from South to North, Locke argued, made a "spiritual Coming of Age" possible (Locke, *New Negro* 7). Even a "race man" like W. E. B. Du Bois found an ancestor figure in a fellow New Englander, Ralph Waldo Emerson; Du Bois's famous "double consciousness" had its source in the same phrase used by Emerson to describe the gap between the "buzz and din" of common life and the precious moments of spiritual illumination. Du Bois would transform that divided self to the psychological split within African Americans of being both Black and American (Bruce 237).

The issue of white influence goes beyond the decades of the 1920s and 1930s: Richard Wright and Theodore Dreiser, James Baldwin and Henry

James, Ralph Ellison and Kenneth Burke, T. S. Eliot, Faulkner and Hemingway, et al. So, what position does McKay occupy in this scheme of what is now seen as "whitewashing"?

We need first to put McKay in another context: the rich intellectual arguments within the 1920s concerning art and the artist. Brooks's "usable past," Eliot's canon of sacred texts, Pound's vortex, Mumford's utopias, Frank's "unanimisme," Bourne's "dual citizenship" ("As long as we thought of Americanism in terms of the 'the melting pot,' our American cultural tradition lay in the past"), Rosenfeld's "Port of New York"—these are only a few of the aesthetic theories swirling about as if in a centrifuge. Ezra Pound was surely on to something when he defined the vortex as "patterned energy made visible," a "cluster . . . from which, and through which, and into which, ideas are constantly rushing" (qtd. in Kenner, *The Pound Era* 146).

The relevance here to McKay lies in his connection to the most famous debate over African American art in the 1920s, that between George Schuyler and Langston Hughes: "The Negro-Art Hokum" and "The Negro and the Racial Mountain." Most critics consider Hughes to be the winner, but given McKay's multileveled arguments in *Banjo* over what it means to be a Black artist, it is doubtful that McKay would find the Schuyler/Hughes debate clear cut, especially since he was also aware of two other texts that appeared in the same year, 1926. Du Bois's "Criteria of Negro Art" and Carl Van Vechten's controversial *Nigger Heaven* contributed to this vortex of "rushing" ideas, all of which appear in *Banjo* to some degree. Van Vechten's Byron Kasson is a college-educated aspiring "Negro" writer who has just moved to Harlem but can't "think of a thing" to write about (*NH* 185). He finds Harlem's low life beneath him, sordid and hostile. He ends up crushed by the world he holds in contempt, ending up in a real-life pulp fiction plot that he disdains in literature. Du Bois pushes the envelope in another direction, arguing that "all art is propaganda," and he wishes to propagate a view of Black life that reflects its best side, not Alain Locke's cult of beauty or McKay's (and Hughes's) gritty Harlem low life.

The question in the Schuyler/Hughes debate centers on whether the "African" or the "American" in Afro-American should be emphasized. Schuyler calls Negro art a fiction since after generations of living in America "the Aframerican is merely a lampblacked Anglo-Saxon" or, put another way, "your American Negro is just plain American" (Lewis 97). Hughes goes in a different direction, saying that he knew a friend who wanted "to be a poet—not a Negro poet," meaning he wanted "to write like a white poet," meaning "subconsciously" that he wanted to be "white" (Lewis 91). Schuyler is collapsing the Negro and American into one, the American melting pot, whereas Hughes champions America as a tossed salad where individual ingredients matter. McKay would probably see something in both arguments, especially since like Hughes he embraces Black life in all its multiplicity, and like Schuyler he recognizes the American in himself (along with multiple other identities). As we have seen in *Banjo*, the question of being an artist is not so simple. Hughes's parable about his friend has a logical flaw: to want to be an artist and not a Black artist does not necessarily mean you want to be white. Ray admired Banjo the Black artist, but he doesn't necessarily want to be like him. For McKay, being an artist means accepting all kinds of literature, but it does not mean denying your racial identity as a Black artist. In fact, your love of the past and the present in all its many colors may even enhance your blackness, as it does in the scene where Ray is sexually aroused by his memory of a Harlem maid while he is pretending to be a white shepherd in Arcadia.

Although we might deplore Schuyler's failure to recognize the horrors of American history when it comes to "Aframericans," he is not wrong to point to an American presence in even the African Americans who chafe the most against white America, the kind who might write "If We Must Die," the kind who though a Jamaican by birth assumes the fierce independence of Emerson's self-reliant American. Here is the reason why *Banjo* never takes a decisive stand on what precisely the word "conjunction" means in terms of the artist. McKay is married to a view that the true artist is protean. Just as it is impossible to confine McKay to being an artist of one particular genre, so is it impossible to put him in a straitjacket as an artist, either as Schuyler's "Anglo-Saxon" (albeit of a Jamaican hue) or Hughes's "white" poet. McKay delights in wearing many hats, sometimes all at the same time.

CHAPTER 4

THE CINEMA AS ROMANCE IN *ROMANCE IN MARSEILLE*

Rex Ingram gave me a job. It was a nice, congenial and easy job. I read a lot of fiction and made a summary of any interesting plots.
—CLAUDE MCKAY, *A LONG WAY FROM HOME*, 272

At the time of McKay's visit to Ingram's film studios in Nice in 1926, Ingram was still considered one of Hollywood's most popular directors, along with Cecil B. DeMille, Erich von Stroheim, Maurice Tourneur, and of course Charlie Chaplin. He had become famous in 1921, not only for directing the World War I epic *Four Horsemen of the Apocalypse* but for making Rudolph Valentino a star in that film. However, by 1926 he had run afoul of the new Hollywood studio system headed by Irving Thalberg. He was a product of the "silent film era, where directors ruled not only the set but the entire production process" (Schatz 35). He lacked the clout of von Stroheim, another rebel, but he "persuaded" film magnate Marcus Loew to "provide him with a studio in Nice," which is where McKay met him (Brownlow 37). McKay was drawn to Ingram because he was an outsider like himself. Besides, Ingram liked his poetry.

Recently critics have pointed to the visual elements in McKay's work. David B. Hobb has referred to the "visual tactics" in his poetry, especially his "North African Panoramas" (Hobbs 194–97). And Stephanie Brown has noted the "abundance of surveillance agents" in *Romance in Marseille*, "operating sometimes independent of each other, sometimes in concert" (Brown 94). But no one has discussed McKay's interest in film, or its relationship to or its presence in his fiction. He defended film as an art form in *Banjo* (1929) in his chapter on "The 'Blue Cinema,'" in which Ray argued that you can't "condemn an art" just because "people make a bad business of it" (*Banjo* 216). In *A Long Way from Home*, he has a four-page appreciation of Charlie Chaplin's genius, especially the "incomparable 'Shoulder Arms'" (117). Allusions to films abound in his fiction, from "Hoot Gibson" Westerns to the Valentino "Sheik" films, to even film magazines which one of his characters is reading in *Banjo*: "The girl was usually reading *Le Film Complet, Mon Cine*, and moving picture novelettes," just the kind Rex Ingram asked McKay read for possible film scripts (*Banjo* 172).

McKay is also aware of movies made for the Black masses. In *Home to Harlem* (1928) Jake and Felice go to a "Negro Picture Theater" in Harlem in which "colored screen actors were all dressed up in expensive evening clothes, with automobiles, and menials, to imitate white society people" (314). McKay knows that a separate Black cinema exists and that, within that cinema, Black people not only emulate rich white folks but even mock them, and the audience is in on the joke. McKay seems to anticipate Langston Hughes's satirical observation that, in Harlem, Black filmgoers are always "laughing in all the wrong places" (Hughes, *Collected Poems* 395). Those "places" would often be scenes depicting an imaginary Black bourgeoisie. This kind of film was standard fare for Black theaters. Jane Gaines observes that "films produced specifically for all-black audiences . . . were created by the black bourgeoisie, often in collaboration with whites, for the entertainment and edification of the group below them," namely people like Jake and Felice (4).

That at least was the specific intention, but in fact, especially in films directed and produced by Oscar Micheaux, there was often another agenda, hidden beneath the melodrama. That would be "the ghost of a second story about life in a racist society," as in the 1927 "Negro" produced silent *The Scar of Shame* (Gaines 15). That "ghost," according to Jane Gaines, complicates the melodramatic plot of the tragic mulatta and the "happy ending" of marriage between two people of the "right" class. *Romance in Marseille* also has a melodramatic format, but its film noir ending turns conventional melodrama into a gothic nightmare. (In *Banjo*, McKay used the anglicized "Marseilles," but in this novel, he used the French "Marseille." I am following his practice when I talk about each novel.)

As editors Gary Edward Holcomb and William J. Maxwell note in the introduction to their excellent edition of *Romance in Marseille* (2020), McKay began his novel in 1929, put it aside in 1930, returned to it in 1932, but gave up on it in 1933, in the midst of the Great Depression (McKay, *Romance*, vii–viii). In the course of writing it, McKay went through two titles, "The Jungle and the Bottoms" and "Savage Loving," before McKay settled on "its most place-bound name" (viii). The new title was a happy choice, not simply because of its focus on a place made famous by Marcel

Pagnol (the Fanny Trilogy—first as plays, then as movies) but for the cinematic possibilities embedded in the word "Romance."

McKay never mentions Marcel Pagnol. *Marius*, the first of the three plays, was performed on stage on March 9, 1929, then made into a film in 1931 (Caldicott 70). Both versions, play and film, were enormously popular in France. McKay wrote *Romance in Marseille* between 1929 and 1932. McKay probably had Pagnol's *Marius*, play and film, in mind when he was writing his novel.

McKay's Lafala is the mirror opposite of Marius. The Black Lafala returns to a racially diverse Marseille a cripple but with money to impress Aslima. The white Marius has wanderlust and wants to sail away from the small community of Marseille, his father's bourgeois life, and his bistro. But unknowingly he leaves behind a pregnant Fanny.

Faced with the prospect of being an unwed mother in a Catholic community, the desperate Fanny marries a man, Panisse, twice her age (*Fanny*, 1932). When he returns to Marseilles, Marius wants to claim his child and Fanny both, but his own father, Cesar thwarts him. However, by the trilogy's end, Marius and Fanny are magically reunited in middle age, thanks to their spoiled, obtuse son and the savvy Cesar who finds a way to bring them together (*Cesar*, 1936). All three films are wonderful soap operas with a specific slant upon Marseille.

In Pagnol's plays and films, not only are his characters white, but he creates a Marseille that is provincial and racially homogeneous. More specifically, Marseille is treated as though it were a small town or village. It is as though McKay's polyglot Marseille didn't exist, something McKay set out to correct in his novel. He saw his novel as a potential film script to rival the sanitized version of Marseille in the film version of *Marius*.

Whether he originally saw his short novel (like the "novelette") as a film script or whether the idea dawned on him as he returned to it is a moot point. Interestingly, in the same year he stopped working on it, he got this encouragement from Langston Hughes in a letter dated September 30, 1930: "Wish you could sell something to the movies and make lots of money. That's what all the white writers are doing. Selling their books months before they come out even" (*Selected Letters* 99). In any event, Arthur Miller's "author's note" to the "story" behind his screenplay for *The Misfits* (1961) points to what McKay had in mind when he wrote *Romance in Marseille*: "It is a story conceived as a film, and every word is there for the purpose of telling the camera what to see and the actors what they are to say" (Miller ix). Throughout the novel, McKay indicates that he is thinking in cinematic terms, but he is also alluding to other visual artists such as Francisco Goya and George Grosz. In *A Long Way from Home*, he connects the dots between Charlie Chaplin, Goya, and Grosz. As we have seen, he compared Chaplin's comic moves to "the sharp lines of Goya," and then singled out "the incomparable 'Shoulder Arms'" for special praise, a film that is "a feat of rapid economical design, as startling as the best of Goya's grotesqueries" (117). Later in that same text, he noted that Grosz's *Ecce Homo*, published in 1922, the same year as Eliot's *The Waste Land* and Joyce's *Ulysses*, captured the "temper and tempo of Berlin of that period" (240). And then he adds this: his "book of drawings is a rare and iconoclastic monument to this closing era even as Rabelais is of the Renaissance." Those "powerful artistic punches," as McKay calls them, were not only satiric, but satire bordering on the gothic. Grosz depicted his subjects—prostitutes, businessmen, captains of industry—literally without their clothes, exposing the gross bodies and behavior. In one portrait, "The Gray Day" (1921), Grosz draws a fat businessman with a flaccid face, and in the background walks a one-armed, cadaverous looking soldier from the Great War, an image McKay would remember in *Romance in Marseille*. In a 1926 painting he called "Drinnen and Draussen" ("Inside and Outside"), Grosz depicts an obese capitalist at a dining table while outside (employing a split screen) a war veteran begs for money. Like his contemporary Otto Dix, Grosz often juxtaposed in his paintings those who profited from the war and those who were crippled or killed in it.

McKay had anticipated both Grosz paintings in his poem of 1919, "A Capitalist at Dinner":

An ugly figure, heavy, overfed,
Settles uneasily into a chair;
Nervously he mops his pimply pink bald head . . . (*CP* 136, lines 1–3)

This nightmarish figure drove "people . . . at their will like helpless sheep" to make a fast buck in the Great War. The last line of the poem is Swiftian: If the earth produces someone like this, "let human beings perish from the earth" (*CP* 136, line 14). We need only remember the famous indictment of humankind by the Brobdingnag king in book 2 of *Gulliver's Travels*: "the most pernicious Race of odious little Vermin that Nature ever suffered to crawl upon the Surface of the Earth" (Swift, *Essential Writings* 397). The descent from DaVinci's Vitruvian Man (Gulliver's praise of English institutions, inventions) to "Vermin" is sudden, as was the disillusionment following the Great War. Little wonder that Swift's reputation as a satirist was revived in the 1920s and 1930s. The grotesque seemed the new normal.

The grotesque is a sharp distortion of the normal. Satirists like Jonathan Swift and Rabelais did not draw a distinct line between satire and Gothic grotesque, nor did Chaplin, Goya, and Grosz. The grotesque could serve a multitude of purposes, as it does in *Romance in Marseille*, whose tenor can suddenly shift from the satiric to the Gothic noir, as its ending clearly shows. Since my thesis is that McKay envisioned his novel as a film script, I want to examine what McKay meant by referring to *Shoulder Arms*'s "economical design" and its "grotesqueries."

Shoulder Arms (1918) begins with Chaplin in character as the Little Tramp, but this time in uniform and training to go the front in the Great War. We see him out of step with everyone else in a marching drill, doing dance steps to someone else's drumbeat. He is so exhausted after this military exercise that he collapses on his cot in a tent.

What follows is a series of comic actions that show this inept soldier as a hero, but the brilliance of the film is to debunk the heroics by exposing them as a dream. There is a point to this other than satirizing the Walter Mitty delusions of the Little Tramp. The film's larger agenda is to expose the Great War as a dream, a nightmare that debunks the belief that this appallingly senseless war was a glorious defense of civilization.

In the film, the normal becomes the absurd as the soldiers attempt to perform civilized acts amid insane situations. One memorable moment in the film is a scene in which the soldiers must sleep in a flooded dugout, acting as though they were getting comfy at home even as they try to keep from drowning. At one point Charlie uses a musical horn as a snorkel as he sinks beneath the water. In an earlier scene, he calmly eats dinner as bombs are bursting behind him in the trench. The inter title calls it "A Quiet Lunch." My favorite scene is Chaplin opening the door to a house in France whose facade is gone, the interior completely exposed and almost demolished, but Chaplin acts out the normal by entering the front door.

During the film, Chaplin saves a beautiful French girl, captures thirteen Germans, steals Kaiser Wilhelm's car, and even captures the kaiser himself, to whom Charlie gives a swift kick in the bum. His fellow soldiers hoist him on their shoulders and proclaim him their hero, as the inter title reads: "Peace on earth ... good will to all." And then Charlie wakes up, and the audience is forced to reevaluate what they just saw, that the movie is a send-up of the kind of propaganda about the war that was current both during and after. The theme of that propaganda was that heroic behavior was possible in a modern, mechanized war and that Americans were fighting to save both civilization and democracy. And, after the war, that they were the ones who won it.

This is what McKay meant by calling the film a grotesquerie, certainly different from Goya's limbless men in his *Disasters of War* and Grosz's bestial figures in *Ecce Homo* ("Behold the Man") but a grotesquerie nonetheless in that its satire becomes dark once you consider the fatuous rhetoric of World War I. The key grotesquerie, of course, is that this noble, saved civilization has enslaved not only the white working class but the invisible African Americans who are being lynched at home.

There is also another way of understanding why McKay saw *Shoulder Arms* as an artistic masterpiece comparable to Goya's *Disasters of War*. The word "grotesquerie" seems to be overkill given the fact that Chaplin's comedy consists mostly of slapstick. But that is precisely the point Chaplin is making: slapstick underscores the insanity of the war itself, as if civilization has suddenly become a caricature of itself. After all, the house Charlie enters through the front door was once a home. Chaplin's antics, however, are double-edged: he himself is graceful in his moves to escape the insanity, whereas the soldiers on both sides are mechanical robots acting out a script designed by madmen.

Here precisely is the paradox underlying McKay's praise of the movie's "economic design." The lunacy of the war is expressed through a tight plot, kinetic energy, and brief images of a world at odds with nature. One scene illustrates both the movie's theme and its method. Charlie has disguised himself as a tree, using the disguise to hide from the Germans and to inflict mayhem on a few of them, but one German soldier chases him into a forest of real trees. As the soldier pursues Charlie through the forest, nature is a backdrop to, and a commentary on, the absurd situation of Charlie as a fake tree and the German as a wound-up mannequin. That pattern of grotesque humans acting out an insane script is one McKay would create in *Romance in Marseille*. Aslima's relationship with Lafala exists within a world in which people prey on one another and is set against what "romance" could mean in another context, one envisioned by Aslima in a Joycean epiphany but doomed to be only a moment's revelation.

Film noir has a long history, much longer than the famous films of the 1930s and 1940s. One filmic device is to begin *in medias res*, which is precisely what McKay does in *Romance in Marseille*. In the novel's first sentences, he gives us a scene in a hospital in which Lafala "lay liked a sawed-off stump and pondered the loss of his legs. Now, more vividly than ever in his life, he visualized the glory and the joy of having a handsome pair of legs" (*Romance* 3). What follows is a flashback, as he "vividly" remembers his African past in which his "dancing" legs were the essence of his identity. That scene is followed in turn by his journey to the docks of Marseille where he meets the beautiful Aslima who captures his heart and then robs him. Shamed by playing the fool, he stows away on a freighter, only to have his legs frozen and amputated when he reaches New York. Following Chaplin's "economic design," McKay gives us this flashback in a few pages.

The rest of the first part is the preface to Lafala's return to Marseille in which the focus is on money: his lawyer's suit against the shipping company, the company's settlement, and the company's revenge against the lawyer who wants half of the money given to Lafala. The five chapters of part one read like cinematic scenes. Their depiction of bad behavior in New York (false friend, corrupt lawyer, powerful corporation) is McKay's use of misdirection; opening scenes in film noir are often at odds with what follows (Vernet 58–59). The novel's real themes will involve the triangular relationship between Lafala, Aslima, and Titin (Aslima's pimp), with subplots occurring in the third part as part of the overall "design." The theme of money, its compensation and its consequences as defined in the first part, will be played out in terms of these three characters. Greed is the defining motif of the first part (everyone, even Lafala, is guilty), and that subject sets the stage for the complicated sexual relationships that ensue when Lafala returns to Marseille sans legs.

In *Romance in Marseille*, McKay used an obvious cinematic technique: cross-cutting, an accepted practice in film production since D. W. Griffith perfected it in *Birth of a Nation* (1915) and *Intolerance* (1916). In the novel's second part, Lafala returns to Marseille a "stump" but a wealthy one. The denizens of low-life Marseille admire him; the men want to bask in his glory, the women want his money, especially La Fleur and Aslima, the competing call girl queens of Quayside. Seeing him rich, Aslima seduces him again and convinces Titin that she is after Lafala's thousands. Titin, however, is suspicious, thinking that Aslima may be playing a double game, and hence the scene in chapter 12 in which the paranoid Titin, thinking that the lovers are betraying him, tries to strangle Lafala in his own room, shouting, "Give me that money or I'll kill you" (66).

So ends chapter 12, with Titin "tightening his hold on [Lafala's] twitching stump." Chapter 13 begins with a sharp cut to Aslima climbing the stairs to Lafala's room hearing Titin's words inside the room: "I'll kill you! I'll kill you!" That is, McKay repeats the scene from another camera angle, changing the mis-en-scene to Aslima's perspective outside the room, the stairwell. Then Aslima enters the room and knocks Titin out with a chair, thereby saving Lafala's life.

What follows is another cinematic moment. Aslima leaves with Titin and protects herself from his wrath by taking the offensive: you ruined our plan to rob Lafala of his money because of your anger and distrust. After this Lafala will never believe me. They return to their room, and there is another cinematic cut. Worried about what Titin might do to Aslima, Lafala has followed them to their room, and as he approaches the door, he hears the two of them arguing. The previous scene is repeated but with Lafala outside the door instead of Aslima.

As Lafala approaches the door, Titin flies out in a rage, not seeing Lafala. Lafala enters to find Aslima laughing at the trick she has pulled on Titin in convincing him that he is the one at fault and not her, but the reader wonders at this point what kind of game is Aslima playing. Does she love Lafala, or is she plotting with Titin to bilk Lafala of his money?

Cross-cutting allows McKay to sustain the mystery. It shows "spatial separation," but by no means does it explain motivation. The "*omnipresence*" of the camera does not mean we know everything: "The narration is unwilling to tell all, but it is willing to go anywhere. This is surely the basis of the tendency to collapse narration into camera work: the camera can roam freely, cross-cutting between locales, or changing its position within a single room" (Bordwell, Staiger, and Thompson 30). A good example of a new camera angle within a single room that sustains the mystery occurs in *Out of the Past* (1947) when Kathie Moffat and Jeff Markham are about to have sex and the camera moves to the French doors with the rain pounding outside. The rain stops and the camera returns to a postcoital Kathie taking the needle from a phonograph record that had been playing the film's sentimental musical motif. The room is now filled with a deadly silence, as Kathie is no longer back lit with Rembrandt lighting. From that point on, the film is permeated with menace as befits film noir. Something similar occurs in *Romance in Marseille*. Aslima has joined Lafala in his hotel room, and before they make love, she tells him that although she has "been a pig all my life," with him, "I feel like "we're clean pigs." Then a paragraph break serves as a cinematic cut, and the scene changes to the morning in which Lafala offers her money for her night with him. She refuses, insisting that she wants to make up for what she has done to him. But the scene ends ambiguously when "we're clean pigs" changes to "we are all pigs" (43).

McKay often has chapters that serve as cinematic cuts. Chapter 9 ends with Aslima not telling Lafala about "what had passed between her and Titin," their discussion to rob Lafala of everything (48). She's afraid that

Lafala will become "suspicious," that he will no longer believe her. Her silence sustains the ambiguity which surrounds her: perhaps she does intend to rob him. Chapter 10 cuts to La Fleur and Lafala in which there is no ambiguity. The scene is a counterpoint to the previous one. La Fleur openly scorns Lafala in the bar (ironically named "Tout-va-Bien"), calling him "Pied-Coupe" ("Stumpy") in front of others and later bragging to her girlfriend that she will take him for everything he's worth (52, 152, fn. 12). The tables are turned when Lafala takes his revenge by throwing her out of his hotel room sans payment. The chapter ends with a cut to Lafala's return to Aslima and with Aslima saying to him "let's go where we can be scratching pigs" (57). Within these chapters are visual motifs and snappy dialogue, especially in chapter 11 when McKay turns the camera to Aslima's momentary vision of freedom and community and Titin's paranoia: "there is the possibility that Aslima might be betraying him with Lafala" (58). All three chapters show the camera moving everywhere but making no moral judgments. In the hotel room, La Fleur and Lafala are equally vicious.

McKay confessed that he didn't quite know what to do with Aslima. On the one hand, she was a femme fatale right out of the pulps, a combination of allure and mendacity, someone very like Brigid O'Shaughnessy in Dashiell Hammett's *The Maltese Falcon* (1930), appearing in *The Black Mask* as "a five part serial running from September 1929 to January 1930" (Penzler 105). Knopf would publish Hammett's novel on February 14, 1930, the same year McKay put his "Romance" on hold (Penzler 105). On the other hand, he admitted that "the Arab girl is growing bigger than I ever dreamed and running away with the book and me" (qtd. in Cooper, *Sojourner* 267). In expanding her character beyond the limits of the femme fatale, he placed her in two different gestalts, similar to what Alfred Hitchcock did in *Vertigo* (1958) with Kim Novak as both Madeleine Ester and Judy Barton. Moreover, McKay seems to suggest that Aslima is a side of himself ("me") as an artist, capable of being an auteur as she shapes scenes and manipulates people. When she sees her competitor in the sex trade La Fleur trying to seduce Lafala, "she sized up the situation immediately and rushed it [*sic*] putting herself between LaFleur and Lafala" (32). What follows is another cut to a scene in which Lafala and Aslima are sharing a meal and McKay has her "moved to a great pity and great shame" over what she has done to him (33). The camera sustains the ambiguity and makes no judgment upon her in juxtaposing two scenes.

In the beginning of their renewed relationship, the focus is on Lafala's passion, his sexual ecstasy. Aslima knows how to exploit it, as she becomes the femme fatale as artist. Aslima promises Lafala that she'll "be a sweet pig to you" (40). Cognizant of the censors, McKay uses this metaphor for their carnality. The pig motif runs throughout the novel; even Titin uses it, to attack what he considers Lafala's greed (65), an irony in that his avarice becomes his sole obsession. Her insistence that "we're *clean* pigs" (my emphasis) suggests a need for redemption, a theme that is embedded in the violent film noir ending (41).

When Lafala returns to Marseille, a rich man but a "stump" (as Titin calls him), Aslima's initial motivation regarding Lafala is threefold, to humiliate La Fleur and to replace her as queen of the sex workers and to rob him again. But we are never quite sure of her motivation. Is she telling the truth when she tries to convince Titin that she's not simply taking Lafala's money for a one-night stand, that she intends to rob him of everything. Convinced, Titin bestows upon her what he considers his highest praise: "You're a brick, a born whore" (48). His own aspiration, he says, is to use Lafala's money "to own a bar" in Marseille (48) that the two of them can run. This infuriates Aslima because she knows he won't marry her since she is a "whore," demanding that the money only comes with marriage: "If I get that money will you promise to marry me before I hand it over? That's the only way I'll feel sure about my share. If we are married! (90).

But there is another side to Aslima. She rebels against Titin's ironclad definition of her as "a brick, a *born* whore" (my emphasis). Responding to Lafala's deep passion for her, she has a moment of transcendent clarity, a vision, "as if her spirit had fled her body . . . in the heart of an antique white-washed city" (60). It's a cinematic moment, darkness changing to light. She wants to tell Lafala her "vision" in order to escape her past and the self that preys on him and the self that is a "born whore." Although she fails to realize this vision of transcendence and community, she is the only one in the novel who has it. It is a vision of "home" outside of time and space, an echo of Prudhomme's poem in *Home to Harlem*.

Although Lafala is the novel's protagonist, Aslima runs away with the story. Lafala is incapable of having her vision. When he thanks her for saving his life, she says the cause "was the vision," and he responds that "you just fell asleep and dreamed a lot" (70). He lives in one world, she in another. He leaves for Africa alone because "the practical side of his nature had asserted itself over the sensual" (127): home to him becomes a place in which he can shine because he has money. Aslima has the vision of a spiritual home but remains homeless in the real world.

This distinction points to the irony of the two of them attending "a romantic sheik picture" in the "respectable part" of Marseille (46). The movie could be *The Sheik* (1921) or *The Son of the Sheik* (1926), but it hardly matters because both are Hollywood love stories. The Sheik himself is not even Arab but is the son of a British father and Spanish mother, so kidnapping, and then marrying, a wealthy, aristocratic American is hardly shocking, especially considering the varied and sordid backgrounds of McKay's characters (born of an enslaved Sudanese mother, "Aslima was born a slave") and the conflicts that result from clashes of caste, class, and ethnicity (44).

Aslima's past continues to haunt her right up to the horrific ending in which she attempts to escape the two "laws" of Quayside that define her: the law that tells her to prey on anyone who is vulnerable and the law that says "Never trust a woman" (33, 48). The first law is the Hobbsian "state of nature" where there are no just laws. The second law is related to the first. No matter what she tells Lafala, she believes that he will not believe her, and that belief becomes a self-fulfilling prophesy. The novel's Gothic ending is tied to both her vision of redemption and community and her despair of ever escaping her past.

The third part begins with a flashback to a new character, Babel, Lafala's friend who stowed away with him but has escaped his fate. It's a flashback as a cinematic cut, as Babel remembers seeing Lafala taken to a hospital on a stretcher. Again, McKay gives us the past revisited from a new angle, an extended mis-en-scene, as we now hear of Babel's misadventures that eventually lead him back to Marseille. The third part introduces us to several new characters: the Marxist St. Dominique, his anti-Marxist friend Falope, the gay couple Big Blonde and Petit Frere. Each has his own story to tell, but they are not digressions. They expand our conception of "romance" in that they place Lafala and Aslima's heterosexual relationship within the context of other passions that range from the political to same-sex relationships.

In terms of what kind of "romance" this story is, the presence of these new characters is a red herring. In chapter 16, Lafala disappears, and the novel seemingly becomes a detective story. The question of what happened to Lafala and who is responsible for his disappearance is McKay's nod to cinematic melodrama.

The solution to this kind of cinematic mystery has no loose ends, as McKay includes characters which further this kind of plot. Babel is arrested for stowing away with Lafala and finds Lafala in jail, arrested by the shipping company in Marseille for the same crime but in reality for causing the company so much trouble and so much money. The original issue in the story returns but now becomes the source of a solution to a conventional mystery. Babel has discovered what has happened to Lafala, so now the problem is how to get him out of jail. A sequence of interconnected events ensues. Big Blonde learns of Babel being in jail, tells St. Dominique, who then visits Babel and learns that "Lafala is here" (99). The smooth-talking St. Dominique then convinces the manager of the company to have both Babel and Lafala released from jail. The ease with which all this is done in a few pages is an expression of McKay's contempt for Hollywood solutions. One final melodramatic question remains: will Lafala take Aslima back to Africa with him?

The new characters in the novel all have their opinions. Big Blonde "was inclined to take the whole thing lightly, saying that Lafala had experience enough to look out for himself" (112). But Babel is worried. Lafala should return to Africa alone and find a respectable wife. Falope calls Lafala a fool for even entertaining the idea. His friend St. Dominique at first thinks Lafala's decision unwise and then later becomes sentimental about the love affair, a nice comic touch considering he is Marxist. These various opinions evaporate in the next scene when McKay cuts to Lafala who "has quite made up his mind about it" (113). He's going to sail away with Aslima.

Still, McKay can't resist drawing out the melodramatic moment. Petit Frere overhears a conversation between Titin and a fellow pimp, indicating that Aslima's plan to rob Lafala is still in play, and La Fleur, after wheedling information out of Babel, sends multiple anonymous notes to stir up trouble, the one sent to Lafala sowing doubts in his mind about Aslima's trustworthiness.

Lafala's decision to leave for Africa alone is an act of closure, a simple solution to a complex situation that removes him from the story. The way Lafala now frames the pig metaphor hints at his decision: the pen traps the pig, excessive joy cloys. Suspicion of Aslima doesn't seem to be the issue here. What Lafala resists is losing control, a striking contrast to the ending in which Aslima loses all control. As a character, he has a part in a melodrama, she in a film noir.

In the novel's last chapter, she hears of Lafala's departure from two of his friends. Her instant despair is rooted in both her affection for Lafala and her guilt over what she has done to him. When she hears Titin rail against Lafala's deception (fleeing with the money, leaving Aslima money which she has withheld), she is aroused to an equal fury. All her complicated emotions are concentrated in a single act, one that explodes Titin's monolithic definition of her as a "brick, a born whore." Titin says that he wished he had killed Lafala that night in his room, and Aslima responds angrily. "Kill him! Kill Lafala? You'd have to kill me first and kill him over my dead body," she shouts. "And drawing the knife she always carried she advanced upon Titin like a madwoman" (129). Although Titin kills her with his pistol and damns her to "Hell," he is the defeated one.

The novel ends in violence, but there is a brilliant "economic design" to the ending. It echoes an earlier encounter between the two in which Titin threatened Aslima with a knife. He had accused her of not being a proper whore, of not giving him the cash she received from Lafala for sex. She counters that this money from a one-night stand is chump change compared with her plan of regaining his trust, and that is the moment when he praises her as being a "brick, a born whore." Titin puts away his knife, but now the knife returns in Aslima's hand as she swoops upon Titin "like a bird of prey" (130). The metaphor suggests that Aslima has morphed into a new self and another kind of artist, one with the inspired madness ("the flashing eyes," the "holy dread") of Coleridge's poet in "Kubla Khan."

The noirish ending adds another dimension to the novel. McKay flirted with the detective story (Lafala's disappearance and what happened to him) and the amorous "romance" format (Lafala's return to Africa with Aslima). The detective story would involve a neat puzzle to be solved, the story of true love, a satisfying conclusion to genuine passion on both sides. Conventional melodrama relies upon emotional moments in which complex moral and social problems get neatly resolved, often in terms of personal solutions. Linda Williams has argued that the essence of melodrama is its "moral legibility," but McKay's metaphor of Aslima becoming a "bird of prey" tells a different story (Williams, *Playing the Race Card* 19). The "prey" (Titin's "born whore") now becomes the predator, and that one act of trying to kill him exposes the whole rotten "social life" of the social structure, which is built upon the principle of predator and prey.

In a recent article, Laura Ryan argues that the novel's ending was "unsatisfying" because it ended in an act of sudden "violence," reflecting McKay's impatience over not getting it published (Ryan 10). I believe the ending works, because it forces us to rethink Aslima's relationship with Lafala, his "practical" decision versus her "vision" and her metamorphosis, and it also makes us take a second look at the novel's first part. The company, the lawyer, the "friend" (Black Angel) are all predators, whereas the true friendships in the third part (Babel/Lafala; Big Blonde/Petit Frere; St. Dominique/Falope) represent the essence of the vision that Aslima has of the spiritual community from which she is excluded. She has one glimpse of paradise, but the world goes on as usual; she commits one horrendous act of revenge, but it is only a small ripple in a huge pond of corruption and indifference—these are film noir themes. Melodrama's "moral legibility" tells a different story. It assures us that there is such a thing as a moral order in God's universe even if good people suffer.

The ending contains another metaphor: Aslima is a "beast" that Titin "would rather capture than slay." And earlier: "He wondered hesitatingly if she wouldn't be getting off too easily with death" (129). He kills her because she is determined to kill him. There is an important distinction here. Titin would rather have her suffer than die. He wants her to know her place, an attitude, as McKay would know from experience, that is fixed in stone, as in "the letter of your law." There is no "moral legibility" in *Romance in Marseille*. That subversive theme is the meaning of the "romance" in the novel's title.

In their introduction to *Romance in Marseille* (2020), a novel never published in McKay's lifetime, editors Holcomb and Maxwell observe that the author's third choice for a title in 1933 was "picturesque and less provocative" (*Romance* xlvii). There are two other reasons to explain why he chose "Romance in Marseille."

For one thing, McKay made a distinction in both *Banjo* and *Romance in Marseille* between the "romance" of Marseille and the "romance" of America. In *Banjo*, "it was America that was for him [Ray] the living, hot-breathing land of romance" (68). What follows is a long list of Dionysian manifestations of that red-hot energy: "Its mighty business palaces, vast *depots* receiving and discharging hurrying hordes of humanity, immense *cathedrals* (my emphasis) of pleasure, far-flung spans of steel roads and tumultuous traffic—the terrible buffalo-tramping crush of life, the raucous vaudeville mob-shouting of a newly-arrived nation of white throats, the clamor and clash of races and the grim-grubbing position of his race among them—all was a great fever in his brain . . . a burning, throbbing romance of his blood" (*Banjo* 68–69). The "romance" of America is Dionysus, but its sinister side is the law of white supremacy, which creates "the grim-grubbing position of his race." Apollonian law (its "letter") denies people of color access to the plenitude within the American scene.

The romance of Marseilles has a different source. In an unpublished letter to Charles S. Johnson, the editor of *Opportunity*, on January 11, 1927, McKay described his response "last summer" to the "life of Negroes in Marseilles" in several contradictory adjectives: "terribly exciting, sad, picturesque, and cruel in many aspects." The reason for this is that "Negroes from every part of the world are flung together there in the old port. Sailors who have lost their ships, many of whom, apparently, never intend to go to sea again. Living on the great breakwater, always bumming, sometimes working and spending their time between the Quartier Reserve and the piers, French, American, English, Portuguese and former German Negroes—all are there." As a dumping ground for Black people from every part of the world, Marseilles illustrated the true "romance" of Europe, only dimly seen in its museums or architecture or history books: "It was as if every country of the world where Negroes lived had sent representatives drifting into Marseilles" (*Banjo* 68).

In Marseilles, Black people really are foreigners, unlike African Americans who are outcasts in their own country because of "your law." No character in *Banjo* could say, as Felice does to Jake in *Home to Harlem*, that "this heah is you' country, Daddy. What you gwine away from it for?" (*Home* 332). Ironically, Black people in Marseilles are a mirror of the modern world, its strange cosmopolitan nature after the Great War: "there was a barbarous international romance in the ways of Marseilles that was vividly significant of the great modern movement of life. . . . The town seemed to proclaim to the world that the grandest thing about modern life was that it was bawdy" (*Banjo* 69). Yet there was a "white-fanged vileness under its picturesqueness," as pimps, "cocottes," guides, thieves, and murderers preyed on the unsuspecting (*Banjo* 69). In this light, McKay would refer to the port city as "sinister Marseilles . . . low-down Marseilles," or, even more explicitly, in his description of the Quai du Port, as "a churning agglomeration of stench and sliminess" (*A Long Way from Home* 261; *Banjo* 13). "Bawdy" is the two sides of Dionysus: life force and death driven.

Perhaps McKay's ambivalent attitude toward Marseilles can be summed up in the oxymoron he used to describe the city, "its cruel beauty" (*Banjo* 68). In any event, it remained for him "Marseilles Motley," the title of a chapter in *A Long Way from Home*. There may be more "social liberties" in Marseilles than in the "United Snakes" (Goosey's coinage in *Banjo*), but there is also more existential angst because there was no strong sense of community. Racism in America, McKay argues, "drives the Negroes together to develop their own group life" (*Banjo* 205) unlike the fragmentary, isolated existence of the characters in *Romance in Marseille*. There is no character in *Home to Harlem*, for instance, quite like "Lonesome Blue" in *Banjo*, whom Ray describes as "an apparition, swaying strangely and mournfully in the square like a fading tree without roots in the soil" (238). A statement like this explains why McKay was so fascinated by Father Divine and his community in *Harlem: Negro Metropolis* (1940).

A second reason has to do with "romance" as a literary genre. As students of American literature know, the word "romance" is a loaded word, and McKay would know this if only from reading his favorite modern author's *Studies in Classic American Literature* (1923). D. H. Lawrence's chapter on "Hawthorne's Blithedale Romance" is especially relevant to McKay's title, his focus on "the brute blood desires" that lie beneath *Blithedale*'s metaphysical trappings (Lawrence 115). There is a connection between the "romance" tradition in American letters and the film noir ending of *Romance in Marseille*.

Hawthorne's subtitle to *The Scarlet Letter* (1850), which Lawrence also discussed in his *Studies in Classic American Literature*, was "A Romance." Hawthorne would elaborate on the word's meaning for him in both his preface to that novel ("The Custom House") and in the preface to *The House of the Seven Gables* (1851). Hawthorne saw the romance writer's terrain as a surreal landscape "where the Actual and the Imaginary may meet" (Hawthorne 29). That landscape is no less "real" than the "real world," a polite fiction for what society accepts as "real." For Hawthorne and McKay, romance is the kind of fiction that exposes "normal" life as unreal. Hawthorne describes the reality of the "romance" world in a brilliant image: "Moonlight" falling upon objects in "a familiar room," he noted in "The Custom House," changes our perception of them, making them unfamiliar, a point made later by Freud in his famous essay "the Uncanny" (1919). The moonlight makes the objects in the room "strange" and remote "though still almost as vividly present as by daylight" (29). Aslima's vision in daylight also turns the familiar into the unfamiliar. The literal procession that she sees changes into "the first gods who emerged out of the ancient unfathomed womb of Africa to procreate and spread over the vast surface of the land. Dancing and dancing down into a deep darkness.... And when they came up into light again the court was transformed into a place of worship" (61). But she can't sustain the metamorphosis of "place" (the "antique white-washed city") into a place of grace, primarily because Lafala lacks the imagination to believe her, or rather that he sees her only in one dimension: the "sensual. In *The Scarlet Letter* Hawthorne holds Hester's "A" in a delicate balance: Is she an Angel or an Adulteress? Is Aslima at the end of *Romance in Marseille* a bird of prey or an avenging angel? Lafala doesn't stay to find out.

As Herman Melville saw, the American Gothic tradition is an offshoot of Hawthorne's definition of "romance." At the heart of Hawthorne's tales, Herman Melville reminds us, is "the great power of blackness ... whose visitations, in some shape or other, no deeply thinking mind is always and wholly free" (374). McKay used his novel as a film script to explore that darkness on multiple levels.

Although the "Romance" in McKay's title is a subtle reminder that his novel belongs to a specific American literary tradition despite its French setting, the novel's violent film noir ending mirrors the dark endings of two movies of 1930: *The Blue Angel* and *Little Caesar*. Moreover, Josef von Sternberg, director of *The Blue Angel*, also directed Marlene Dietrich in another film released in 1930, *Morocco*, in which she plays a chanteuse/prostitute, as she does in *The Blue Angel*. She, as Amy Jolly, tells Tom Brown (Gary Cooper), who is in the French Foreign Legion, that there is a "foreign legion of women too, but we have no uniforms, no flags and no medals . . . and no wound stripes when we are hurt." Earlier, von Sternberg would focus on a sympathetic low-life prostitute, Mae (Betty Compson), who tries to drown herself, in his dock movie *The Docks of New York* (1928), and on Bull Weed's (George Bancroft) flashy mistress, "Feathers" McCoy (Evelyn Brent) in his gangster movie *Underworld* (1927). Thus, McKay had a background of popular culture to work with as he was writing *Romance in Marseille*, as well as the early German noir films of the 1920s: *The Cabinet of Dr. Caligari* (1920), *Nosferatu* (1922), and *Dr. Mabuse the Gambler* (1922)—films that were all offshoots of greatest "grotesquerie" of the century, the Great War.

Romance in Marseille has an even more vital connection to popular culture: its connection to the pulps, specifically to *The Maltese Falcon* (1930). Dashiell Hammett's chilling novel is also a "romance" in the Gothic tradition that Melville saw in Hawthorne's stories. The black bird, the statuette that all the characters are pursuing, has a history, as Casper Gutman tells Sam Spade. In exchange for Malta, Gozo, and Tripoli, the Knights Templar were to give to Charles V of Spain each year a black statuette encrusted with jewels. One was lost at sea, and Gutman, after searching for it for some seventeen years, has traced the lost and stolen bird to the United States. The "dingus" turns out to be a worthless piece of lead, but it is one over which many lives were lost.

The mayhem within the novel proper is only half the story. There is another transatlantic history embedded in the history of the falcon. Charles V was one of the founders of the slave trade, ordering in 1518 that Africans be shipped to the Americas as slaves. A third manifestation of corruption were the Crusades in which the Knights Templar became rich, for, as Gutman said, "the Holy Wars . . . to the Templars were largely a matter of loot" (*Maltese* 124). What the falcon statuette symbolizes is greed that travels from the Old World to the New World, involving both past and present, another version of Paul Gilroy's Black Atlantic.

It is this pulp theme that connects Hammett's novel with McKay. Hammett's black bird is Lafala's money—almost everyone is after it. The three parts of McKay's novel are tied to that pulp theme; it's what gives the novel its "economic design." The pulps let history in through the back door. *Romance in Marseille* links the matter of "loot" to the theme of slavery and its legacy. "Loot," after all, was the reason for the slave trade, the cause of its human cost. Lafala's amputated legs has a history in the Atlantic slave trade.

Consider the novel's first part, set in New York, seemingly having little to do with rest of the novel set in Marseille. True, Lafala's condition has its origin in Marseille (Aslima's treachery), but the focus is upon the sympathetic American "friend" and the morally responsible white lawyer. In reality, of course, "Black Angel" and the lawyer are only interested in Lafala in terms of what they can gain from his plight. The lawyer strikes a hard bargain with both Lafala and the shipping company: a fifty-fifty split with Lafala of the hundred thousand dollars from the company. What ensues is both high comedy and a serious theme. Angered at having to pay out an enormous sum, the company uses the law against the lawyer. It has "stipulated" only "a certain sum" for the lawyer, not 50 percent. Its representative says, taking the high moral ground, "I am here to protect this man's rights" (21). It is precisely the argument the lawyer had used in court to get the settlement.

McKay's point is that "rights" are a convenient cover for greed, echoing Gutman's language to Spade—"plain speaking ... clear understanding ... equitable"—to lull him into revealing where the black bird is hidden (109). "Rights" are central to the American Constitution, as in the Tenth Amendment of the "Bill of Rights" that ensure that the "rights" of the States are protected, a linguistic blind to protect southern slave holders. The "Dollar Line" is the American shipping company that docks in Marseilles in *Banjo*, McKay's wry take on both the ominous economic dynamo of United States after the Great War and international capitalism. Titin's greed is only small beer, as is La Fleur's and the others, but McKay's point is that capitalism trickles down from top to bottom.

As an expression of modernism, *Romance in Marseille* connects high and low, a theme familiar to fans of Raymond Chandler. Foreshadowing Chandler, McKay noted in *Home to Harlem* that the "underworld" was intertwined with the world of respectability, and of course we see that often in *Romance in Marseille*. In the novel's third part, the shipping company tries to take its revenge on Lafala for challenging the system by throwing him in jail, using the laws of "civilization" to do so. It had appealed to individual "rights" earlier in its legal complaint against Lafala's lawyer, but now the laws of civilization trump those "rights." "Romance" exposes the contradiction, the underlying darkness. Pulp fiction is at the bottom of the literary hierarchy, but its "romance" is at the heart of McKay's novel.

The novel's pulp ending and the metaphor of Aslima as a "bird of prey" transcend the limits of the classic detective story. As Jerold J. Abrams notes, "there is a 'way out' in the [Sherlock] Holmes stories, and there is absolutely none in film noir" (Abrams 75). Aslima's metamorphosis from prostitute to "bird of prey" puts life into Hammett's black bird. McKay wants us to remember her as someone from his great poem, "If We Must Die," not dying passively like "hogs / Hunted and penned in an inglorious spot" but "fighting back" (*CP* 177–78, lines 1–2, 14). In death, she is no longer a "sweet pig."

Too bad Lafala is not there to see the transformation, but then *Romance in Marseille* has the "economic design" of film noir. Gestures of defiance and acts of good faith are lost in silence in the sinister city, just as the history of slavery and its legacy go unnoticed and unrecorded, with the exception of the pulps. At the end of the brilliant film noir *Out of the Past* (1947), Ann Miller never finds out the truth about Jeff Markham after his death—that he was innocent of the crimes he was accused of, that he was not running off with Kathie Moffat. The Kid lies to give Ann a life, but what hovers over her in the movie's final frame is the huge white courthouse, a symbol of McKay's "the letter of your law." That courthouse blots out not only her life and Jeff's but Kathie's as well, for her story remains untold. In his excellent book on film noir, *More Than Night*, a title McKay might have chosen for his own novel, James Naremore notes that in *The Maltese Falcon* "the rara avis turns out to be just as counterfeit as the characters" (Naremore 52) What McKay's ending underscores is the "void" at the center of a Western civilization based on the principle of reason. Predator and prey turn law and human rights into a fiction.

CHAPTER 5

"THAT STRANGE PLACE"

Claude McKay's *Gingertown* as a Modernist Short Story Cycle

For there was an American miss
Who dreamed of an African kiss
But her little brown knight
Did not know how he might
So unrealized was her bliss

—MOORISH LIMERICK, PREFACE TO CLAUDE MCKAY'S "LITTLE SHEIK" (*GINGERTOWN* 260)

The 1920s saw the short story cycle emerge as a modernist form. Inspired by Anton Chekhov, James Joyce's *Dubliners* (1911), Sherwood Anderson's *Winesburg Ohio* (1919), Jean Toomer's *Cane* (1923), Hemingway's *In Our Time* (1925), and Faulkner's *These Thirteen* (1931), McKay used the idea of the cycle or collection as a counterpoint to the idea of a master narrative, especially suspect after the carnage of the Great War. McKay singled out both *Winesburg* and *In Our Time* as works that survived "the vast international cemetery of this century" because they were modernist texts that critiqued modernity (McKay, *Home to Harlem* 227; *A Long Way from Home* 251–52).

Winesburg may have inspired McKay to name his collection *Gingertown* because, as both titles suggest, place is significant for both authors. Jennifer J. Smith has called attention to the "persistence of place" as a distinguishing feature of the American short story cycle (Smith 37–59), but *Gingertown* poses a special problem since, in this collection of twelve stories, half are set in Harlem and New York and the other half, except for the last two, are set in Jamaica. The structure of McKay's collection is much closer to that of Anderson's second collection of stories, *The Triumph of the Egg* (1921). Here, Anderson varies the location of his stories between village and city, no longer focusing exclusively on the village as he did in *Winesburg*. Moreover, he bookends *Triumph* with prose poems that comment on his stories. Similarly, McKay prefaces the first story of his collection, "Brownskin Blues," with his poem, "The Harlem Dancer," from his book of poetry, *Harlem Shadows* (1922), and he begins his last story, "Little Sheik," with a "Moorish Limerick." Like Anderson, McKay frames stories with textual commentary from another literary genre. Moreover, "The Harlem Dancer" serves as a preface to the entire cycle of stories.

The last two stories in *Gingertown*, "Nigger Lover" and "Little Sheik," are set in Marseilles and Tangier, respectively, and there is a reason for this change of place. At the center of *Gingertown* are "Truant" and "The Agriculture Show," two stories that in tandem serve as a transitional moment that takes the reader from one place, New York City, to another, the rural life of Jamaica and beyond—to cities that are even stranger than New York. These two stories also serve as a diptych in that like a camera eye they bring the major themes of the entire text into focus. These themes are not those, as critics have argued, that focus on the juxtaposition of the urban with the pastoral, but rather those that arise from "the spirit of place" giving meaning to human lives.

McKay's aesthetic strategy is not limited to a comparison of six stories with six stories in terms of place. He also uses the last story in the first six stories, "Truant," to comment on the first story, just as he will use the last story in the collection's second half, "Little Sheik," to comment on the collection itself. In addition, the stories work as a sequence, each building on the one before and commenting on the one after, but also, as Robert M. Luscher has said of short story cycles, they create small circles within the larger short story cycle (Luscher 150, 154).

In stories like "Crazy Mary" and "The Strange Burial of Sue," set in the village life of Jamaica, McKay was clearly influenced by Anderson's small town "grotesques," but it would be Anderson's modernist method of linking stories through patterns of imagery and metaphor that would intrigue McKay. As students of *Winesburg* know, the repetition of hands, doors, and walls links stories in which characters struggle to express themselves or escape some kind of confinement. So too, especially in *Gingertown*'s New York/Harlem stories, McKay will use tropes from "The Harlem Dancer" to push forward his narrative, ending in "Truant" which casts a critical eye on a city and nation that both enthralls and entraps.

"The Harlem Dancer" that prefaces *Gingertown* is itself a brilliant poem that combines a Romantic/modernist image—the dancer and the dance—within a traditional literary form, the Shakespearean sonnet. Its themes, metaphors, and imagery foreshadow those in the Harlem/New York section of *Gingertown*:

> Applauding youths laughed with young prostitutes
> And watched her perfect, half-*clothed* body sway;
> Her *voice* was like the sound of blended flutes
> Blown by black players upon a picnic day.
> She *sang and danced* on gracefully and calm,
> The light gauze hanging loose about her form;
> To me she seemed a proudly-swaying palm
> Grown lovelier for *passing* through a storm.
> Upon her swarthy neck black shiny curls
> Luxuriantly fell; and tossing coins in praise,
> The wine-flushed, bold-eyed boys, and even the girls,
> Devoured her shape with eager, passionate gaze;
> But looking at her falsely-smiling face,
> I knew her self was not in that strange place. (my emphasis)

The narrator perceives that the dancer is self-contained within the dance: "Grown lovelier for passing through a storm." The allusion here may be to Hemingway (the dancer like Pedro Romero in *The Sun Also Rises* holds "his purity of line through the maximum of exposure"), but the image of the dance itself is possibly indebted a line from W. B. Yeats's "Among School Children," which reads, "How can we know the dancer from the dance?" (Hemingway, *Sun* 172; Yeats 214). The answer is that we can't. In the moment of the dance, the dancer is the dance, or as Frank Kermode puts it precisely in *The Romantic Image*, "for as long as the dance lasts the dancer cannot be distinguished from it (92)." According to Kermode, the modernists appropriated this image from the Romantics as a mode of resistance, no matter how temporary, against the chaos of modernity.

Although the narrator sees her dance as a self-contained "organic movement" (Kermode 70), as a concrete act that expresses a vision of a world elsewhere, she is not dancing alone. Her partner is the poet in that he articulates in words what she expresses through space. In other words, they are both artists, but he is the poet as *vates* whose visionary poem counters the finite "gaze" of the spectators.

The beauty of her dance is like "words in a special language" (Kermode 81). The girl's dance not only reconfigures the "strange place," it is also an answer to Anderson's prose poem that prefaces *The Triumph of the Egg*. Anderson's "Dumb Man" is looking for words to tell his stories, to give his characters words to express themselves: "If I could say the words, I would sing the story" (*Triumph* 203).

These three tropes from "The Harlem Dancer"—dancer and dance, place and "strange place," gaze and vision—serve as the building blocks for the structure of McKay's Harlem/New York section of *Gingertown*.

In the opening story, "Brownskin Blues," both the song and the dance are no refuge for Bess in Harlem. From the American South, she danced in road shows as a young girl, but she now finds herself in the big city dancing in a cabaret. She has a boyfriend (Jack) who loves her, another (Rascoe) that she has "kept" for two years but who now fancies another (Teresa) with lighter skin.

Yet it is the setting of the cabaret in which she dances and sings that defines her predicament: "The ceiling was covered thick with *artificial* autumn leaves in which were imbedded clusters of tiny *electric* bulbs" (3) (my emphasis) The cabaret replaces the street as the "strange place," but Bess lacks the Harlem Dancer's inner resources ("the holding of [the] purity of line") to keep chaos at bay.

Although Bess is a favorite in the cabaret, McKay distinguishes her dance from that of the Harlem Dancer by its explicit sexuality. Bess both sings and dances, yet the sexual innuendo of song is expressed in the dance as a "Wicked Wiggle" which elicits coins from the admiring males. The setting (artificial leaves, electric lights), the dance and song linked with sex and money—no wonder Bess describes her performance in the cabaret as "working" (8). These themes, performance as spectacle and labor for hire, highlight themes that appear in the story "Highball." In a larger sense, the distinctive features of McKay's Harlem, and those of the larger metropolis of which it is a part, are capitalism and its impact upon race.

Bess is vulnerable despite her commercial success. Skin color disrupts the dance, cripples the dancer. Teresa walks in the door with Rascoe on her arm, and she immediately focuses on Bess's "eyes," and that gaze from the light-skinned Teresa is devastating. It stops Bess in her tracks, ending her dance and song. At first skin color's connection to capitalism is not apparent, but it soon will be. Refusing to continue her dance and song, and fired by the manager, Bess isolates herself in her room, believing that only a light skin will win back Rascoe, especially after Rascoe in a subsequent encounter calls her a "dam' black sow" (17). Visiting her favorite beauty salon, she starts reading the advertisements for bleaching cream in the Black press, appearing even in the militant *Crisis*, and they convince her with their promise that "bleaching's sure in style" (22). Yet the suffering she endures when she applies the bleach to her body turns her dream of a garden of refuge into a Technicolor nightmare: "a mighty red jungle of blazing trees. Burning, blazing until they were reduced to a mass of strange flowers with red lips and fiery tongues..." (23). Bess scars her face so badly that no cabaret wants her, and she finds herself with "a scrubwoman's job (25)." Although McKay gives us a happy ending—Jack believes that love is more than skin deep—the story's simple but direct point is that capitalism is insidious in that it uses skin color to promote self-hatred.

In the extraordinary story that follows, "The Prince of Porto Rico," hubris destroys the dancer. As a newcomer to Harlem, Manuel is called the "Prince" because of his sartorial splendor and his way with women. He believes that he is destined to dance through life, but he misreads his new environment. A barber and a dandy, he mistakes his outward appearance, especially his clothes, and his savoir faire as tools of power and control. "I never did let love make a fool of me," he says: "Love is easy" (40). He's just the opposite of Bess, believing it beneath a man's dignity to get jealous over a woman. What he doesn't consider is that, as an immigrant to Harlem, he doesn't know the territory.

Thus, he assumes that when he meets Tillie at a "parlor social," she is what she says she is: a "grass widow" whose husband is out of town. His own vanity blindsides him, as it does George Willard in Sherwood Anderson's *Winesburg* story "An Awakening," but its violent albeit grotesquely comic ending is a nod to Hemingway. As Frederic Henry says in *A Farewell to Arms*, when asked if he had done "any heroic act" during the bombardment, "I was blown up while we were eating cheese" (*Farewell* 55).

Unknown to the Prince, Tillie's husband, Uriah, works nights in town. Tillie, who never lets grass grow under feet, is currently seeing someone named Hank at Bella's "buffet flat," but when the Prince shows up, she dumps Hank for the fashion plate. The jealous Hank leaves a message for Uriah that another man is kicking in his stall—and that very night. Uriah rushes to his apartment just as the Prince has changed his fancy clothes for what he thinks are Tillie's "pink pyjamas" and has acquiesced to her desire to "dance a little" before they make love (49).

It turns out to be the dance of death. As Uriah rushes into the room, he sees the Prince's stylish "reddish-brown suit and orange tie" on his pricey "Morris chair," a symbol of his own hard work to keep Tillie in the fine "satin" kimono which she is wearing. He reads the Prince's clothes not only in terms of Tillie's infidelity but as symbols of one social class exploiting another: "Silent that suit but, oh, so eloquent" (53), especially as it lies upon his chair, a symbol of what a working-class stiff like himself cannot afford.

Although the Prince escapes out the window onto a fire escape, he is wearing Uriah's pajamas and has no shoes. Twice humiliated by clothes, Uriah pursues and guns the Prince down in an "open lot," a no-man's-land of "broken bottles and empty cans," images of his ignominious fall from former splendor (54). The story's great power lies in the meeting of separate lives whose temporary connections are unpredictable and traumatic, similar to the "social life" of Hemingway's "The Killers."

In the story that follows, "Mattie and Her Sweetman," the dance is at the center of the story. Living with a much younger man, and supporting him, Mattie attends a "parlor social" with Jay, her peacock lover who brags that he "ain't soft and sissified with no women," even with the woman who is keeping him (61). Over course of the evening, Mattie keeps asking Jay to dance, but he repeatedly refuses her and becomes so annoyed by her requests that he calls her a "black woman," the ultimate insult in "Aframerica" (63). To compound the insult, he boasts of the new suit that Mattie has bought for him, at the same time that he is dancing with a younger woman.

Like the previous story, clothing is a silent object that speaks loudly. Furious that Jay has both ignored and mistreated her, Mattie leaves early, carrying with her the overcoat that she has bought for Jay. At story's end, he is literally left out in the winter cold as Mattie refuses to let him in her apartment, throwing his old clothes out the window—the "rags" of his suit made into a "bandana" to house "his old greasy cap, his old shoes, and the remains of his silk shirt" (70–71). Jay's naked condition is a variation on the story of the emperor's new clothes. At the parlor social, clothing is his cover and his persona. The last line of the story has Jay heading toward Lennox Avenue with sleet blowing in his face, as "the wind *sang* around his rump" (71) (my emphasis). The dancer is bent over with the bends, as the freezing wind is the only song he hears. Richard Wright would use that frightening image of the wind in the last line of *Lawd Today!* (circa 1934–36).

"Near White" is both a "passing" story and a story about what Theodor Adorno calls the deception of the "moviegoer, who perceives the street outside is a continuation of the film he has just left" (Adorno *Dialectic* 99). In the case of Angie Dove, it's not a movie but a dance "craze" that beguiles her.

White enough to "pass," Angie soon delights in the white world and all its gaudy glories, reluctant to return to Black Harlem, even with its society balls for the mulatto elite. The light-skinned "Negro" male who has introduced her to life's forbidden fruit has skipped town on short notice, but having acquired the taste for adventure into the white world, Angie travels one night outside the Belt to a vaudeville house on Broadway. There she meets a white man, appropriately named John West, who assumes she is as white as she appears. Together they go to a dance palace in which she links the dance with access to a "greater world" (86).

John West wonders why she will not let him escort her home, concluding that her parents must have entangled her life in an unwanted sexual alliance: "This is the modern world," he tells her: "You don't have to marry anyone you don't like" (92). But as Angie discovers, modernity is not as open as the dance palace makes it seem. When Angie asks, what if you met a "quadroon girl or octoroon, could you still love her?" John says he would rather "love a toad" (102).

Shocked and bewildered by his brutal response, she rushes home, haunted by the word "toad," but McKay's satire cuts two ways. Although West's remark undercuts his professed liberalism, the "toad" in Angie's garden is the reality behind her own vanity. Setting herself above others, seeing modernity's surface as substance—she has turned her dance into a vaudeville farce.

The story that follows, "Highball," centers on song rather than dance. Its protagonist, Nation Roe, was an obscure blues singer in Baltimore who finds himself an overnight success on Broadway: "That was Nation's achievement" (108). The story's focus is less on what fame does to his music, making it palatable to a white audience, than on what it does to him. He divorces his simple but charming Black wife for a trophy wife, Myra, a flashy but vulgar white woman who swills down booze like a pig, waddles like a duck, and behaves like a "coarse cow"—McKay uses all three metaphors (117, 128, 132) to express Nation's blindness. The highballs that Myra drinks are the perfect symbol of the commercialized city that spawns her. The name "highball" implies sophistication, but it is only booze and ginger ale.

McKay underscores the city's culture industry by the white people who become Nation's friends, especially George Lieberman, "the successful black-face actor" (110). Although George is critical of Myra's piggish behavior, his role as an "actor" is fake; his claims to depicting Black life depend on appearance. Behind the grinning black mask is the grinning white face—a double fakery because George is Jewish—a man negotiating an American identity through blackface. Like Jacob Rabinowitz (Al Jolson) in the first sound movie *The Jazz Singer* (1927), blacking up is a performance that says in essence that putting it on means you can also take it off (Rogin 417–53).

George is a white version of Nation, who has allowed his music to be watered down to suit white taste. And the racist Myra becomes a nastier version of George—she and her friend Dinah refer to Nation as a "prune" (136). At story's end, Nation becomes a man without a friend, without a wife, and without a nation. Lost in an existential void, he "bellowed like a wounded bull" (138). In this bullfight, there is no matador to dignify his spiritual death.

"Truant" is the last of the New York/Harlem stories. The stories that precede "Truant" all help to emphasize the centrality of this sixth story in the collection. The first five stories emphasize the city's magnetic force in creating a destructive myopia in the self, seen especially in Angie in "Near White" and in Nation in "Highball." In "The Prince of Porto Rico," the dapper barber thinks that life in his new island home will be like that of his former island home, yet Prince discovers that, if "love is easy" there, dying is easy here—all too easy, if you can't read the street signs.

"Truant" also begins with the illusion that the city is easy to read. Barclay Oram and his wife Rhoda attend a New York stage show celebrating family life, "clean vaudeville," which Rhoda finds "pretty nice" (139, 140). This is the city under the moral law of white America, the diversity of the city reduced to a happy white Irish family: "Father, fat and round like a chianti-bottle, skips into the picture and up leaps boys and girls and mother with baby. The Merry Mulligans!" (139). Old vaudeville is a mirror of the real city—its promiscuous, bawdy, raucous, diverse spirit (bears, dwarfs, acrobats, juggling, magic acts, et al.) is the city's heart—and a metaphor for McKay's short story collection.

It is this Dionysian energy that attracts Barclay to New York, the "enchantment . . . of Stone and steel! Steel and stone! Mounting in heaven-pursuing magnificence" (152). Even nature seems out of place in this world of the Dynamo and "vertical towers": "A tree seemed absurd and a garden queer in this iron-gray majesty of man's imagination" (152–52). Ironically, its alien "majesty" ("Where factories grow like jungle trees") heightens and focuses his memory of the past: "The steel-framed poetry of cities did not crowd out but rather intensified in him the singing memories of his village life. He loved both, the one complementing the other" (159). His response to the city is a prose version of "The Tropics in New York."

But what is truly fascinating about this "strange land" of New York is that it is also "a great city of great books" (153). For Barclay, love of "book knowledge" becomes a "hunger," and he becomes "enchanted by the words: University, Seat of Learning" (154). It is there that he meets Rhoda at dances hosted by the university, which "he had found more enchanting than the library" (155). He loved dancing with her "all the time," and loving her results in her pregnancy and his leaving school to support a family. Life for Barclay begins to imitate art—the bad art of the Merry Mulligans.

The thing about Rhoda that seduces Barclay is also what attracts him to the city—its promise. It was "her mouth [that] made me marry her . . .

the full large mouth that was mounted on the ample plane of her features like an exquisite piece of bas-relief " (151). That sculptured beauty on the architecture of her face was also sensual when it spoke: "her ripe-ripe accent and richness of laughter." The mouth itself had an "almost unbearable sweetness, magnetic drawing, sensuous, exquisite, a dark pagan piece of pleasure" (158). "That mouth," Barclay thinks, "was the enchanting thing about her" (150).

Although enchantment is what first drew him to the city, both the city and Rhoda's enchanting mouth turn into something sinister in which he begins to feel "like a bee that darts too far into the heart of the flower and, unable to withdraw, dies at the bottom of the juice" (156). Rhoda's mouth threatens to engulf Barclay. That closure extends to the enclosed space of the Pullman train where Barclay works as a porter, and which becomes another metaphor for the city.

When the train is in movement, Barclay can identify with the cities and their freedom, yet when Barclay sees the train as a job to support Rhoda's desire for respectability and for her family to become like the Merry Mulligans, the train becomes a jail. Even the wonderful cities he visits become tainted: "Washington reminded Barclay of a grave" (145). Rhoda's "large mouth" begins to lose its charm, becoming something grotesque—"she chewed her gum as if she were eating food, opening her mouth so wide that people could see the roof" (140). The dances at the university are replaced by the enclosed space of home—hence the pun on Rhoda's "roof."

The next day, Barclay becomes a "truant" from his job as second cook on a Pullman car run to Washington DC. In a larger sense, it is truancy from the "purchasing power" the job gives him to pay for "wife, child, flat, movie, food, liquor . . ." (143). Given a ten-day suspension, he is chastised by Rhoda, who reminds him that for ten days they will not have means to support both the family and "our social position" (150). Almost overnight, the city's poetry, its "piling grandeur," the architectural image that he once saw in Rhoda's mouth, is replaced by the city as suffocating enclosed space, underscored for Barclay in the story's opening scene by the subway in which people are "penned up like cattle" and at story's end by the liberty bonds that he finds in his trunk, which he was forced to buy during the Great War "to make the world safe for Democracy" (141, 161–62).

Barclay chooses to leave wife and child not because he hates his family but because he and his family are being transformed into the Merry Mulligans. Although it is tempting to read this story's ending as autobiographical, its layered themes reveal a tension between a love of family and a love of city—and a fear of being entrapped by both.

"Truant" is a bridge to the "The Agricultural Show" and the stories that follow in the second section of *Gingertown*. Although the collection's second section reflects a radical shift to another world, Jamaica, this is not the unpolluted world of the pastoral. "The Agricultural Show" alludes to Virgil's *Georgics* rather than his *Eclogues*. Although Barclay, in his disgust for capitalist New York, sometimes longs for the "green intimate life that clustered round his village" (152), "The Agricultural Show" is not set in the village of his pastoral fantasy. McKay shows Jamaica to be far more complicated in its social network of desires and aspirations than New York. Or rather, both places have not escaped modernity. As McKay himself said, there is no such thing as "Negro life in its pure state," not even in Africa. And, he added, "I don't believe that any such place exists anywhere upon the earth today, since modern civilization has touched and stirred the remotest corners. I cherish no Utopian dreams about any state of society" (Cooper *Passion* 137).

"The Agricultural Show" is not only his send-up of a "pure state" of society, but it also illustrates the idea that city and garden are never completely divorced from each other. In placing "Truant" and "The Agriculture Show" at the center of the collection, the sixth and seventh stories, respectively, McKay created a diptych in which the tropes of garden and city are interwoven. Since music and dance are themes in all the stories, the collection is a kind of symphony or musical medley in which garden and city are interchangeable motifs.

If there is a pastoral theme in "The Agricultural Show," it is expressed by the adolescent Bennie who begins and ends the story and who innocently perceives that the show reflects his brother's intelligence and integrity in creating it. The brother, Matthew, however, is not so innocent in his motivations. Educated in the city, he is the village druggist who has introduced German music to his church (e.g., Beethoven and Bach) and whose "Show" is his urban dream of bringing prestige to the village and of advancing his own social aspirations.

Matthew makes two clever social moves on the colorful Jamaica chessboard—one is to convince the governor of the island to bless the show with his presence and the other is to persuade the prosperous Mr. Andry to hold the show on his vast estate, Naseberry Park. To everyone's surprise, the governor accepts because he wants to be seen a man of the people, and Mr. Andry agrees to Matthew's proposal because he wants to advance the social ambitions of his two daughters.

One delicate irony in the story is that the "Show" becomes a spectacle that overshadows the native products of the village world that it celebrates.

This is Michael North's thesis in reverse. It will be the Jamaican village and not New York that puts agriculture behind glass. As the show slowly develops into a reality, others more socially powerful than Matthew will use it to advance their own interests. Eventually, not only will city, town, and village play a part in the show's promotion, but as agent of the British crown, the governor will head the parade.

Another subtle irony is that the social and genetic makeup of Jamaica is hardly homogeneous. Even the members of the village cannot be called "pure." The parson and his wife Madam Daniel are "Aframerican"; Mr. Andry, of uneducated peasant stock, has grown up in Central America and has returned to Jamaica a wealthy man with a wife of "Spanish, Indian, and Negroid blood" (172). Without any social pretensions himself, he has two daughters who do and who present him with a dilemma. A self-made man with dark skin, his only claim to respectability is his money, but in a society that valorizes light skin and social antecedents, especially British, that is not enough. It is enough, however, to prevent Matthew from entering the front door of his palatial estate. Though highly educated, Matthew is not only unmistakably Black but also poor.

Andry's daughters are not the only daughters with social ambitions. The other aristocrat in the area is Busha Glengley (who will play a prominent role in McKay's *Banana Bottom*), an Irish adventurer and the Banana King of Gingertown who has multiple illegitimate children and five children by his common-law wife, the Widow Clavale. Two of his three daughters went to "the best ladies college in the colony," and the youngest one was educated "in England." So here is the conundrum for the daughters of both families. All want some kind of social status, something their money cannot buy. Yet fortunately for the Andry daughters, their mother was of mixed blood, so they are not dark like their father but of a "reddish" hue. And fortunately for the Glengley daughters—and McKay's irony here is as sharp as Jane Austen's—their mother dies "conveniently" right after the "youngest Miss Glengley had finished her education" (178). Now daddy can be referred to as a "widower" and not the sire of bastards. The Agricultural Show thus becomes the perfect opportunity to move into "the inner Sanctum of Respectability" (178), especially now that the governor himself has elevated a lower art form of the peasants into a high social affair.

The rest of the story deals with the machinations of the Glengley daughters to recenter the show upon themselves. They seek out Matthew in his drugstore, posing as charitable aristocrats happy to lend a helping hand: "And just as they were about to drive away Miss Glengley remembered that the governor might want to have supper in Gingertown after the show and that they would be delighted to place their home and service at his disposition" (180). They might also have remembered to have invited Matthew to that dinner, but it would take the governor himself to jog their memory—he would insist that Matthew attend the garden party held by the daughters of an Irish adventurer and a former barmaid of Kingston.

The comedy continues at the show itself when the wife of the village parson and an American to boot (Madam Daniel) seizes the opportunity to thrust herself into the limelight. Her husband had been invited to sit on the stage that hosted the governor, and his wife followed right after him. At first both the Glengley and Andry daughters "tittered" at her social faux pas, but when she remained sitting with the other dignitaries on stage above the rest, the laughter turned to "an envious glare" (187).

McKay's satire focuses on human nature—its tendency to one up the other—but it also takes into account the matrix of a specific society. As anthropologist Peter Wilson has observed of Caribbean culture, the twin poles of "respectability" and "reputation" reflect two different value systems within it. Both systems operate dialectically, but neither one is completely separate from the other. The influence of the colonizer upon the colonized creates a value system from without, a system run by the inflexible laws of respectability. Such a system shapes a class structure that is both undemocratic and arbitrary. For the gods seem to bestow respectability by chance; yet chance is fate: light skin, a fortunate marriage, a lucky birthright. Here the white man's values are primary.

In contrast, reputation arises from within the indigenous culture (Wilson 153). Although there are different kinds of reputation—a good carpenter, a good scholar, a good schoolteacher— it is located in the idea of equality. Anyone can attain it. However, no matter how secure a person's reputation is, it can always be compromised by respectability. In creating and organizing the show, Matthew's reputation is secure, yet others parade their respectability to prey upon his handiwork. Thus, when McKay refers to the crowd at the show as "a charming country multitude," it is a delicate critique of the "pure" pastoral, for there is no such thing as a "charming country multitude" as a single entity. Rather, as Wilson notes, using a metaphor from Booker T. Washington, Caribbean culture is like a barrel of crabs—those trying to climb up and out on the backs of others and those pulling others down who are trying to get out.

The story's ending combines both respectability and reputation to give us a satirical perspective on the day's events. Bennie is basking in his brother's glory, looking with his mother at a photograph of Matthew with the governor. Both admire "Matthew's big work in that little village of Black people. Of his talent for getting along with big people" (190–91). Bennie admires the purity of Matthew's act, putting on the show, whereas the mother sees the context in which the two men are portrayed, the photograph. Bennie reminds his mother that the governor even bowed to her, and yet the mother's response is telling: "yes, sonny, but it is nothing to lose your head about. . . . The Bible said, Ethiopa shall stretch forth her hand to God" (191). The show's importance pales beside a female heavenly city that will not be contaminated by a photograph taken to promote the Governor's worldly interests. The mother's response is not that of a sentimental old woman but rather of one wise enough to recognize that nothing in the earthly city remains "pure."

"The Agricultural Show" forces a rereading of the Harlem/New York stories. In "Brownskin Blues," Bess thinks that life can be made simple by changing the color of her skin. Urban media—newspaper advertisements, radio, songs—are forms of thought control that paralyze her own human experience. It is not that the city is simple in itself, but its "Culture Industry," as Adorno calls it, is all pervasive. The city simplifies life for Bess because she allows it to, and she pays for her failure to read the urban scene, a theme repeated in "The Prince of Porto Rico," "Near White" and "Highball." Self-absorbed, Angie in "Near White" can only perceive the white city beyond Harlem as "her new world . . . a vast pleasure-world" that her near-white skin entitles her to (81). She models her dreams of escape on the title of a popular fad, the "Butterfly Craze." She becomes the pastoral butterfly she claims to despise, flitting from one tawdry pleasure to another. Angie's epiphany that she is only a "toad" in John's garden is comic not tragic because her views of the city never rise above the superficial. In "Highball," Nation Roe's music is direct and powerful, yet once he moves into the white world, he wants to be sophisticated—hence his white wife. The irony is compounded when he discovers that his "sophisticated" white wife is a vulgar booze hound and that his white friends want him to remain a simple, uncultivated darky.

For McKay, urban complexity tends to devolve into a parody of pastoral simplicity, compromising both the artist (the dancer) and their art. In contrast, Barclay in "Truant" recognizes that the city is also the world's library, its poetry and life force, and his perception of these urban facets evokes his heightened involuntary memory of a world he thought he had left behind. But what he comes to see is that the city can betray itself, simplifying its vitality and complicity becoming the Merry Mulligans. McKay entitles his collection *Gingertown* in that this "town," for all its comic faults, is a more complete realization of human diversity and "culture" than capitalist New York.

"The Agricultural Show" is a delicate parody of pastoral simplicity, as suggested by the word "Show." It's a village facade or performance that hides the complex social maneuvering going on behind the scenes. "Crazy Mary," the story that follows, takes a dark, penetrating look at the reality of village life and its intersection with city culture. What the story illustrates is McKay's point that "modern civilization," and by this he means city culture, has "touched and stirred the remotest corners" of human existence and that "Negro life in its pure state" is a fiction (Cooper, *Passion* 137).

As a young woman, Miss Mary has studied in Gingertown and returns to her village a talented sewing-mistress. The local schoolteacher courts her, and the village expects their marriage only to be shocked by a mother who accuses him of having seduced her young daughter, Freshy. Miss Mary is an educated, even worldly, woman, and meeting with the daughter, she gets Freshy to confess that the schoolmaster has not touched her. She repeats this, "in her refined way," to the church's congregation. All goes well until Freshy's mother stands up and claims that Miss Mary forced her daughter to confess and, in addition, that Miss Mary herself has had an affair with the schoolmaster (197).

Although the schoolmaster "quietly" leaves the village, he reappears later as a city dude from Colón, accompanied by a "saucy" wife, "dressed in an extreme mode of the Boston dip of the day" (200, 201). He is welcomed back into the community. Moreover, McKay tells us that before the scandal broke, he was a talented cricket player and "organized a cricket club" in the village (194). These small details of village "social life" are a reminder that city culture is already present in the rural community, and it has an influence.

Freshy's later promiscuity—having three children with three different men "before she was nineteen"—calls her sullied innocence into question. But the real issue is not who did what to whom but rather the community's divided behavior toward Miss Mary. When Freshy's mother accuses Miss Mary of having premarital sex with the schoolmaster, it divides the village into male and female camps, the women saying that Miss Mary is no longer a virgin, the men insisting she still is. The tolerance that once existed in the village for "deflowered" virgins is now swallowed up in village politics.

Caught between these irreconcilable forces, Miss Mary becomes a village character, or as McKay puts it, with quiet irony, "the village folk settled down into familiarity with her as a strange character" (200). She becomes "strange," not because she is a monster but because the community has become one. As a man, the schoolteacher can flee the village for the wider world, and then return with a fashionable city wife, whereas Miss Mary's life is confined to a community that refuses to recognize its own contradictions. When Miss Mary sees her former lover and his new bride emerge from a church service, she confronts them both with a "lecherous laugh" (201). She then proceeds to throw herself over a waterfall, the ultimate gesture of contempt for a community that refuses to know her or to know itself.

The story, "When I Pounded the Pavement," that follows "Crazy Mary" is a city story, yet its link to "Crazy Mary" is the theme of law. The presence of the moral law in Miss Mary's village shatters the false boundaries that separate city and village, for the villagers' behavior in "Crazy Mary" echoes a judgment upon the city that McKay had made elsewhere in "Truant," that the city's ironclad moral law "held humanity gripped in fear" and killed compassion (160–62).

This distinction is made clear in McKay's autobiographical sketch "When I Pounded the Pavement." The sketch is the central panel of a triptych that includes "The Strange Burial of Sue," the story that follows "When I Pounded the Pavement." The three stories taken together illustrate Luscher's point about short story sequences having small circles within the larger short story cycle. Within "When I Pounded the Pavement" is a moment that symbolizes the theme that links all three stories: the invasion of the city into private lives and the disruption that ensues.

The significance of "When I Pounded the Pavement" lies in the title. "Pounding the pavement" refers to McKay's brief stint as a policeman in Kingston, a soul-killing job of deadening routine. In a mockery of the Ten Commandments, everyone was expected to follow the "book" written by the Irish cop who was their boss. The ultimate dark comedy of the job is its parody of an idealized village community: "Outside my office work we did everything in common, drilling, eating, bathing, dressing, sleeping, even the ceremony of the watercloset" (208). As in McKay's *Constab Ballads* (1912), the mechanical drilling or "a-trampin'" that the recruits have to endure is juxtaposed with the dance or in one case with the music of a marching band that inspires the townspeople to 'dancin' with a glad shout" (*CP* 86, lines 3, 12; 99, line 1). The title refers to an unnatural world in which men pound, but nature dances (*CP* 54, line 18; 128, lines 43–48). Or more precisely, as the story indicates, the marching both disguises and reveals the cruelty of impersonal law.

Being a cop in the city means intruding upon people's lives for officious, petty, and sometimes vicious reasons. In a defining moment, the narrator realizes that he has been part of a plan to entrap a person who is the political adversary of someone who seeks political power. The incident is both grotesquely comic and terrible.

Stationed outside a servant girl's room, the narrator is expected to arrest her clandestine lover in the act. Finding the door locked, he and the two owners of the house step through the open window like thieves themselves. Awakening the lovers by tearing away the sheet that covers them, the narrator reluctantly arrests the man only to discover later that this man's political career is ruined by the tabloids, that he is also given six months' imprisonment and twenty-one lashes. As did McKay, the narrator retired from the constabulary.

The story that follows, "The Strange Burial of Sue," a story that James Weldon Johnson told McKay was "one of the finest stories I have ever read," also pits city law versus village tolerance as its major theme (JWJ to CM, September 30, 1933). The story's real center, however, is Sue, a free-hearted woman caught in a mesh of village politics and male egos.

The story begins with a young man named Burskin berating Sue in the Grog Shop, a male-dominated world. The men in the shop know his story—how his jealousy of the city-slicker from Panama, Johnny Cross, is the true motive for his vilification of Sue. Sue is married to a good man, Nat Turner, whom she truly loves and who accepts her promiscuity, as does the village because she fulfills "the peasant-folk idea of goodness.... Which means she was kind" (223). She is more than kind—she sees people through their illnesses, even nursing Turner's first wife and others through a smallpox epidemic.

The village tolerates Sue's promiscuity as long as it remains hidden, but once Burskin publicly accuses Sue of adultery, the village becomes moralistic. Soon the local but city-educated parson gets into the act and denounces Sue's "fornication" from the pulpit. Village tolerance disappears, and Sue finds herself alone and bereft as urban law, male bluster, and female gossip drive her to work herself to death. Law, church, city—these become insidious forces that erase the memory of Sue's good deeds.

Her burial is "strange" because the men who have killed her spirit fight over her even in death, and the village women, who know Sue's real character as "kind," are stunned into silence by male vanity and arrogance. In the funeral sermon, the parson damns her soul to hell, but Burskin erupts in histrionics, crying out that "If Sue gone a hell I gwine there too" and threatens to throw himself into "her open grave" (245). Chaos ensues. Only Turner keeps his composure, banishing the parson and reading the sermon over Sue himself.

Amid the noisy confusion of the burial, Turner asks those "who had anything to say in favor of Sue to say it" (245). The women who once gossiped about her now remember her "generosity" (245) and "say" it, but of course it's too late. The language of law has spoken from the pulpit, only confirming what malice has done to the language of the village itself.

The key moment in the story lies in the grog shop's opening scene, and McKay's return to it later on. Although the men disapprove of Burskin's tirade against Sue, they do nothing to stop it, and the women who hear it from the street, "stopped to listen and passed on, ashamed and afraid for themselves" (222). Although Sue rushes into the grog shop and batters Burskin senseless, it's a pyrrhic victory. Burskin's voice is Sue's life laid bare, made "public" (236). Hence when McKay returns to the grog shop later in the story, he describes Turner's "wrath" as taking a legalistic turn—he would "bring Burskin before the judge" (236). The men in the grog shop, when they saw "the silent change in Turner, his profound anger, [they] could not say a decent word to him about the matter" (236). When Turner does bring a lawsuit against Burskin, he files one in turn against Turner. The "decent word" is replaced by legal script. Sue dies at the hands of city justice, male authority, and female fear.

The three stories taken together—"Crazy Mary," "When I Pounded the Pavement," and "The Strange Burial of Sue"—not only make a unit within *Gingertown* but point to a subtext within "The Agricultural Show," the potentially explosive relationships involving city and village that McKay's delicate comedy keeps hidden.

"Nigger Lover," the story that follows Sue's travails, is about as far from the world of the Jamaican village as one can imagine, but it does focus upon a woman. Set in the polyglot seaport town of Marseilles, the story deals with the raw, violent but culturally rich world that McKay writes about in *Banjo* and *Romance in Marseille*. The title of "Nigger Lover" is racially loaded, "correctly translated," McKay insists, from the French "*l'amie des Negres*" (248). But being linguistically "correct" is grossly misleading, as McKay says: "literal translations are often words" that are inaccurate in terms of real meaning, similar to the "letter" that kills the spirit (249). In American slang, especially in the American South, the phrase "nigger lover" is damning: it refers to someone who is a racial traitor. "Nigger lover" is pejorative, damning, literal; a friend of the Negroes reveals friendship, compassion, openness, charity.

Consider how the patrons of the waterfront bar view this old woman, a prostitute who is fond of Black sailors. What McKay tells us is that her affection for Negroes has its source in a romantic encounter with a Negro in her youth. It is a moment in the past that defines her life in the present.

Her story is both sentimental and profound, one that uses the trope of a whore with a heart of gold to explore the serious themes of memory and loss. McKay, who cites Charlie Chaplin in *Banjo* (*Banjo* 216) as evidence that cinema has the potential to become a serious art form, reworks a sentimental moment from a Chaplin film, *City Lights* (1931), to make a serious statement about human attachments. In Chaplin's film, a blind girl thinks that a handsome aristocrat paid for her successful eye operation. Her sight recovered, her romantic fantasy remains. Will the handsome aristocrat ever return to marry her? Her fantasy is shattered by the sudden, shocking presence of Charlie and the revelation that it was a ragged bum who paid the bill—and with stolen money. The brilliance of Chaplin's ending lies in its ambiguity—what will the girl do, reject Charlie or accept him? Either way, reality shatters her illusion.

In McKay's story, the narrator recalls a time when a young prostitute took a Black sailor to bed in desperation because her rent is due, only to find the next morning after he has left that he has given her three times the money owed her. The sailor's generosity leaves its mark upon her, yet there is an ambiguity behind the gift, as in the Chaplin film. The sailor at first thought "how he might slip out without leaving her anything at all" (257). This also recalls Marcel Pagnol's popular play *Marius* (1929), which was released as a film in 1931. Young Marius unknowingly leaves a pregnant Fanny to set sail from Marseilles to lands unknown. Like the character Nigger Lover, Fanny, too, is left with memory and loss.

Why is this story in a collection of stories whose two settings are New York and Jamaica, primarily Jamaican villages? There are two reasons: one specific, one general. Unlike Sue in the previous story, the people in the seaport bar recognize the authenticity of Nigger Lover's life; her shameful name is also her badge of honor. Despite the transient nature of bar life in Marseilles, the sailors on some level respond to Nigger Lover's passionate attachment to homeless men. In contrast, the homogeneity of village life in "The Strange Burial of Sue" can turn on a dime, revealing both intolerance and vicious injustice. The pejorative phrase "Nigger Lover" that gives the story its name takes on another meaning—the one who remains firm in her devotion, truly "*l'amie des Negres*."

The collection ends with the subtlest of McKay's stories, "Little Sheik." The story is prefaced by a "Moorish Limerick," fit counterpart to the "The Harlem Dancer," the poem that prefaces not only "Brownskin Blues" but the volume itself. McKay pretends to diminish its significance by calling poems of this kind "nonsense poetry" or "trifles strung on fine threads of incidents that spring and sparkle like fountains out of the life of common folk" (260). These poems are often "rakish and ribald," reflecting the Moors' "sense of the ridiculous" (260), but by calling these poems "fountains,"

McKay is referring to a symbolic object that he has valorized in his poetry. The "fountains" are folk art that inspire the artist who works in print.

Looked at closely, the poem foreshadows themes in the story that express a huge divide between the Western and African worlds. On the surface, the story is simple: an attractive unnamed American girl in Tangier hires a young native to show her the town. She fantasizes about him, naming him "little sheik," with an echo of the Rudolph Valentino movies (*The Sheik*, 1921, and *Son of the Sheik*, 1926) that captivated American audiences in the 1920s. She charms him and he becomes her guide without having a license and at the end of the "incident" is thrown in jail for "six weeks" (273).

Referred to as "Miss U.S.A.," she is an ordinary American girl delighting in an adventure, but this is precisely what makes her so deadly (267). She walks through Tangier in a cloud, fantasizing about a complex world she knows nothing about: "she felt like one passing in a dream through the scenes of the thousand nights and peopled them again in her fancy" (262). When she thinks about her "little sheik," she puts him in a Valentino movie, only changing the cinematic plot: "With a flash of thought of those very moving pictures of sheikdom she wondered if the role would not here have to be reversed and she herself kidnap her brown idol out of that barbaric fairyland and make a getaway in her coupe across the desert" (268). However, the next day, when she finds out what has happened to her "sheik," her fantasy concerning her young guide "seemed like a mere shadow over a dream" (272), and she "upbraided herself for her indiscretion and that very day she jumped into her coupe and quit that charming town where she had hoped to make a long stay" (273).

McKay looks at her "indiscretion" in a more serious light. She enters another culture with preconceived Hollywood notions about it, wreaks havoc, and then leaves. Her actions are more serious than an "indiscretion," and the town is much more complicated than "charming." The person she fantasizes about ends up in prison. Her "unrealized ... bliss" is trivial compared with her total blindness of the culture she has entered, and she has left with the same ignorance she came with. In his poem called "Tanger," McKay focuses on a theme in the story, "tourists" who buy "souvenirs" in the city's marketplaces, ignorant of Tangier's rich cultural history and of its tortured past in which Morocco had been fought over by European powers (*CP* 225, II, lines 9–10).

"Little Sheik" is less a story about cultural confusion than it is about the consequences of cultural entitlement. The nameless girl's sense of superiority comes from an America that has no sense of its own transience, its own mortality, or, as McKay puts it, describing her reckless act of drinking from the town's "fountain": she had "faith in the magic of beauty to exorcise microbes" (263). McKay underscores the naivete of "Miss U.S.A." in his poem "America" with its echo of Percy Shelley's "Ozymandias." Blinded by its own hubris, America cannot foresee that "Time's unerring hand" will someday sink its "priceless treasures" into the "sand" (*CP* 153, lines 13–14).

McKay's final story and the "Moorish Limerick" are fitting conclusions to a collection of stories that began with poem about a Harlem girl dancing in "a strange place" but longing for a world elsewhere. The American girl in "Little Sheik" reflects the sinister side of America's longing for a world elsewhere. She is a symbol of American imperialism; she carries a cultural baggage of entitlement and a view of the world defined by Hollywood.

Equally significant, "Miss U.S.A" casts a shadow over the six stories set in Harlem. This last story makes us look back on the first half of *Gingertown* as we begin to recognize the pernicious effects of white American ideology on Black life, its debilitating consumer culture, middle-brow attitudes, and its inflexible racism. The British presence in "The Agricultural Show" is just another flower in the multicolored garden of Jamaica, and, as *Banana Bottom* illustrates, it is not always negative. Bita's English education, especially her love of its literature, complements her homegrown understanding, but Barclay's love of ideas, his identification of New York with "books," is overwhelmed by the ubiquitous and insipid "clean vaudeville" of the Merry Mulligans. The American girl of "The Little Sheik" is not evil but obtuse, and for McKay that may be worse than evil. The Brits knew exactly what they were doing when they invaded other countries, forcing their culture on other people, but white Americans live in a kind of cloud cuckoo land, inflicting emotional and physical damage on those lower down, all the while insisting that theirs is the best of all possible worlds.

CHAPTER 6

HOME IN THE HIDDEN SPACES

W. E. B. Du Bois's *Dark Princess* and
Claude McKay's *Banana Bottom*

She told them that the only grace they would have was the grace they could imagine. That if they could not see it, they would not have it.
—BABY SUGGS IN TONI MORRISON'S *BELOVED* (1987)

In his review of *Home to Harlem*, an indignant Du Bois wrote that after reading "the dirtiest parts of its filth I feel like taking a bath," causing an angry McKay to accuse Du Bois of reducing all art to propaganda and being incapable of understanding "the art of life" (Cooper 244). *Home to Harlem* was published four months before Du Bois's novel *Dark Princess*—time enough for Du Bois in his novel to add to his critique of *Home to Harlem*. Matthew Towns (his co-protagonist) tells a minister that the Harlem cabaret they will visit will "either be tame or nasty" (*Dark Princess* 64). And Perigua, a character from Jamaica filled with blind rage, blows himself up while trying to blow up a train.

McKay would respond the next year with *Banjo* (1929), and as William J. Maxwell has perceptively noted, each novel is "transnational" in its outlook (Maxwell, "Banjo meets the Dark Princess," 170–83). Yet I want to argue that McKay's more studied response to *Dark Princess* is not *Banjo* but *Banana Bottom*. In *Dark Princess*, Du Bois would be the visionary; in *Banana Bottom*, McKay would become the anthropologist. Du Bois would split his female protagonists between Sara Andrews and Kautilya, the princess from India, the first the master of "real life" within the world of Chicago politics; the second, the voice of the "dream," a platonic version of real life. Sara sees Black people in Chicago in terms of a voting bloc, something to be manipulated; the princess sees people of color in global terms, noncitizens within nations who need to recognize their unity in order to free themselves from white domination. Du Bois would depict a divide between the "dream" and "real life," whereas McKay would argue that Jamaica, the setting of *Banana Bottom*, is a multilayered culture, each layer infiltrating the other. When McKay discusses Jamaican society in *Banana Bottom*, he is looking over his shoulder at the Du Bois who wrote *The Philadelphia Negro* (1899). He wants to challenge Du Bois on his own turf. In his groundbreaking study, Du Bois the sociologist talked incisively about African Americans in terms of social facts and statistics, and McKay would depict his Jamaican characters as intimately connected to the cultural matrix of its complex society.

Yet as Wayne F. Cooper notes, McKay always felt an ambivalence toward Du Bois because *The Souls of Black Folk* (1903) was a formative influence upon him as a young man (Cooper 244). This line from Du Bois's great book must have especially resonated with McKay: "Why did God make me an outcast and a stranger in my own house?" (*Souls* 5). In *Banana Bottom*, McKay would answer that question by creating a character who would, in her journey toward selfhood, turn that house into a garden.

A daughter of a drayman, Bita Plant is adopted by two English aristocrats and educated in England. When she returns, the peasantry reminds her of her past as the aristocrats plan her future. Although caught between two worlds, Bita will harmonize the two, allowing McKay to marry both high and low instead of splitting them into two as does Du Bois in *Dark Princess*. Bita will combine Sara's pragmatism with the princess's idealism; there won't be a division as there is in the *Dark Princess*.

Du Bois would use Dante's *Divine Comedy* to structure his novel, his dark princess acting as a Beatrice to Matthew, whereas Bita would become her own Beatrice. Nonetheless, the two novels have more similarities than differences. Each novel employs what T. S. Eliot in his essay on Dante calls a "disciplined kind of dreaming" (Eliot, "Dante," 209)—McKay using his favorite Romantic poets for that source and Du Bois focusing on the sequential pattern of the *Inferno*, the *Purgatorio*, and the *Paradiso* as his epical *Commedia* moves from darkness to light.

The first section (of four) of *Dark Princess* is called "Exile," echoing Dante's banishment from Florence for the last twenty years of his life (1301–1321). That theme is central to the *Commedia* beginning with Dante the pilgrim finding himself lost in a dark wood at the beginning of the *Inferno* and being told by Cacciaguida in the *Paradiso* that his "exile" would mean he would have "to leave those things you love most dearly" (canto 17, line 57). *Dark Princess* begins with Matthew being told by the dean of the medical school at the University of Manhattan that "white woman patients" will not have "a n----r doctor delivering their babies" (*Dark Princess* 4). Banished from his beloved obstetrics, he finds himself that night in Dante's dark wood, walking until dawn in the alien city. Later, he is asked by someone on the ship taking him to Germany "where he was going," and he responds tellingly: "I don't know." When the princess asks for his address after he saves her from an unpleasant encounter with a white American, he writes "Matthew Towns, Exile, Hotel Roter Adler" (5, 17).

For much of the novel, he remains a wanderer in an obscure world, first involving himself with a revolutionary to wreck a train, then becoming a corrupt Chicago politician. The first lands him in jail, the second places him in purgatory. The difference between the two, as it was for Dante, is that purgatory is for the contrite. The low point for Matthew comes when he tells a woman who wants him, as a Black politician, to improve the working conditions for Black women and children, and he brutally responds that he can do nothing for her, that he is "not responsible for this world, madam" (146–47).

Making money through corruption doesn't bother him as long as he can acknowledge it as simply Sara's pragmatism. It is the sloppy edges of pretending that it's something else that disturbs him. He becomes haunted by the princess's face, especially her eyes. Because he has not forgotten her, she can remind him that he is "responsible for this world," that she can deliver him from this "purgatory" because a spark of her presence remained (226). Later he expands upon the symbolic significance of his memory of her: "The only thing that was able to lift me from cynical selfness, organized theft and deception was that finest thing within me—this love and idealization of you. If I had not followed it at every cost, I should have sunk beneath hell" (263). Du Bois underlines the princess as Dante's Beatrice when Matthew remembers his lynched Pullman Porter friend Jimmie. That bleak memory is countered by his memory of the princess who "came down from heaven and opened the gates of hell" (304). And earlier, when she appears out of nowhere at what was to be Sara's triumphant soiree for Matthew the cynical politician: "I came to save your soul from hell" (209).

In Du Bois's novel, however, the Beatrice figure is not gender specific, for Matthew in a curious irony (since he himself is so lost) serves as a salvation for the princess. When he meets her in Germany, she invites him to a conference of representatives of Pan-African and Pan-Asian nations, several of whom are skeptical of Matthew's presence. They cannot believe that the Negroes of his nation, the United States, are capable of throwing off mental servitude. Yet for the princess, Matthew becomes a beacon of "light," symbolizing the possibility that the "wallowing masses often conceal submerged kings" (34). She herself has lived a sheltered, privileged life in India, singled out by fate as one of the chosen, but in the second half of the novel she chooses to sink to the lower depths of poverty and exhausting menial work in London and America to find out if Matthew's belief in the Black proletariat is justified. This is not welcome news back home. An emissary from India chastises Matthew late in the novel, saying, "She gave up everything and went down into the depths . . . stooping to raise the dregs of mankind; laborers, scrubwomen, scavengers, and beggars, into some fancied democracy of the world! It is madness born of pity for you and your unfortunate people" (298, 300). As Matthew becomes a rising Chicago politician, the princess rises because she sinks. Her true nobility emerges when she identifies not only with the "wallowing masses" but with Matthew's unlettered, impoverished mother in Virginia. What will not be lost on McKay, however, is Du Bois's bifurcated cultural canvas and his fairy tale ending in which the marriage between two members of the Talent Tenth is at odds with his democratic theme.

Du Bois strengthens the princess's identification with Beatrice with a precise visual image: their eyes. The princess's eyes restore Jimmie's butchered face. On one page in *Dark Princess*, they are mentioned three times, blinding Matthew with their penetrating beauty: "great wide orbs of darkening light" (15). Later, when reunited, he looks at her "magnificent face," defined by her eyes: "he wanted to see her eyes, the eyes that he had never forgotten since he first looked into them, eyes that were pools of mystery and revelation, misty with half-sensed desire, and calm with power" (219). Similarly, Virgil, Dante the pilgrim's guide through the underworld, describes Beatrice as having "eyes of light more bright than any star" (canto 2, line 55). In *Paradiso*, Dante singles out "those lovely eyes" as "the source of bliss in which my gaze finds rest" (canto 14, lines 131–32), and as he ascends in terms of his vision of her and heaven, he "beheld / new brilliance in her eyes, such purity, / such ecstasy, her countenance was now/ more beautiful than it had ever been" (canto 18, lines 54–57). And as always her "eyes" are associated with light, the dominant visual image of paradise. Again, T. S. Eliot is relevant here: "Dante's is a *visual* imagination. It is a visual imagination in a different sense from that of a modern painter of still life: it is visual in the sense that he lived in an age in which men still saw visions" (Eliot, "Dante" 209).

Du Bois repeats this idea in his "Envoy" to *Dark Princess* when he asks, "Which is really Truth—Fact or Fancy? the Dream of the Spirit or the Pain of the Bone." It is as if, in asking this question, he is not only remembering *Home to Harlem* but explaining why he subtitled his novel "A Romance." McKay, too, as we have seen, will call his Marseille novel a romance, but his idea of a romance is the pain of the bone that lies beneath the surface of things, a noir treatment of reality. *Banana Bottom*, too, has its dark moments, but they are contained with a texture of a complicated social reality, a garden world with real toads.

Dark Princess has plenty of toads, especially in the sections dealing with Chicago politics. Sammy Scott wheels and deals in Chicago's Second Ward as a small-time Black politico as well as a "super-businessman . . . selling the right to gamble, keep houses of prostitution, and commit petty theft to certain men, white and black, who paid him in cash" (110). But the most fascinating character within this masculine world is Sara Andrews, "thin, small, well-tailored" and totally ruthless: "she . . . had a good intellect without moral scruples" (109, 114). She begins as Sammy's secretary then becomes his partner because of her intelligence: "she could put a lie through the typewriters in so an adroit way that it sounded better than the truth and was legally fireproof" (112). Her most distinctive feature is her "straight gray eyes," an attribute and color associated with her throughout the text and standing in contrast to the princess who dresses down and cuts her beautiful hair, but the "steadfast glory of her eyes showed unchanged" (111, 209). As a foil to the princess, Sara is always sartorially impeccable, but her grayness is a liminal color, neither this nor that, suggesting her moral ambiguity.

The brilliance of Du Bois's brutal portrait is that he also admires Sara. A woman of color (though she can pass for white), she creates that hard exterior to keep the world's cruelties at bay. And she's a fighter, defeating all the obstacles in front of her (prejudice, school, men) to achieve what she has with Sammy, the possibility of political success. Du Bois calls her "an artist," creating her polished persona from scratch, but he also sees her major flaw: "she failed in greatness because she lacked the human element, the human sympathy" (192).

It's more than that. She can't see beyond the moment, the confined space of the immediate environment. Those "gray eyes" are myopic. They only see what is in front of them, never beyond. They are the eyes of a wolf or Dante's "she-wolf" (*Inferno*, canto 1, line 49). She's a predator, a pure pragmatist whose "incontinence" (like that of Dante's "she-wolf") is her bottomless passion to rise to top. At one point, she drops Sammy for Matthew, seeing the latter as having a better chance for becoming the first Black man sent to Congress. She believes she can control Matthew, her first major mistake because he is still haunted by the "dream" (136) that the princess symbolizes for him, the belief that the two of them can make a better world beyond the narrow world of Chicago politics. Sara is another source for McKay's Bita in *Banana Bottom* besides the Princess. Bita will not only become the Beatrice to her own life, but she will also become an "artist" by making her own life a work of art but with "the human element, the human sympathy."

Sara's tragedy is that she chooses hell. As Dorothy Sayers says of Dante's *Inferno*, "nobody is ever *sent* to Hell. Men go there of their own will" (47). Phillip H. Wicksteed puts it another way: "Dante sees exactly what the sinner *chose*, and conceives of the Divine justice as giving him that" (67). When Sara appears in the courtroom for her divorce from Matthew because she can no longer control him, Du Bois describes her in terms of her favorite color. Her clothing reveals her artistry and her blindness: "She had on a gray tailor-made suit, with a plain sheath skirt dropping below, but just below, her round knees. There was soft gray silk within and beneath the coat. There were gray stockings and grade suede shoes and gray chamoisette gloves. The tiny hat was gray, and pulled down just a trifle sideways so as to show sometimes one and sometimes two of her cool gray eyes" (292). Now one, now two: Du Bois incisively shows how Sara uses her gray eyes and her well-tailored clothing to manipulate others and her immediate environment, the courtroom. But her enormous power within a confined space is always limited by both the space and her passion. Her reason for marrying Matthew is the same as the one for divorcing him, "enlightened self-interest" (138), but there is nothing "enlightened" about her "self-interest." Her pragmatism is a kind of darkness in which the "gray" turns into a spiritual blackness.

Du Bois's play on "light" reveals the fallacy of her success. Her idea of enlightenment is the opposite of "light," the image always associated with the princess and Dante's Beatrice. "Enlightened" only means raising self-interest up a notch. When she agrees to marry the corrupt Sammy with his "tobacco-stained teeth," his dental imperfection reveals the flaw in her sartorial splendor (294). Her choice of "damnation" is different from the non-choice that Black women have in Du Bois's *Darkwater* (1920). In his brilliant essay, "The Damnation of Women," Black women endured "the crushing weight of slavery . . . under it there was no legal marriage, no legal family, no legal control over children" (98). Sara has a choice, but it is illusory. Although she expresses her independence within the newly emancipated decade of 1920s and the Harlem Renaissance, her choice is circumscribed by her "tobacco-stained" aspirations. In *The Souls of Black Folk*, Du Bois points to the myth of "Atalanta" as "not the first or last maiden whom greed of gold has led to defile the temple of Love" (65). In stooping to pick up the prize, Sara picks up a rotten apple.

In *Banana Bottom* (1933), McKay describes a reverse pilgrimage for Bita Plant. After spending seven years in England, she returns to Jamaica under the guardianship of Malcolm and Priscilla Craig. At thirteen, Bita had been raped by Crazy Bow, but Malcolm Craig, who came from a long line of white, Christian missionaries, and his wife Priscilla choose to save Bita by sending her to England to be educated like a lady. Her "cultivation" in the mother country would, they hope, repair the consequences of her deflowering. At her return, the Craigs, whose Free Church centers the town of Jubilee, now expect Bita to be a member of their family and to take her place, despite her dark skin, among the colored, "cultured" elite of the island. Her status as an aristocrat of color and her English education link her with the princess, but while Bita will find harmony between her peasant heritage and her European "improvement," the princess will see conflict. She cannot reconcile her love of England, especially for her "tutors," from her desire to emancipate India from England's rule (231, 256). As *Banana Bottom* unfolds, Bita's imagination will incorporate English education with a native culture that she will see for the first time.

Like the princess, Bita is always the object of somebody's plans for her. The battleground lies somewhere between Bita's feeling that "I am myself," as she tells Hopping Dick, and the Craigs who "had made her what she was" (*Banana Bottom* 100). McKay often expresses his major theme in spatial terms: Hopping Dick asks her if she won't find Jamaica "too small" after living abroad, but Bita's response is telling: "I believe I could live anywhere there's air to breathe and space for free movement" (44). At first, on her return, she finds a world of contested space, from Black Belle and the Choirsters who musically challenge her, to Yoni's jealousy of her because of Tack Tally, to Priscilla's plans for her, to Marse Arthur's brazen attempt at rape. Jamaica's cultural landscape is a confusing chess board, and not all the pieces are black and white.

Yet ultimately Bita's journey home will be circular in a positive way, for, to paraphrase the now famous line from T. S. Eliot's "Little Gidding," she will "arrive where [she] started / And know the place for the first time." What Bita discovers, to her amazement, is that her life has not gotten any simpler after her return home but has become more complex: the boundary lines confusing, the claims upon her contradictory. Even better lines from Eliot to explain Bita's "exploration" of her home are those from the last stanza of "East Coker":

> Home is where one starts from. As we grow older
> the world becomes stranger, the pattern more complicated
> Of dead and living. [http://www.paikassociates.com/pdf/fourquartets.pdf]

The simplicity of her past belongs to a child's memory. As an adult, she will confront a world that has been there all along only as a child she lacked the maturity to see it. Before Bita can know the place of her childhood for "the first time," she will have to learn what words like "flowering," "planting," "cultivation" and "culture" mean for her, metaphors that run throughout McKay's text, and, for that matter, Du Bois's earlier novel, *The Quest of the Silver Fleece* (1913). Zora, Du Bois's female protagonist in that novel, anticipates Bita. She too symbolizes a marriage of high and low, of native Black culture with ever expanding white cultures (DC and Europe).

In her rough journey toward self-knowledge, Bita will find out that true "cultivation" is no easy task. McKay uses the word in both the sense of tilling the soil and of refining and improving the human estate. Often, he puns upon this word and plays with its various meanings—well-tended plants and animals, education (formal and informal), culture (high and low). For instance, "generations upon generations of Northern training in reserve, restraint and Christian righteousness had gone to cultivate" Priscilla's face, "a face fascinating in its thin benevolent austerity" (16). That kind of cultivation leads Priscilla, at one point in the novel, to condemn Bita in her own mind for dancing at a native "tea-meeting": "Bita was as atavistic as her race. A branch of the same root and the deceptive lovely flower would wither to seed a similar seed. . . . All the money she had spent would be wasted, all her planning and thinking and careful cultivation come to naught" (92). But Bita is not that kind of girl. At the novel's end, she combines the best of her native soil with the best of her education in England. It is this true inner harmony that allows her to make an intelligent choice of mates within a very complex Jamaican society.

For Jamaica is no simple pastoral world. On one level, her deflowering is a metaphor for what has happened to Jamaica itself—it has been raped by English colonists. That primal act of violence, however, is disguised in spatial terms by the geographic pattern of the town of Jubilee, where the Craigs have their mission. Although the Craigs are descendants of a long line of abolitionists who tried to reform the Anglican Church, they are members of the English elite, and thus their church (the mission) and the town of Jubilee, which Malcolm's ancestors had founded, is described in terms of a proper English garden, with just the right touch of ordered variety: "From the porch [of the mission] it was a precious view of the community that had *sprung up* (my emphasis) around the church on the hillock. Below there were three neat parallel streets containing the oblong edifices of the Wesleyan Church, the courtyard with its big yard, the post office, the dry-goods store, with one street curving uphill suddenly, at the top of which was the rectory half hidden by tree ferns and lime trees, and in between the grey-white gable-end cottages set in their flower gardens" (34). This "neat" pattern is set against the house and garden of Jordan Plant, Bita's father:

> It was a framed house of six rooms and a veranda and fixed upon stout cogwood pillars sunk deep into the earth. Set a little way back from the village road, there was a flower-garden front full of heavy-scented hot-country flowers growing untidily thick together.... Anty Nommy loved flowers and had a wonderful hand with them, but she had no sense of space and patterns in a garden, so the flowers grew all ways, struggling and blooming over and under one another. From the back of the house Jordan's vegetable and fruit garden went sliding green and fat down to the river. (51)

McKay is not setting one urban-garden pattern against the other but making an argument for both. Priscilla's mistake is her myopia—she sees the "mission" as the architectural structure (and the ideology it expresses) as the one that should dominate the town instead of being only another flower in the garden. Jordan's garden is full of "flowers" that "grew all ways, struggling and blooming over and under one another." They are a microcosm of Jamaican society, the deflowering of Jamaica resulting not in a destruction of native culture but a renewal of it in hybrids.

This is something Bita will have to discover on her own. What surprises Bita on her return is that her island is both familiar and unfamiliar, both home and not home. It is a variegated social and political landscape of class divisions, gender conflicts, religious differences, and racial hierarchies that she will have to navigate. It is also an interwoven, geographic landscape of city (Kingston), town (Jubilee and Gingertown) and village (Banana Bottom). And there are other smaller, spatial units: the grog shop next to the Jubilee market, a male-centered world whose misogynistic gossip has its religious counterpart in the demonic religion of the Obeahman of Banana Bottom ("Obi-God of Evil") whose claustrophobic dwelling was "a large long cave" on top of which was "an arch . . . overgrown with cutting grass, wild fig trees, and orchids" (134–35). This is a far cry from Squire Gensir's "bungalow," a "spacious place" that Bita loves to visit. Within is his library, his piano, and his sheet music, and like his candid personality, "the house opened with large French windows on a level with the sills looking over the Banana Bottom valley to the mountain chains beyond" (119).

It is significant that Banana Bottom stands at the crossroads where the road to Jubilee and Gingertown meet. Bita finds herself at a crossroads, returning to Jamaica as a product of English culture but attracted to the native culture of her past. Where does Bita fit in? Educated in England, she now has a new status in the Jamaican class system. She is the dark-skinned daughter of a prosperous peasant, but suddenly she has had greatness thrust upon her from the outside by two white, English aristocrats. As a Black theology student educated in Kingston, Herald Newton Day would have never considered her his intended if the Craigs had not made her their "experiment."

The pitfalls and contradictions Bita confronts are remembered by McKay himself. The world he left behind for the large cities that beckoned to him from Kingston's docks was just as messy, complicated, and difficult to understand as any Paris, New York, or London. One reason for this is the outside influences within Jamaica that complicate the inner sociological dynamics of both peasant life and the English presence.

Those outside influences are not of a piece. There is the Irish adventurer Busha Glengley, the English Evan Vaughan (baker turned factory owner turned fundamentalist preacher), and the Indian and Chinese coolies—these in addition to the cultured Craigs. The Craigs are not the only elements within the Christian circle of influence. The Craigs belong to an abolitionist offshoot of the Anglican Church, which makes their Free Church at Jubilee less formal than the official Anglican Church in Kingston. Paradoxically, the natives are attracted to the high church of their former slave holders because of its rich ceremony, whereas the Free Church that fought for their freedom has only their token allegiance. But all religious ties, as Evan Vaughan's opportunistic revivalism attests, are literally dependent on the weather. With the drought, he created a brand-new religious atmosphere.

This stock market of religious influences is only a small part of the total package that makes up the diversity and confusion of Jamaican life. Moreover, the stocks are never stable, continually mixing into new combinations so that one day Vaughan's stock is high, the next day the Craigs', the next day the Obeahman's. With Tack Tally's suicide, stock in the Obeahman plummets (even he cries out to Christ in despair), just as the church of Malcolm's father drops in value when he tries and fails to have the peasants get a better price on their coffee beans. 'No good deed goes unpunished" is a saying that should have originated in McKay's Jamaica.

Part of the problem, discussed earlier in the chapter on *Gingertown*, lies in the sociological presence of two different value systems: one based on reputation, the other on respectability. Put simply, respectability is tied to skin color (light), class, even chance (Priscilla choosing Bita to become "a precious flowering of a great work"), whereas reputation is something earned, as illustrated by Jordan Plant's rise from drayman to landowner (11). Though often in conflict, both systems are never completely separated from the other.

For instance, Busha Glengley's octoroon bastard son, "Marse" Arthur, thinks that his money and color permit him to rape Bita, even though she now has a privileged status because of her English education and her connection to the Craigs. Arthur thinks color trumps "reputation," her English education, an opportunity Bita was given (chance) and then earned. When Bita rejects him, he calls her a "n----r" gal, trying to humiliate her by reducing her to her dark skin. Jubban jumps to her defense, pummeling Arthur to the ground. Color is supposed to defer to color—but not this time. He is only Jordan Plant's drayman and dark like Bita, but he also has a sterling reputation because of his mastery of husbandry. He is responsible in great part for Bita's father's prosperity.

Another example of the confused boundary lines within Jamaican society occurs in Kingston right before Bita's marriage to Jubban. Both Bita and Belle Black are furious because of the treatment they received from a "respectable" hotel when an octoroon employee refuses to rent them a room. Belle then deliberately picks a fight with a "light-skinned person" in a bridal shop, telling her that "in de country where ah come from you got to show some'n moh'n a li'l turn colour to make class. You got to be somet'ing. You got to hab somet'ing" (299). Belle is exaggerating; color is just as important in the provinces as in the city, as the presence of the Glengleys illustrates.

A bounder like Tack Tally illustrates this perfectly. He presumes to impose himself upon Bita not only because of his light skin but also because of his "American" ways picked up in Colón. Tack is an example of outside and inside influences merging in a negative way and, as such, is a foil to Bita. That Tack dresses to perfection but has no home of his own (reluctantly living in a rundown shack with his mother) contrasts with Bita, who will plant herself in her father's house to create an intimate space all her own.

But the best example in the novel regarding the dialectical relationship between "respectability" and "reputation" occurs in a comical passage in a grog shop in Jubilee in which the gossiping males bring up the subject of Bita's sexual life. We need to set the stage here. The guys in the grog shop, from the lofty position of their bar stools, have just been talking about Gracie Hall's fall from her father's grace. Gracie's family has pretensions to middle-class gentility, but Gracie, who had lived in the "city," has cast off provincial restraints, and when the merry-go-round came to Jubilee, she participated in the "common peasant" pleasures by riding on it. Her father is furious because his daughter has damaged his respectability. In his anger, he knocks her off the mechanical horse upon which she was riding, much to the delight of the "ballad-mongers" of Jubilee who write a song that puns upon Gracie's "ridin'day" (along the lines of the rock and roll hit "Mustang Sally"). Her fall from the merry-go-round is also a fall in her reputation.

That the literal metamorphoses into the figurative serves as a preface to the grog shop gossip about Bita. The merry-go-round is not just a sexual metaphor but also a version of the wheel of fortune. The Craigs' marriage plans for Bita, as a symbol of her new respectability, are in jeopardy, according to one grog shop philosopher.

Before Herald Newton Day disgraces himself with a "nanny goat" (as he is about to give a sermon on "personal purity"), Bita puts herself in danger by flirting with Hopping Dick, a flamboyant but penniless dandy. This becomes a source of amusement and argument for the men in the grog shop, with one fellow, called "the little one," claiming that Hopping Dick doesn't stand a chance with someone as high up and cultured as Bita. Then a character known as "the tall one" responds, and his response consists of a series of parallel circles that touch upon the novel's major themes. In answer to the objection that Hopping Dick has no "chance" to make it with Bita, the tall one says:

> Gawd made man an' then woman from man, accordin' to the Bible. An' Gawd put an O in woman. But dere's no O in man. Now dere's an O in the reading and figuring a life and woman is in both a them an' both ways. So you nebber can tell about a woman whedder her is in the readin' and figuin' side a life an' when you come to any man an' a woman, well, you jes' cyant tell nuthin' at all. An' when a man tell you him is gwine mek a woman doan' you start a-crying him down an' say him cyant, becausen de woman is high up an' stylish an' nice-speakin' an all. Fer de leetlest thing can mek a woman fall, when a man can get away wid 'most anyt'ing an' still stand 'pon his feet. (107)

The richness of this passage goes beyond the bald statement that the "O" of a woman's vagina makes her vulnerable. The shift in meaning occurs in the fourth sentence: "dere's an O in the reading and figuring side a life and woman is in both a them an' both ways." Human experience involves perception ("reading") and interpretation ("figuring") and this results in our attempt to understand experience by putting a circle around it. The comedy here is that the circle is often too small or too large or doesn't fit "at all," which then causes the tall one to admit that when it comes to "any man an' a woman" we don't really know a thing about them. Moreover, a woman is an enigma. A man never knows "whedder her is in readin' or figurin' side of life." He then tries to recover his argument by saying "de leetlest thing" can bring a woman down, whereas a man stands on level ground.

But note that men in the novel are also brought down by "de leetlest thing"—music for Crazy Bow, purity for Herald Newton Day, anger for Tack Tally, sexual desire for Arthur Glengley. If a woman is teetering like Gracie Hall because she stands upon the "O" of society's prescriptions, or if she is shaken and disgraced like Yoni Legge by the "O" of her vagina, men do not escape the consequences of sexual desire, as the double entendres of the novel's title suggest. Men are equally ruined by their "tools." Jubban gives Arthur Glengley a sound thrashing, Tack Tally commits suicide, and Herald Newton Day loses everything. In shifting the emphasis from female to male, the passage becomes an exegesis in small of the novel itself.

One major theme is that, when it comes to sexual desire, anything can happen to both male and female, and most of it destructive. Marriage attempts to regulate desire but often ends by confining women like Bita to the enclosed circle of respectability. Bita finds herself at one point caught between the two poles of desire and law (marriage), between Hopping Dick and Herald Newton Day—and Priscilla who stands behind him. Bita's marriage to Day would complete Priscilla's "plan" (109) of exposing a Negro to "cultivation." This circle around Bita becomes more and more like a noose.

In the tall one's speech, McKay puns on "figuring," for the word points to figures of speech as modes of understanding—hence riding the merry-go-round shades into sexual riding, McKay implying that we do not live on one simple plane of existence. Priscilla attempts to put a "figure" around experience, but the value of that figure depends upon an accurate "reading" of the text of experience. Her misjudgment of Day, her attempt to enclose Bita within the boundaries of class and Christian morality are her undoing. Throughout the novel, acts of interpretation abound, and even the admirable Squire Gensir (based on McKay's friend and mentor Walter Jekyll) doesn't escape McKay's critical eye.

Despite his anthropological interest in native life, Squire Gensir unconsciously romanticizes it because of his great fondness for the natives. They have done, he believes, what civilized people have found impossible to do, "to eliminate the inessentials that militate against plastic living" (120). By "plastic," he means "flexible." The natives are free because they are able to live deliberately. Yet when Day's sodomy occurs, Squire Gensir is baffled, just as he is baffled by the peasants' worship of both the Christian God and Obi, the African "god of evil." McKay notes of Gensir that "being an enthusiast of the simple life, he was like many enthusiasts, apt to underestimate the underlying contradictions that may inhere in his more preferable way of life" (176).

By the end of the novel, Bita has rejected the imposition of a single pattern on either Jamaican society or on her own life. What she does embrace is "clear thinking," which she calls "the most beautiful of all things" (314). She has reached this conclusion by reading Blaise Pascal, the seventeenth-century French philosopher who, like the tall one, was fascinated by the image of the circle.

Georges Poulet has observed that Pascal gave a new reading to the medieval maxim that "God is the center of everywhere and the circumference is nowhere" (Poulet xi). Pascal saw the terrifying implications of this thought, for he believed himself lost in the "infinite immensity of spaces." If the universe is a circle, we can never know its boundaries, yet "through space the universe encompasses me and engulfs me *like a point*" (qtd. in Poulet 39). According to Poulet, Pascal believed that humankind is "powerless to give himself any points of reference, without a hold on any world larger than the narrow circle of his island or his cell" (33). McKay's reinterpretation is to show that Bita's "island" is no more or less "narrow" than any other "circle." Life in New York, as "Truant" illustrates, can be as circumscribed as any life in Banana Bottom.

What Bita discovers in the novel's conclusion is that "clear thinking" means freeing herself from both society's suffocating circles and the circular nature of desire. In the course of the novel, a number of false circles have encompassed Bita: as an object of Priscilla's "pet experiment" (211), as a helpmate for Herald Newton Day, as a trinket for Hopping Dick's vanity, as a convert to Evan Vaughan's fundamentalist Christianity, as a Black wench for Arthur Glengley's lust. Bita has had to come to terms with them all, even with the admirable Squire Gensir's "contradictions."

Yet "clear thinking" also means finding an expanding circle that does not terrify her with its "infinite immensity of spaces." When she marries Jubban, her deceased father's "drayman," she incurs society's disapproval but plants herself on solid ground (and not on the "O" of her vagina). Paradoxically, embracing the local expands her conception of culture to include her London education, her intellectual life given to her through books. As Bita herself reflects, "her music, her reading, her thinking were the flowers of her intelligence, and he [her husband] the root in the earth upon which she was grafted, both nourished by the same soil" (313).

She focuses upon specific lines from Pascal: "la vraie morale se moque de la morale; la morale du jugement se moque de la morale de l'espirit" (314) ["True morality laughs at the moral. The morality of judgment laughs at the judgment of "l'esprit"]. The French "l'esprit" can be translated as either "spirit" or "mind," and both apply in terms of what Bita is rejecting, whether it be Yoni's Dionysian truth of the vulva (her name in Hindu means "vagina") or the narrowed-minded truth of Priscilla's rigid Christianity.

Mark Helbling perceptively notes that McKay does some selective editing on this passage from Pascal, "failing to complete Pascal's last line— 'l'espirit, qui est sans regles' [the spirit or mind that is without rules]" (116). The Penguin translation puts it this way: "The morality of judgement has no time for the random morality of the mind" (212). The missing "sans regles," Helbling argues, allows McKay to simplify Pascal to focus on Bita's final belief that "clear thinking" is the basis of happiness. Yet "true morality" is always, to a certain extent, ad hoc, or as Hopping Dick puts it at Bita's wedding: it is a "happy day" when one gets the right person in the right way, "but nobody knows 'bouten dat in de beginning" (303). "Clear thinking" for Bita means taking into account the organic nature of human experience.

McKay has Squire Gensir tell Bita that the lines from Pascal that she likes were "more Pagan and Stoic than Christian" (314). Their Pagan side is reflected in the distinction Pascal makes between two types of intelligence—each potentially narrow but each potentially insightful. That is, his view of "la vraie morale" and "la morale du jugement" occurs in the context of his discussion of "the mathematical mind" versus "the intuitive mind." The "mathematical mind" wants life circumscribed by definitions and principles, but it has trouble with the quotidian world— ordinary everyday experience with all its contradictions and paradoxes.

In contrast, "the intuitive mind" judges "at a glance," but has difficulty moving beyond facts and hence often embodies them in concrete societal laws and customs to simplify experience. It travels along a horizontal line, abandoning verticality. "The mathematical mind" suffers from the opposite defect—it often wanders in Swift's Laputa-land. Although he leans toward the "intuitive," Pascal argues for an intelligence that takes the best from both types of cognition. The truly moral is above the petty definers of morality but is still moral. It is not the "intuitive" pragmatism of the fundamentalist preacher Evan Vaughan who used a drought (fact) in Banana Bottom as a cunning opportunity to control others. Judgment then is an intelligence that uses reason but is not bound by ratiocination. It uses intuition but is not seduced by selfish motives (Pascal 212).

Given the context of Pascal's distinction between true morality and morality by the book, and true judgment versus the "random morality of the mind," McKay left out the "sans regles" because the conclusion that Bita arrives at is that the true "rules" of morality and judgment arise from an awareness that life is fluid and not fixed. Coleridge's theory of the Imagination is relevant here: "the repetition in the finite mind of the eternal act of creation of the infinite I AM." It takes what the "finite mind" perceives and "dissolves, diffuses, dissipates, in order to recreate" (Perkins 452). True morality and true judgment are the products of "clear thinking" as recreated and renewed perceptions in a continuum, but, as Hopping Dick puts it, nobody knows anything about this "in de beginning."

Recreating experience is precisely what the "ballad mongers" do when they reconstruct Gracie Hall's fall by giving it a new spin in a new story. They are putting a new circle of interpretation around a previous one. This speech act is a form of carnival according to M. M. Bakhtin: an interpretation that reinterprets an interpretation. They have done this with Bita's rape ("Crazy Bow was first"), which the Craigs have tried to cover up with an English education, and with Yoni's pregnancy, which she claims was caused by an angel: "There's an angel hovering round, / Look out, sister, look out" (272)! This ability to turn experience into storytelling of multiple dimensions is what Squire Gensir admires in Jamaican folk culture, and it is what Bita sees as the source of true "cultivation," the ability not to deny experience but to embrace it and reshape it in terms usable for the future.

As long as "everything is explained . . . by definitions and principles," the world makes sense to the "mathematical mind" (Pascal 212). But if the world can no longer be understood in terms of a priori definitions, the "mathematical mind" operates "sans regles," that is, arbitrarily. Conventional morality, on the other hand, is the "intuitive mind" as "good sight" embodied in stone (Pascal 210). Priscilla Craig's view of Bita is an example of this kind of "mathematical mind" and a conventional morality, which Pascal sees as the negative side of the "intuitive mind" (210). She wishes to impose a circle around Bita in terms of a superior education (Western), a superior culture (England) and a superior church (the Free Church). She refuses to recognize the values of other cultures and other moral and artistic perspectives. For her, the artwork of Africa is savage and demonic, an indication of her narrow view of the African presence in Jamaican life.

Her dependence upon definitions results in a comic, arbitrary view of Africans. She calls Bita a "nymphomaniac" because Bita refuses to stop seeing Hopping Dick (221), but she rejects the definition of "kleptomaniac" for the Jamaican ladies who steal her knitting needles because "kleptomania" (228) is a nervous disorder peculiar to the higher civilizations. Since Priscilla sees Africans as naturally libidinous, she is ready to apply a sexual "mania" to Bita but decides that "stealing" is a more appropriate term for the African ladies of her sewing circle. Kleptomania is a European disease and not applicable to those of the lower orders.

There is, however, another interpretation of Bita's "nymphomania" that is more accurate in describing Bita. It is expressed by Anty Nommy's mispronunciation of the word "nymphomania" to "nymph fer manaxe," suggesting that this verbal mistake is a form of "figuring" that arises from "reading" the text in a new way (221). Anty Nommy is unconsciously calling attention to what has been suffocating Bita since her return from England: she has been living under the axe of someone else's definition of her, especially by the men on the island such as Tack Tally, Hopping Dick, Arthur Glengley, Herald Newton Day, and even Malcolm Craig. Her mispronunciation takes an "axe" to those definitions.

Consider the Craigs' intentions for her. By giving her an English education and marrying her to the cultivated Harold Newton Day, these two can lead their people into the promised land of the Christian faith and the traditions of Western civilization, especially its inheritance of the Enlightenment tradition.

Day's middle name is significant. He has Isaac Newton's "mathematical mind" in that his sermons are mostly definitions, abstractions. He reduces the biblical Psalms to a collection of simpleminded homilies for living the "pure" life and ends by having his body below the waist revolt against his narrow, "mathematical" circumscription of experience. Defiling himself with a goat (the medieval symbol of lust) illustrates McKay's great lesson that life cannot be strait jacketed into perfection—religious, mathematical or otherwise— such as defining Jamaican life as "pastoral."

But McKay's point regarding Day is more subtle than the id rearing its ugly head. Day's first sermon to the common folk of Banana Bottom has as its theme the "watchman" passage from Ezekiel 3:16–21, the basis for the famous spiritual and the equally famous novel by James Baldwin, *Go Tell It on the Mountain* (1953). In biblical text, the Lord tells the "Son of Man" that he, Ezekiel, is a witness and a "watcher" over his people. In the sermon, Day arrogates to himself the perfection that belongs only to God. The focus of his watcher is not on protecting these unlettered peasants but on claiming superiority over them. The echoing of Day's "watchman" motif in the novel's ending reestablishes the biblical humility that goes along with "clear thinking." Bita has chosen for a husband a simple man of the people; she has watched, over time, his true worth and her choice has created an invisible city for them both.

Bita's coming of age has not been an easy process, and McKay was probably thinking of Pascal's aphorism that immediately follows the "la vraie morale" passage: "The body is nourished gradually. Ample food but little substance." Bita refers to Pascal's "gem" as "a thought like food" (314). Her "vraie" education has occurred "gradually"; her education in England was only the first stage of her intellectual development, "ample food" but of "little substance" if it only exists within the context of Priscilla's plan to remake her an English woman of color (Pascal 212).

For Coleridge, the creative act involves both "reading" and "figuring" in terms of Bita's personal perceptions (The Primary Imagination), or what Squire Gensir calls "plastic living," and in terms of artistic creation (The Secondary Imagination), the ability of the folk imagination to reshape a Mozart melody into a native song, or to take a European dance like the minuet and change it to a popular dance called the "mintoe" (123–24). But there is also such a thing as creative reading as well as creative living or the creative act.

At the novel's conclusion, Bita "recreates" William Blake's poem "The Little Black Boy" (267) in terms of an original interpretation of that great Romantic poem. It is an act that defines her as no longer John Locke's passive perceiver but as Coleridge's creative reader. On the surface, the poem seems to be saying that the young Black boy desires his "soul" to be "white," and thus, Bita thinks, it should not be read by an impressionable young person who would fail to see the levels of irony in the poem. But Bita now understands the poem's thematic complexity because she reads it through the lens of two cultures. She sees that the mother's voice in the poem creates a fiction of color, a color scheme, to protect her child from the world's injustices until he is old enough to understand them. Because she does not want him prematurely consumed by hatred, she tells her child to "shade" the white boy "from the heat" until they are both freed from the black cloud and the white cloud that hover over them.

The important line in the poem, which Bita repeats in her reflections, is that both the Black boy and the white boy live under a "cloud." They will only enter the "golden tent" when the cloud is removed. The cloud is death, the white sepulchre; it is the letter that kills the spirit, and to protect her son from the letter of the law, the sepulchre, the mother spins a fable of love—her son must love the white child so that he will grow up to be whole. It is only then that the son will be able to face life's injustices.

Bita can see the poem's "la vraie morale" because she has become a creative reader of her own life. In reading the poem, Bita reconstructs her own childhood, remembering her father's love and protection, especially after her rape by Crazy Bow. She realizes that all the men that she has loved—her father, Squire Gensir, and Jubban—have shared something of his integrity. True "cultivation," as Squire Gensir said to Busha Glengley, is not a matter of class but character, and character itself depends on the "reading and figuring" of life. People who self-destruct like Crazy Bow, Tack Tally, and Herald Newton Day lack this ability. Crazy Bow is swept away by his music (Dionysus), as he was swept away by his lust when he raped Bita as a young girl; Day by his abstract plans for perfection (Apollo). Neither has Bita's "clear thinking." She returns home to marry Jubban because she now feels at home in the world: "She thought how the finest qualities of mind or brain or heart were the attributes of only the rarest spirits, who may spring like flowers in the commonest as much as the most exclusive places, in the proud domain as well as the peasant's lot and even in hothouses. How then could any class or people or nation or race claim a monopoly of a thing so precious and so erratic in its manifestations?" (266). The sentiment about common life alludes to the Romantic poets, but it also points to a hidden theme of *Banana Bottom*: the possibility of creating a city in a garden, a garden in a city.

Cultivation in the broader sense of improving the human estate is tied to the motif of dancing. Those who disapprove of dancing like Herald Newton Day call it a low form of human behavior. "I don't care about popular music. It doesn't stir me. I think it a shame that such a noble thing as music, should be put to such degrading purposes as dancing" (172). The African masks terrify Priscilla with their "satanic power"; she dreams of them "dancing around her," grinning and surrounding her in a "dancing fury" (199). Even Bita succumbs at one point to the "satanic power" of the dance, becoming a different person in the "religious ecstasy" of the Great Revival (250). The Dionysian element of the dance is always present, as when Black Belle implicitly links Bita's dancing at a public picnic with Yoni's "dancing someways in de bush" with Tack Tally (85). However, dance as an ideal creates a delicate balance between passion and artifice.

That balance through dancing becomes a means by which McKay establishes Bita as his ideal. Bita likes all kinds of dances, even the more formal "waltzes and minuets." Although she prefers "the native group dancing," those dances, "in a more artificial atmosphere," are pleasing (84). McKay is using "artificial" here in the older, eighteenth-century meaning of that word—it is synonymous with "artifice. There are, in other words, all kinds of artistic expressions. At the novel's end Bita embraces "her music, her reading, her thinking" as "flowers of her intelligence" (313), flowers that are not at odds with the flower of her husband, Anty Nommy, and her native garden. For her, the transformation of the "minuet" into the native's redefinition of that dance as the "mintoe" (literally the "little toe") is comparable to what she has done with her life. The natives have taken an English dance and made it their own, recognizing the delicacy of the original even as they transform it into something else. McKay sees this act as a microcosm of what Jamaican society, at its best, does with the legacy of colonialism.

Perhaps the most perfect moment of balance and harmony for Bita occurs when she dances with Hopping Dick at a house party to which members of all social classes are invited. Here, dance becomes a perfect expression for the momentary merger of two cultures and the merger of two very different people. The dance moves from the polished "mahogany" floors of light-skinned Jamaican gentility to the grass plot of a multicolored house party: "And as Bita stood up to Hopping Dick (who perfectly acted the role of his nickname that night), hands poised in the air and she pirouetting around him to the fiddling of the native translation of the minuet, she felt it was a happy choice when the native tongue turned that name to mintoe" (196). But the dance is momentary, and Dick is "acting" out a part because he has a part to play in the dance. In life outside the dance, Hopping Dick is a threat to Bita's sense of herself. Dance is one thing, life outside the dance another. The O in woman is also Obi, the God of evil, of excess, and Bita has to learn to harmonize Apollo and Dionysus. Her sophisticated reading of Blake's poem, seeing its levels of irony, is the culmination of her total education.

In a sense, her creative reading of Blake's poem reflects a kind of communal intelligence. After her rape by Crazy Bow, Bita had become the subject of a song, the village ballad makers creating a satirical ditty that turns the cruel act into comedy. No matter how much you dress her up in "silk" and "gold," and although "the prince may come after," you cannot deny that "Crazy Bow was first" (14). The song deflates "respectability," by linking the high with the low, a marvelous contrast to Priscilla's song "praising God from whom all blessings flow" which, in reality, praises her own "work" by taking the low and making it high by sending the disgraced Bita to England (13). Later, when Bita returns from England, the song satirizing her is "remembered in the hills again" (30). It is not merely remembered but recreated, McKay hinting that the women have shifted the emphasis from male to female. The song is now sung with "all honour to Bita" (30). Not only did she have the pluck to triumph over adversity and to reenter communal life without arrogance, but she had the good fortune to have rich benefactors. The song reflects communal wisdom but is also, like art, to be reinterpreted in terms of changing circumstances.

The song about Gracie Hall, however, continues to subject her to ridicule because, unlike Bita, she has not changed. Like Bita she is sent to a larger world than Banana Bottom, but unlike Bita, she has never learned to read and figure. Her parents sent her to Kingston to become a seamstress, and, seduced by urban liberty, she forgets, as her father does not, about her "respectable" position as a member of the middle class in Jubilee. On the one hand, it is mere bad luck that she is disgraced for her ride on the merry-go-round; whereas Bita dances at a village tea-meeting where all the classes mingle but does not suffer for it. On the other hand, it is Bita's active engagement in the dance that changes the dynamics of the moment: "And she danced forgetting herself, forgetting even Jubilee, dancing down the barrier between high breeding and common pleasures under her light stamping feet until she was one with the crowd" (84). Gracie passively sits on the moving wheel; Bita makes the wheel move—and becomes part of it. Her mind dances with Pascal at the book's end.

Pascal's comments on "la vrai morale" is prefaced by the line: "True eloquence has no time for eloquence" (212). The novel ends with Bita's reflection upon her English education, that it has not been a waste because true "eloquence" involves both her love of Square Gensir's library and Anty Nommy's vernacular. Perhaps Squire Gensir has the final word on what nourishes: "Everyone borrows or steals and recreates in art" (McKay, *Banana Bottom* 124). The key word is "recreates," which is precisely what Bita has done with her own life once she returns to Jamaica, taking what she has been offered and reshaping it into something new. This is what the folk community did with her rape by Crazy Bow: "Crazy Bow was first." The song represents a kind of communal wisdom, both cruel and comic. Like satire, it is cruel because it exposes the fact that marriage to Herald Newton Day or Priscilla's "experiment" will not cover up the brutal truth. It is comic because it softens the blow of the rape through communal laughter, especially when the Jamaican women reinterpret the song "with all praise to Bita."

The distinction Squire Gensir makes between what is original and what has been "recreated" can take a personal turn when Bita says that "I am myself" and that she "was trained . . . to be" (100). Or as Squire Gensir puts it, your English education was "something to fit you into a rigid pattern" (121). The "I am myself" is not fixed but fluid and organic, and the "was" in the self the Craigs had made is a false self because it *is* fixed. We see Bita's rebellion against this fixed self when she lets her anger dictate her behavior. She convinces herself that she loves Hopping Dick because Priscilla is against him. Her response to Priscilla is an example of the negative side of the "intuitive" mind, one that responds only to the emotional moment. Her maturity comes when she frees herself completely from Priscilla and becomes her own agent.

One part of the redefinition involves her choice of Jubban as her husband, a choice that outrages polite society. It is a choice that reflects a new self, a new perspective. Romantic love, Bita decides, is an "exotic imposition, not a real intrinsic thing that had flowered out of the mind of her race" (313). Her true reading and figuring entail a love that spreads outward like Pascal's large circle: "whose center is everywhere." That space is one that contains her memories of the past and her future with Jubban, Anty Nommy, and her child, who, in the last sentence of the novel, is already showing the "strength" of his mother.

What the novel's ending reveals is not a conclusion to a good story but an ongoing organic process, not the static world of a product, but the minuet endlessly being transformed into the mintoe. Bita falls asleep reading Pascal's *Pensees*, but she is awakened by her son's voice and Anty Nommy's exasperation with him: "Showing you' strengt' a'ready mi li't' man. Soon you'll be l'arnin' fer square you' fist them off at me" (315).

Here is the right balance between permanence and change. Bita's son is named for her father, but her son's engagement with the world will be like hers—an ongoing fight on many levels. The learning process will involve a recognition of the world as a series of expanding circles. At the end of *Banana Bottom*, Bita has renewed her life by reconfiguring it, by seeing both the "miraculous in the common" (her marriage to Jubban) and by understanding that her London education has not alienated her from her culture but has given her a new appreciation of the infinite variety of its concentric circles.

CHAPTER 7

GANGSTERS IN CONTEXT

Harlem Glory and *Amiable with Big Teeth*

> The realist in murder writes of a world in which gangsters
> can rule nations and almost rule cities.
> —RAYMOND CHANDLER, "THE SIMPLE ART OF MURDER," 1944

The recently discovered *Amiable with Big Teeth*, which was written around 1940 and published in 2017, is set in a specific time in Harlem's history and world history. It begins with Italy's invasion in 1935 of Ethiopia and Harlem's reaction to that momentous event. A second invasion, however, is the one with which the novel is most concerned: the invasion of Harlem by the Soviet's popular front. The novel treats both invasions as power grabs by two sets of gangsters.

Chandler's observation in this chapter's epigraph is relevant here because the background of McKay's novels not only involves the specific historic moment of the 1930s but World War I, the setting on the home front of *Home to Harlem* and the time frame of 1919 for the publication of "If We Must Die." Chandler served in World War I (the only survivor of a bomb that blew up the rest of his platoon), and his point about "gangsters" ruling nations underlines the thesis of Adam Hochschild's most recent study of America and "the war at home" in *American Midnight* (2022). Hochschild's history of America in the war and after is the most thorough study to date of the "police state" created by President Wilson. Wilson said he wanted the world made safe for democracy but made a world unsafe for those who disagreed with his war program. McKay calls his comrades "kinsmen" in "If We Must Die" rather than African Americans because the gangsters who now ruled the nation lumped all dissenters as the enemy: "Striking workers, radical suffragists, and African

American migrants were all, at some point during the war, referred to as 'pro-Germans'" (Capozzola 201).

Hochschild points to the extraordinary number of government agencies that emerged during the war to police the nation's citizens: The American Protective League, the Bureau of Investigation (the "Federal" added later), the Committee for Public Information, whose whole purpose, according to its founder and director, George Creel, was "the fight for the *minds* of men, for the 'conquest of their convictions'" (qtd. in Kennedy 61). Creel also designed the "Four Minute Men" whose sole aim was to flood all possible public venues to preach the gospel of the great "Crusade." Hochschild has an impressive list of venues in addition to "movie houses": "Rotary and Kiwanis luncheons, county fairs, Indian reservations, women's clubs, churches, synagogues, labor union meetings, band concerts, between innings at the World Series, revival tents, and some 500 logging camps" (174). If Creel wanted to control the hearts and minds of Americans, the American Protective League wanted to monitor American bodies. According to Ronald Schaefer, "APL members impersonated federal officers, opened private mail, wiretapped telephones, recorded conversations with dictaphones, broke into offices, conducted searches and seizures, and delivered materials they uncovered to the Justice Department's Bureau of Investigation" (17). One architect of this repression was Albert Burleson, the postmaster general, who went on a censorship rampage, denying mailing privileges to all subversive publications that dared to criticize the war effort. Eventually, Hochschild notes, "Burleson would ban from the mail virtually the entire socialist press," using the Espionage Act and the soon to follow Sedition Act (1917) as justifications for his decisions (138). The passage of both acts not only stifled all dissent but permitted atrocities such as lynching and the deportation of dissidents of all persuasions, resulting finally in the infamous Red Scare of 1919. The key element of this new dispensation was the rise of the "security state." As Christopher Capozzola notes, "increasingly, Americans articulated their political obligations not to many things but to one: the state (16)." During the war, the ultimate safeguard of the state was surveillance, or as Capozzola puts it, America became "The Surveillance State" (201). People, it was believed, needed to be "watched."

Burleson's ire was specifically directed at *The Masses* whose editor was Max Eastman, McKay's personal friend. When *The Masses* folded, Eastman revived it as *The Liberator*, and McKay became a coeditor and a leading contributor. The FBI never forgot or forgave McKay's radicalism, hounding him for years and keeping a voluminous file on him (Holcomb 24–26).

When McKay has Bugsy in *Banjo* refer to the United States as the "United Snakes," he is no doubt thinking of the FBI's "surveillance" on him, but he is also remembering the gangster world of absolute power created by the surveillance state during the war. The "united" points to the difference between gangster crime and individual crime. The gangster is part of a gang. He may be the alpha male in the gang, but his presence is part of a collective, now the government of these "United Snakes." Curiously, Hollywood itself expressed the connection between gangsters and the government. The Hays Code of 1934 insisted that movie gangsters either die or go out cowards, but the new "G-Men" in the cinema of 1930s who replaced the gangsters simply repeated the same "theatrics of violence," this time within a socially approved moral framework (Clarens 129).

The thesis that government could be permitted to sanction violence was expressed by Randolph Bourne in his posthumously published essay entitled "The State" (1919). Bourne had been an admirer of John Dewey's pragmatism, but when he saw that Dewey, along with other leading American intellectuals, had capitulated to the wartime hysteria, he despaired over America's future. In "The State," he depicted the dark side of "The Beloved Community," Josiah Royce's positive view of America's future and the supposed end result of Dewey's pragmatism, the intelligent interaction of children and adults with their environment. But that "environment" was now tainted by government control, or as Attorney General Thomas Gregory "boasted" during the war, "It is safe to say that never in its history has this country been so thoroughly policed" (qtd. in Hochschild 189). In his novel *1919*, John Dos Passos would refer to Bourne as a "ghost" that would not go away, quoting the most famous line in the essay: "War is the health of the state" (Dos Passos, *USA* 449–48). What war allowed was not only violence against its own citizens but surveillance as intimidation, thereby foreshadowing modern critics of culture like George Orwell, Louis Althusser, and Michel Foucault.

In "The State," the "Beloved Community" had a demonic double, as "the nation in wartime attains a uniformity of feeling, a hierarchy of values culminating at the undisputed apex of the state ideal (Bourne 361). Bourne refers to the state as a "mystical conception" that lies dormant because it doesn't exist as a concrete reality like the country and its people, which are made up of a multiplicity of concrete realities that cannot be easily categorized (359). Once war is declared, however, the state rises like Lazarus from the grave to swallow up the government and its citizens who then act with a single voice and with a monolithic force. The state proceeds to stifle all dissent, coercing its citizens, through a kind of "spiritual alchemy," to act in total concert (356). That "alchemy" is a sleight of hand, a form of magic, emotional theater—all in the service of an invisible god. Although the state enlists its citizens' loyalty primarily through patriotic appeals, forms of intimidation are important elements in this melodrama, especially fear, paranoia, and hatred of a demonized other. The flag as a symbol replaces the country with its diverse ethnic strands and classes. Blind loyalty replaces civil liberties and freedom of speech, as the state becomes a monster with one all-seeing eye like some grotesque cyclops.

Bourne's essay reads at times like a gothic novel in that the historic moment of America's entry into the war repeats the buried but horrific nature of America's history. World War I didn't just change America (killing progressivism and liberal thought) but also brought to the surface a pattern of history that most historians have ignored. Although Bourne never uses the word "gangster," the ruling classes in America—be they plutocrats, captains of industry, or the Southern "slaveocracy"—have behaved like gangsters, using crisis situations to intimidate others and to disguise a love of power.

Love of power driving human behavior is an important theme in book two of *Gulliver's Travels*. The myopic Gulliver assumes that power rather than greed would appeal to the King of Brobdingnag. He is shocked when the king refuses his offer of gunpowder that "would have made him absolute Master of the Lives, the Liberties, and the Fortunes of his People" (Swift, *Gulliver's Travels* 398). The king was shocked by the carnage that gunpowder was capable of: the effects of gunpowder, said Gulliver, could "batter the strongest Walls to the Ground; sink down Ships with a thousand Men in each, to the Bottom of the Sea; and when linked together by a Chain . . . divide Hundreds of Bodies in the Middle, and lay Waste all before them." Swift seemed to be predicting the horrors of the twentieth century.

It is a scene like this that revived Swift's reputation in the 1920s, when, in the eyes of many, Swift changed from being a misanthrope to being a modernist. Gulliver's "gift" to the king in the 1920s became the Pandora's box of the Industrial Revolution whose new technology made industrialized death possible in the Great War. In 1917, it seemed to many that the war could only end with complete extinction on both sides. As we have seen, McKay called it "the vast international cemetery of this century" (*Home to Harlem* 227).

Mass murder would find its way into the pulps such as Dashiell Hammett's *Red Harvest*, serialized in *The Black Mask* in 1927, in which by the end of the novel all the gangsters in "Poisonville" kill each other. The Great War and American pulp culture were intimately connected. As Paula

Rabinowitz astutely notes: "in America, modernism cannot be separated from kitsch, mass culture, vernacular, and other popular forms" (*American Pulp* 35). Langston Hughes would remind McKay of this in a letter: "The New York theater, the part that hasn't gone black, has gone in for gang warfare and underground stuff, and is producing some amazing lifelike and tremendously entertaining pictures of modern Chicago and Tenth Avenue scarcely less melodramatic than the reality" (LH to CM, September 13, 1928, *Selected Letters*).

McKay would be more interested in gangster movies rather than New York's theaters. The violent ending of *Amiable with Big Teeth* would echo the grotesque final scenes of the famous triad of gangster movies of the early 1930s—*Little Caesar* (1931), *Public Enemy* (1932), and *Scarface* (1932)—and possibly the ending of the African American film, *Dark Manhattan* (1937), a Black reprise of *Scarface*. He would also be influenced by other gangster films, notably Josef von Sternberg's *Underworld* (1927) and possibly Oscar Micheaux's *Underworld* (1937).

McKay was certainly no fan of Hollywood. He is quite explicit in one "Cycle" poem: "I hate what Hollywood means in every way" (*CP* 250, line 14). And yet he makes this shrewd observation in another "Cycle" poem: "Hollywood is our first and greatest source / Of education, greater than our schools, / Hollywood's talents chart our national course . . ." (*CP* 249, lines 1–3). In the same poem he juxtaposes Hollywood's fantasy factory with the grim reality of Black American "cities where our blood / Congeals on pavements whence the terror springs" (*CP* 249, lines 11–12). That stark image has its source not only in what McKay has experienced on Harlem's streets but also what he has seen in Weegee tabloid photographs and Hollywood's gangster movies.

McKay would also be aware of Bertolt Brecht's play, *The Three Penny Opera* (1928), and its film version (1931). In both play and film, the gangsters, Mack the Knife and Peachum, are not only capitalists but fight over political control of the city. The source of Brecht's play is John Gay's *The Beggar's Opera* (1728), in which the connection between the gangster and the politician is made even more specific. Gay's target is Robert Walpole, England's prime minister (1721-1742) whose political power seemed so absolute and corrupt that both Henry Fielding and Alexander Pope would expose him as a gangster in 1743, in, respectively, *The Life and Death of Jonathan Wild, the Great* and the final version of *The Dunciad*. Pope's mock-epic poem was also in Walter Jekyll's library (McKay, *A Long Way* 13).

Like the endings of the Hollywood gangster movies, McKay's final scene in *Amiable with Big Teeth* reverses the gangster's path to worldly success.

In that last scene, the Leopard Men kill Maxim Tasan in a ritualized killing because they see Tasan as "an evil influence upon the community" (265). McKay is using a conception of satire here that has its roots in Africa, in a primal communal response to something infectious in the tribe that has to be removed. In *The Power of Satire: Magic, Ritual, Art*, Robert C. Elliot points to a ceremony on the Guinea coast in which a tribe singles out an evil presence that must be "cleansed" (78). The Leopard Men throw Tasan off a tall building. He crashes to the ground, "dashing his brains among the garbage of the neglected Harlem pavement" (269). It's a pulp ending. The ambitious Rico (Edward G. Robinson) in *Little Caesar* dies in the same garbage-strewn world that he came from.

Tasan's violent descent is the direct opposite of his meteoric rise; the "garbage of the neglected Harlem pavement" deflates the hollowness of his inflated, Communist rhetoric: "we are implacably, historically and eternally in the service of humanity" (55). What he intends to do to Professor Koazhy happens to him, his ironic fall being the reverse of his rise, the ironic ending of almost all gangster movies. Or as Pamela (Gladys George) says about a dead Eddie (James Cagney) at the end of *The Roaring Twenties* (1939) "He used to be a Big Shot." Eddie dies on the semivertical stairs of a church.

In *Home to Harlem*, Ray thought that someday he would like to write like the great "satirists" of his age: "Bernard Shaw, Ibsen, Anatole France, the popular problemist H. G. Wells" (225). In one of McKay's "Cycle" poems of 1943, he asks "for a Mencken upright on his feet, / To blast the smugness of the black elite" (*CP* 245, lines 13–14), but the satirist he evokes in *Harlem Glory* and *Amiable with Big Teeth* would be the great eighteenth-century English satirist Jonathan Swift and his target would not only be "the black elite" but those of all stripes who prey upon Harlem's citizens. Swift was capable of both the light touch and satiric sledgehammer, the one finding a place in *Harlem Glory*, the other in *Amiable with Big Teeth*. The Horatian satire in *Harlem Glory* puts the more sinister Juvenalian satire of *Amiable with Big Teeth* into perspective.

When McKay turns to *Amiable with Big Teeth*, the focus narrows to the big teeth behind the amiable smile. As McKay said in another "Cycle" poem, he preferred the "old bandits that I know" to the sinister "new gangsters" of the Russian Revolution "who eloquently profess / All things to all men which they can't bestow" (*CP* 254, lines 6–8). This distinction between "old bandits" and "new gangsters" marks the difference between *Harlem Glory* and *Amiable*. There was a certain innocence about the bandits of Harlem's numbers racket in that the vice was simple, direct, and obvious: greed. The "new gangsters" were after higher stakes, universal power.

Like Dashiell Hammett's *Maltese Falcon*, McKay's plot in *Amiable with Big Teeth* works by misdirection. Hammett begins his novel with Miss Wonderly's lies and Archer's death, but what soon emerges is Casper Gutman and the falcon statuette that everyone is after. In the course of novel, Archer becomes an afterthought, as Wonderly metamorphoses into the enigmatic Bridget O'Shaughnessy and the "dingus" (the statuette) reveals its deadly history of slavery and greed in the New World. When the bird finally appears, it turns out to be lead and is not encrusted with valuable jewels. The "wonder" of Miss Wonderly is as fake as the statuette, just as the "wonder" of the "green breast" of New World in *The Great Gatsby* became the Valley of the Ashes.

McKay begins his novel with high comedy, as though *Amiable with Big Teeth* will be another *Harlem Glory*. The envoy from Ethiopia, Lij Tekla Alamaya, has arrived in Harlem to urge its citizens to support his tiny African country against Italy's Fascist aggression, but he is upstaged on the podium by Professor Koazhy who stands beside the envoy in the flamboyant "uniform of an Ethiopian warrior" (9) and gives a long speech on African history. He rouses the crowd to a patriotic pitch, asks for a twenty-five-dollar donation from each member, and ends in Peixota's home not as a charlatan but as a genuine hero. Assembled in Peixota's house, in addition to the garrulous Koazhy, are his socially striving wife Kezia and his ditzy daughter Seraphine. The novel begins as though it could be a potential screenplay for a screwball comedy in the style of 1936's *My Man Godfrey*, albeit with a political theme.

Yet there are two other figures in Peixota's house who will become major players in the novel's emerging political conflict: Dorsey Flagg and Newton Castle. As an executive member of "Hands to Ethiopia," an African American organization whose sole purpose is to aid Ethiopia, Dorsey is a foil to Castle, who, it soon becomes apparent, is an attack dog for the novel's most sinister figure, Maxim Tasan, a Soviet agent, who promises a utopian future for all, but who seeks only power for himself. He declares that "the Soviet state has abolished race and color," but the "state" in the novel is Bourne's gangster State (*Amiable with Big Teeth* 55. All citations are to this edition). He will accuse Peixota of being a "gangster" because of Peixota's criminal past, but that past is small beer compared with Tasan's international schemes. Tasan's plan for Harlem, to control its hearts and minds, echoes a parallel theme in *Home to Harlem*. The Soviets are only the most recent player in Black Harlem's short history who intend to reduce it to a colony.

Pablo Peixota's gangster past serves as a foil to Tasan's gangster present. A former Harlem numbers kingpin, he is now "a wealthy man" because he has become a major figure in Harlem's real estate market. McKay sees him as a person who could only exist in Harlem's fluid social space: "Perhaps nowhere else in America but in such a community could the former promoter of a gambling game arrive at such a position of power and respect" (26). In other words, some gangsters are better than others, just as some social worlds, no matter how flawed, are better than false utopias.

As a leading Harlem citizen, Peixota has become chairman of "Hands to Ethiopia." The "White Friends of Ethiopia" make the same claim, but since they are dominated by the Soviet presence, they secretly intend to subsume the "Hands" under their banner and thereby inflict the Soviet ideology upon the Harlem populace. Although a novice in world politics, Peixota sees a connection between his past and the Soviet gangsters. As he tells the envoy from Ethiopia, Lij Tekla Alamaya, "I know enough of the game from my experience with the diplomats and fixers of what they call the underworld" (250). By this time, he already knows what the "White Friends" are up to: power and control. The "White Friends" want world domination, nothing so petty as "underworld" domination.

Although Tasan is at the sinister center of global gangsterism, McKay withholds his presence until certain local matters become established regarding Italy's invasion of Ethiopia. The articulate Flagg and the schoolteacher turned activist Castle meet at Peixota's house to devise a strategy to help Ethiopia fight the Fascists, but it soon becomes clear that the real fight is at home. At first it seems that the African American Castle is the only spokesman for the Soviet-backed popular front. He wants to oust Flagg from the African American based Hands, labeling him a follower of Leon Trotsky and a Fascist, but both Flagg and Peixota become aware that Tasan is the real force behind the White Friends organization. Peixota begins to see that "Maxim Tasan wanted power over the life and thought of his people, to turn their mind toward Soviet Russia as a Promised Land" (61). And Flagg is even more specific, that as a voice for the Soviet Dictatorship and the real power behind the Popular Front, Tasan is an "incorrigible gangster" (76).

Castle remains a comic figure throughout the novel, a vicious little gnat whose left-wing ideology is compensation for his small physical stature and his deep-seated insecurities. It's Tasan who is truly scary. His is a politics of power in which anything is permitted as long as it succeeds. He steals Tekla's letter from the emperor in order to control and disgrace him, uses Seraphine to get at her father, stages an arrest of Peixota to dredge up his "gangster" past, and manufactures a fake "princess" from Ethiopia in order to muddy the political waters of Harlem.

One theme in the novel is the tension between the local and the global. The *Labor Herald*, the voice of the Soviets, calls Peixota "a gangster and racketeer," as does Castle who refers to him as "that gangster Peixota," who "thinks he is big bug" (154, 127), but the irony of the metaphor, as Flagg notes, is that the ex-numbers emperor Peixota has little knowledge of "the tug-of-war power politics which is spreading out over the world, even to Harlem to spread confusion among our people" (122). Peixota is only a little bandit, to use McKay's phrase, whereas Tasan hides behind the inflated rhetoric of the "perpetual promise." His slogan, "All the World aboard the Popular Front," has its counterpart in "The World is Yours" advertisement for Cooks Tours that Tony (Paul Muni) takes for this future in *Scarface* (237).

Here, satire, crime novels, and gangster films meet. Dorsey Flagg deflates Tasan's utopian pretensions by saying that expecting "the Popular Front to protect Democracy" is "as fantastic as the idea of an incorrigible gangster and lawbreaker starting a campaign for legislation to make the nation safe for legality and honesty" (76). There is an obvious echo here of Wilson's inflated promise "to make the world safe for democracy" while he destroyed it at home. Like Wilson, Tasan hides his racism: African Americans are "chicken feed," in the scheme of things and Harlem a "minor theatre . . . altogether inadequate for his ideas" (89, 260). As a gangster who wears a utopian mask, he embodies the Faustian dream of wanting more and always wanting more—the dark side of capitalism, which is less about money than it is about power.

As Luc Sante notes, the distinction between "mystery fiction" and crime fiction is crucial in terms of the theme of power. Classic detective novels "attribute a superior logic to virtue," turning "the pursuit of evil into a civilized and bloodless game" (Sante 18). Thus, power resides with virtue. In contrast, crime fiction "acknowledges that law tends to be an attribute of power, rather than virtue, that its exercise can be messy and its boundaries ambiguous," as McKay had made clear in "I Pound the Pavement" (Sante 18). The two worlds—the law and the gangster—have power in common. Like Wilson, Tasan makes claim to a "higher law" than one which would address the specific problems of African American life, but that law, as Sante notes, hides another motive.

The famous gangster movies of the 1930s are also about power. The gangsters in these films, be they Rico (Edward G. Robinson) in *Little Caesar*, Tom Powers (James Cagney) in *Public Enemy*, or Tony (Paul Muni) in *Scarface*, love wealth and what comes with it—sexy women (with the exception of Rico who seems to prefer Joe Massara), flashy clothes, gaudy dwellings—but their real passion lies elsewhere. The neon sign for Cooks Tours saying "The World Is Yours" in *Scarface* is the beckoning symbol that drives all three men. That the sign is flashing from a tall building and outside of Tony's reach is the Tantalus nightmare.

But the real comic irony in all three movies is that the "World" is defined by each gangster's limited imagination. Tony only wants to extend his power to Chicago's North side; Rico to "Little Italy" on Chicago's North side, and Tom to being a highly paid henchman for "Nails" Nathan's beer empire. When a gang member praises Rico for "getting up in the world" (Burnett 205), the title of both novel and film come to mind: *Little Caesar*.

What all three gangsters get is a literal fall from what they desire. Tony descends the stairs of his bulletproof apartment to meet a hail of bullets (or in the alternative ending demanded by the Hays Code, he drops through the scaffold to his death on the gallows). The already murdered Tom Powers falls flat on his face, tied to a mattress, as his brother opens the door to their home, and a diminutive, unshaven, and disheveled Rico dies by machine-gun fire as he hides behind a windblown, desolate backside of a huge billboard. Dwarfed by the billboard, his descent to Lilliputian status is what turns this gangster film into satire. Tasan's descent into "the garbage of the neglected Harlem pavement" repeats this theme (269).

In *Gulliver's Travels*, Swift would expose absolute political power as a cultural nightmare, as he would elsewhere in *The Drapier's Letters* (1724-1725) and *A Modest Proposal* (1929). Swift's satire of the Laputan philosophers in Book Three of *Gulliver's Travels* begins with a mild attack upon the philosopher kings of the flying island who literally do have their heads in the clouds. They are so engrossed in speculative thinking, especially mathematics, that they need what Swift calls a *flapper* to bring them back to tangible reality. The flapper boxes the individual philosopher's ears or eyes, depending upon the multiple occasions of being in "danger of falling down every Precipice," or "bouncing his Head against every Post; and in the Streets, of jostling others, or being jostled himself into the Kennel" (Swift, *Essential Writings* 413).

All of this is great fun, slapstick comedy at its best, but Swift refuses to leave his satire at this level. There is a secondary satire regarding the island that flies above the people below. We discover that the philosopher kings of Laputa not only neglect their citizens' welfare, but their political relationship to them is one of terror. At any time, if the subjects below (read Irish but also the poor) are rebellious, the island can descend, blocking out the sun and rain. If the subjects are really truculent, the flying island can descend by threatening those below with the fear of crushing them.

This is not always a good idea in practice, however, since those below have learned how to bring the island itself crashing to the ground. As George Orwell saw, Swift saved his serious attack on totalitarianism for book three of *Gulliver's Travels*.

In any event, what began as Horatian satire ends as a dark dystopia, a political system run by those whose only knowledge of the polis is abstract and theoretical and subsequently without mercy. Swift ends his comic treatment of Laputa with a story about a woman married to its prime minister (read Robert Walpole) who escapes to live with a "old, deformed Footman" below who beats her. The gullible Gulliver sees this as an example of the inexplicable "Caprices" of Womankind," but Swift's satire has larger implications (*Essential Writings* 417). The prime minister's indifference to his wife reflects the flying island's indifference to the people below it. That, of course, explains Tasan's relationship with Harlem.

This is a perspective that goes beyond Walter Jekyll's library. The 1920s saw the proliferation of pulp magazines like *The Black Mask*, and the 1930s would be the decade in which Dashiell Hammett, Raymond Chandler, James M. Cain would transform pulp fiction into literary art. In "The Simple Art of Murder" (1944) Chandler would say that the best of crime fiction uncovered a "hidden truth" about American life, and he would credit Hammett for leading the way but then would then add: "Hammett was the ace performer, but there is nothing in his work that is not implicit in the early novels and short stories of Hemingway" ("Simple Art" 18, 14). McKay had earlier said that Hemingway had "quickened and enlarged my experience of social life," and he made it clear that the "social life" was American: "a certain quality of American civilization that is not to be found in any other distinguished American writer" (*A Long Way* 252). As we have seen, McKay had applied Hemingway's keen analysis of American "social life" to Harlem in *Home to Harlem*, especially as it concerned Jake and Ray as homeless men.

Citing Gertrude Stein, Fredric Jameson notes that Chandler's detective fiction belongs to a distinctive American reality, one essentially ad hoc as opposed to "the lived routine and continuity" of English life, whereas "American life, American content . . . is a formless one, always to be reinvented, an uncharted wilderness in which the very notion of experience is perpetually called into question and revised, in which time is an indeterminate succession out of which a few decisive, explosive, irrevocable instants stand out in relief" (Jameson 627). *Home to Harlem* charted a pattern of "a few decisive, explosive, irrevocable instants," but they were scattered throughout a text that often read like a romantic, picaresque romp. As he told H. L. Mencken, "the harsh reality" of Harlem life was draped on the "romantic skeleton" of the picaresque motif (*Letters in Exile* 133). It was a dystopia in disguise. *Amiable with Big Teeth* pulls no punches, and McKay focuses on African American history as an endless cycle of "promises and then disappointment and destruction" (Whitehead and Jenkins).

In *Amiable with Big Teeth*, both the Ethiopian envoy and a Soviet agent show up as "irrevocable instants" and change the dynamics of Harlem life, one asking for help, the other bringing the plague. Although Tasan's death is an exorcism of a disease that infects the community, his corpse is different from the "corpse" in the classical English detective story. As W. H. Auden notes, the "corpse" in the English village is "shockingly out of place, as when a dog makes a mess on the drawing room carpet" (Auden 408). It is "out of place" because it is at odds with the pastoral "daily life" of the village. By finding the person who put "the mess" on the clean carpet, the detective returns the village to a state of "grace," to a state of innocence that existed before "the mess" got there. In McKay's fictional Harlem, the "mess" is already there, awaiting the next messiah who promises to clean it up.

Amiable with Big Teeth has its comic moments, but its core is dark. McKay's other unpublished (and unfinished) gangster novel, *Harlem Glory*, was written earlier—around 1937—and was more akin to the cinematic genre of the 1930s screwball comedy. In *Harlem Glory*, McKay makes use of the side of Swift that Dr. Arbuthnot saw when he told Swift that *Gulliver's Travels* was "a merry work" (qtd. in Quintana 142). In *Harlem Glory*, McKay's protagonist Buster South is a kind of Gulliver moving through, and adapting to, various landscapes ranging from the numbers racket in Harlem to the enormous confidence game practiced by "Glory Savior." In *Amiable with Big Teeth*, McKay moves from Dr. Arbuthnot's "merry" satire of Lilliput's six-inch emperor (the "Delight and Terror of the Universe") to the Brobdingnag King's angry rejection of Gulliver's gift of gunpowder and his dark laughter at Gulliver's patriotic description of his brutish homeland (*Collected Writings* 340, 397). That distinction sums up the difference between McKay's two gangster novels: the "merry" satire with which he treats Glory Savior and his band of worshippers versus the savage indignation that he directs toward Maxim Tasan and his global thugs, Stalin and the Soviet Union.

Unlike Bita Plant in *Banana Bottom*, Buster South is hardly a character at all but rather a vehicle through which McKay can explore the transition of Harlem from the Roaring Twenties to Harlem of the Great Depression.

When Buster comes north to Harlem as part of the great migration from the South in the 1920s, he attaches himself to Ned Rose, a Black numbers runner. When an irate "citizen" murders Ned because his bank goes bankrupt, Buster joins his savvy wife who takes him to Paris, but even she can't stay solvent and commits suicide, leaving Buster to return to a very different Harlem in the next decade. By this time the white gangsters have taken over the numbers racket and Buster is down and out until he meets up with the cult of Glory Savior. The novel at this point sharpens its satiric intent, both as it highlights Glory Savior as a confidence man but also as it exposes the gullibility of his followers. What gives the satire its punch is McKay's dual perspectives: tolerant exposure and slapstick comedy.

McKay's source for Glory Savior can be seen in his history of Harlem of the 1930s, *Harlem: Negro Metropolis* (1942). In that book, McKay spends a long chapter, nearly forty pages, on Father Divine, his religious cult, and his stunning rise to fame in Harlem and even to national prominence. Although McKay satirizes Father Divine, the Peace Mission does still exist as a church and is considered an important precursor to the civil rights movement.

McKay is especially fascinated by Divine's finesse and by the devotion of his followers. He never quite calls himself a god but always hints at it: "I am here, there, and everywhere. Dial in and you shall find me. Aren't you glad?" Does the "dial" refer to the radio or the phone? In either case, modernity is a tool Father Divine uses to reshape old-time religion. The "Divinites" respond by calling him "Father" or seeing him as "the second incarnation of the Christ" (*Harlem: Negro Metropolis* 37, 44). His "apotheosis" had its origin in a judge who mysteriously died after sentencing Divine to jail for being a public nuisance, and his followers took this a sign of his divinity. Ironically, this could only be read in a newspaper.

McKay never says that he is a phony, leaving us to make the connections. Besides, McKay acknowledges that he does many good things for the suffering people of Harlem, providing soup kitchens, cheap rooms, and spiritual comfort during the Depression. But McKay is amused by the good Father's way of hiding his finances from public scrutiny. In Divine's "Kingdom there is (1) no sex, (2) no race, (3) no color, (4) no money" (45). As private individuals, his followers do make money in the outside world, but when they "deposit" that money with him, it is never "recorded" because it does not exist. His "angels" are above mundane concerns, and their "individuality" is subsumed in the "collective servitude and strict discipline in every domain of life with one man as supreme dictator" (48). The dictator, however, is benevolent and more fool than knave. McKay's portrait of Divine and his cult occurs within the context of high comedy, the approach McKay takes in *Harlem Glory*.

Also behind *Harlem Glory* is Swift's comic analysis of the "madness" of Peter and Jack, the founders of Popery and Puritanism, respectively, in *A Tale of a Tub*: "When a Man's Fancy gets *astride* on his Reason, when Imagination is at Cuffs with the senses, and common Understanding, as well as common Sense, is Kickt out of Doors; the first Proselyte he makes, is Himself, and when that is once compass'd, the Difficulty is not so great in bringing over others; a strong Delusion always operating from *without*, as vigorously as from *within*" (*Tale* 171). Swift's "Digression on Madness" in *A Tale* aptly fits Glory Savior and his followers. They repeat "glory" as if the word made sense and was not, as Swift puts it, a series of "long Hums" causing the "whole Assembly of Saints to sob to the Musick of one solitary *Liquid*" (*Tale* 271, 279). Swift depicts the mesmerizing effect of the Chant of the Saints to be linked to their "Systems," either the one created by Jack or the one asserted by Peter who because he is the oldest son in the parable of Father's coat believes himself to be "*God Almighty*, and sometimes *Monarch of the Universe*" (*Tale* 115).

Swift claimed that the aim of his satire in *A Tale of a Tub* was to ridicule folly rather than to expose vice. Although he depicts the excesses of Jack and Peter in terms of their arrogant "madness," they are more comical than sinister. Nevertheless, McKay hints of how a comic view of Glory Savior as dictator can easily morph into the sinister Maxim Tasan, and again *A Tale of a Tub* helps to explain this shift in perspective. The Allegory of the Coat in Swift's satire sheds light Maxim Tasan. Peter and Jack in *Tale of a Tub* reject the simple instructions in their father's will regarding the care of the coat: the coat is "very plain" and quite serviceable and should not be meddled with (*Tale* 82). The two brothers proceed to meddle: Peter embroiders it, Jack rips it apart. Peter's improvements become the dogma of the Catholic Church. Jack's removals become the basis of the Protestant Reformation. One is to the right, the other to the left, but in Swift's allegory the two brothers are often mistaken for one another: "Insomuch, as nothing was more frequent than for a Bayliff to seize *Jack* by the Shoulders, and cry, *Mr. Peter, You are the King's Prisoner*. Or, at other Times, for one of *Peter*'s nearest Friends, to accost *Jack* with open Arms, *Dear Peter, I am glad to see thee, pray send me one of your best Medicines for the Worms*" (*Tale* 199). Tasan masquerades as a revolutionary, but behind the mask is a right-wing thug.

Glory Savior's "liquid" use of "glory" as elevated nonsense is, on a lower key, similar to Tasan's repeated utopian refrain that the popular front will level the playing field for everyone. Nevertheless, Glory Savior lives in a world of his own, like Jack and Peter. He begins his sermon by shouting "Glory all souls!," and the response of his followers circles back to himself, "Glory Savior" (McKay, *Harlem Glory* 76). Although he continues with a list of sins committed by those outside his realm, sounding like Gulliver's verbal rampage once he's fallen under the spell of the Houyhnhnms, ("that gin-guzzling, card-playing, numbers-gaming, skirt-chasing, sex-salted gang of fast men and women"), there is no mention of empire in his speech. Rather his focus is upon himself as "glory" personified. Referring to another soul he has saved, he says with a straight face, "My glory struck like lightning and he could not resist" (76). Glory Savior is a small-time charlatan, the artist as a local confidence man.

McKay's satire centers on an individual enamored with himself and his sexual potency ("My glory is all-penetrating.") and on someone whose game is a "holy racket" (83) but whose cult is hardly a political system meant to coerce others—hence the comic ending in which his white consort Glory Queen intends to cuckold him with Buster. Glory Savior is like the Laputan philosophers who live so much in their brains that their wives have no trouble conducting extramarital affairs because no one is minding the store.

The ending of *Harlem Glory* would fit nicely with Swift's satire of the egghead philosophers. Glory Savior is so caught up in his personal glory that he doesn't know that Glory Queen is chasing after Buster. When she is thwarted, she fears exposure and utters a line that recalls Rico at the end of *Little Caesar*: "Poor Glory Queen! What will become of me now?" (112). Rico says, famously: "Mother of Mercy! Is this the end of Rico?" The comedy of both endings lies in the characters referring to themselves in the third person. McKay debunks the myth of the self's reinvention as a second self by noting that Glory Savior was originally a guy named Robert Byrd who once operated a now defunct employment agency and that Glory Queen was once a nonentity in the white world who, as a rich white woman, saw an opportunity to find fame in the Black world.

The satire in *Harlem Glory* has minimal impact beyond self-exposure. In *Harlem Glory*, Buster sees little difference between the numbers racket and Glory Savior's cult (80). As long as it stays on the level of a "racket," it is no real threat to Black life. In *Amiable with Big Teeth*, the stakes are higher. The novel begins with Fascist Italy's invasion of Ethiopia and the various political responses in Harlem to that global event. Here gangsterism as a global racket dwarfs Glory Savior's local nation.

McKay makes three connections between *Amiable with Big Teeth* and *Harlem Glory*. Tasan says contemptuously of Father Divine that "he's easy to handle, for he stays in his field" (131), implying that he's only a minor irritant when it comes to persuading Harlem's Black citizens to join the popular front. As the model for Glory Savior in *Harlem Glory*, Father Divine's presence was central, but here he is pushed to the sidelines because McKay is after bigger game. Pablo Peixota is no longer a numbers big shot; his former racket takes a backseat to gangsterism on a large scale. Even Buster makes an appearance in *Amiable with Big Teeth*, albeit with a different last name, as the proprietor of "The Airplane," a cabaret that survived Prohibition. Cults, numbers, the cabaret scene—these Harlem institutions are subsumed in *Amiable with Big Teeth* within a global network of international intrigue, military intervention, and political revolution.

In his biography of McKay, Wayne F. Cooper notes in passing that McKay and George Orwell led parallel lives. "Through the 1930s," both retained a left-wing perspective, but both "became increasingly disillusioned as the decade advanced" (*Sojourner* 346). Both saw, as Orwell put it, that the Comintern was simply "an instrument of Russian foreign policy" (*Collected Essays* 1: 349). The turning moment for Orwell would be his experience fighting for the Republic in the Spanish Civil War. For McKay, his disillusionment was more gradual, but *Amiable with Big Teeth* arrives at the same conclusion as *Homage to Catalonia* (1938). The Communists fighting on side of Spain's Republic wanted to control the outcome of the war: it was they "above all others who prevented revolution in Spain" (*Homage* 57). Despite their disillusionment with the politics of Soviet Russia, McKay remained a Marxist, and Orwell never stopped believing in Socialism.

Their parallel lives existed on several planes. Both men tried to be policemen, McKay in Jamaica and Orwell in Burma, and both found that service in their respective political systems intolerable. Orwell soon became disgusted with British imperialism, coming "to regard [it] as largely a racket" (*Collected Essays* 2: 23), and McKay could not stomach orders that framed innocent people ("When I Pounded the Pavement"). Each believed that the city had sacred places: libraries, cathedrals for McKay, pubs for Orwell—and that these places were threatened by monolithic political institutions (*Collected Essays* 3: 43–47). Each shared a hatred for cant and poverty. Ray's ruminations on the subject of poverty in *Banjo* were similar to Gordon Comstock's in *Keep the Aspidistra Flying* (1936): poverty kills creativity. Each saw that you can't go home again, as demonstrated by Jake in *Home to Harlem* and George Bowling in *Coming Up for Air* (1939), and each believed that if there was any hope against authoritarianism, it lay with the "proles." Orwell said that "language . . . suffers when the educated classes lose touch with manual workers," (hence his love of "animated conversation" within Pubs), confirmed by McKay in *Home to Harlem* and *Banjo*. Orwell saw "obscenity" as "a kind of subversion"; Chaucer's "'Miller's Tale' is a rebellion in the moral sphere, as *Gulliver's Travels* is a rebellion in the political sphere" (*Collected Essays* 3: 285). They both liked sexual jokes, ballads, and stories in popular culture. Orwell believed that the comic postcards of Donald McGill, found in any "cheap stationers' windows," had the appeal of the "music-hall world" (*Collected Essays* 2: 164–65). In *Home to Harlem*, Jake recites a bawdy ballad about a sailor named "Bullocky Bill," but he couldn't remember all the lyrics (*Home* 293)—which of course couldn't be published anyway. What really connects them, however, was their admiration for Swift, especially *Gulliver's Travels*.

Orwell said that "if I had to make a list of six books which were to be preserved when all others were destroyed, I would certainly put *Gulliver's Travels* among them" (*Collected Essays* 4: 220). In *Animal Farm* (1945), he would use Swift's beast fables (the Spider and the Bee in *A Tale of a Tub*, the Yahoos and Houyhnhnms in *Gulliver's Travels*) to expose the totalitarian regime of the Soviet Union. The death of Tasan at the paws of the Leopard Men is a spin on a Swiftian beast fable. McKay describes Tasan as a "furry little animal, a ferret," who has teeth that bite, and the "Leopard Men" kill him (53). His attack dog spokesman is Castle, just as Squealer finesses Napoleon's speeches and actions in *Animal Farm* (1945). At the end of Orwell's satire of a utopia gone wrong, the animals can't tell the difference between the pigs and the humans, just as Tasan at first passes himself off as a "White Friend" of Harlem. As gangsters who thirst for power, pigs and humans, thugs and ideologues, are interchangeable.

Power, especially that which inflicts physical pain, is the major theme of *Nineteen Eighty-Four* (1949): "if you want a picture of the future, imagine a boot stamping on a human face—forever" (Howe 118). This image not only has its origins in the pulps, but it echoes the politicians of Swift's Laputa who, if the natives below are disobedient, can threaten to stamp out their faces by lowering the island. Orwell thought that "Swift's greatest contribution to political thought . . . is his attack, especially in Book III, on what would now be called totalitarianism" (*Collected Essays* 4: 213). The basis of his gangster dystopia, says O'Brien in *Nineteen Eighty-Four*, "will be the intoxication of power," physical and mental (118). Tasan's grand scheme to control the world is not through "traditional politics" but through "power politics as a religious ecstasy gripping and sweeping people off their feet to imagine that they could find social salvation in a pharisaism such as "Soviet Russia is a Workers' State" (116). One reason that African Americans in

Harlem are receptive to such a catchphrase, as Tasan astutely sees, is that they have no "consolidate" economic life and hence no "political power." Tasan wants to erase an imagined Africa in Harlem and replace it with a utopian noplace.

Tasan is a thug in a revolutionary's clothing, comparable to the brutal O'Brien who deceives Winston Smith into thinking that he is sympathetic to those who rebel against Big Brother. In both *Amiable with Big Teeth* and *Nineteen Eighty-Four*, McKay and Orwell associated totalitarianism with, in Orwell's phrase, "the modern gangster outlook" (*Collected Essays* 2: 186). He complained that Yeats's poetry did not acknowledge the new reality, that the world was not governed by spiritual aristocrats but by "murdering gangsters" (*Collected Essays* 2: 274).

But this raises a question concerning McKay's and Orwell's relationship to the pulps. Both saw the Great War as a watershed that brought forth new authors with a new outlook, but neither wrote "A Simple Art of Murder," which depicted a Dashiell Hammett as a new kind of modernist. Although their taste in literature was expansive (Orwell liked both Henry Miller and T. S Eliot), their lists of important new writers after the Great War such as James Joyce and D. H. Lawrence were not proletarian writers. McKay told James Weldon Johnson that *Home to Harlem* was "a real proletarian novel," but he did not consider himself a proletarian novelist, despite his Marxism. He might write a "proletarian novel," but that would not be the only kind of novel he would write. And although Orwell thought that proletarian writers forced other writers "to look at things that were under their noses" and that the proles themselves "reinvigorated" the English language "from below," he too never thought of himself as a proletarian writer (*Collected Essays* 2: 43; 3: 27). Nor did either one see himself as a pulp fiction hack. So why the "gangster" theme?

Their ambivalence toward the pulps can be seen in Orwell's critique of the "socks on the jaw" school of modern literature (*Collected Essays* 1: 444). American writers are most guilty of "this kind of disgusting rubbish," which usually features "the 'he-man,' the 'tough guy,' the gorilla who put everything right by socking everybody else on the jaw" (*Collected Essays* 1: 220, 478). He reserves his real loathing for an American novel entitled *No Orchids for Miss Blandish* (1939), written by James Hadley Chase. Orwell focuses on the "sordid" and "brutal" subject matter, which he describes in great detail: "The book contains eight-full dress murders, an unassessable number of casual killings and woundings, an exhumation (with a careful reminder of the stench), the flogging of Miss Blandish, the torture of another woman with red-hot cigarette ends, a striptease act, a third-degree scene of unheard-of cruelty and much else of the same kind" (*Collected Essays* 3: 217). Some of the horrors described above would be part of the torture done to Winston and Julia in *Nineteen Eighty-Four*. Orwell disapproves of the narrative excess in this kind of novel, branding it gratuitous cruelty, but what if gratuitous cruelty belongs to the social fabric of the future? In discussing another Chase novel, *He Won't Need It Now*, Orwell uses a frightening image that he will use in *Nineteen Eighty-Four*. Chase's hero "is described as stamping on somebody's face, and then, having crushed the mouth in, grinding his heel round and round in it" (218).

In this book review, Orwell draws a contrast between a gentleman burglar in the *Raffles* stories, who though a "snob" lives by a moral code, and the "cesspool" of Chase's *No Orchids* whose only code is "the pursuit of power" (217). Orwell returns to that theme two more times: "in *No Orchids* anything is 'done' so long as it leads on to power" (220–21). He then draws a connection between this pulp novel and the age in which we live: "in his imagined world of gangsters Chase is presenting, as it were, a distilled version of the modern political scene" (223).

Yet what Orwell refuses to acknowledge, as Chandler does acknowledge in "The Simple Art of Murder," is that a pulp novel like *The Maltese Falcon* can be a new modernist genre that exposes the political scene for what it is. Orwell in fact hints of this possibility when, in reviewing Rudyard Kipling's writings, he compares "the nineteenth-century imperialist outlook," to the "modern gangster outlook" of 1942 fascism. They are "two different things" (*Collected Essays* 2: 186). If that is the case, why not admit to a new kind of literature that expresses the difference, especially when totalitarianism's aim is to not only control the future but to rewrite the past—that is, to deny "the very concept of objective truth" either in the past or the future (*Collected Essays* 2: 136). In his famous essay "Politics and the English Language" and "The Principles of Newspeak" as an appendix to *Nineteen Eighty-Four*, politicians in charge of the polis reshape the language to rewrite the past in order to control the future. What the pulps do, as Chandler implies, is present violence in the present as a reminder that violence has always been a part of American history and the history of civilization. The pursuit of Hammett's "dingus" in *The Maltese Falcon* is not just the passion of avarice in the present but a reminder of "the pursuit of power" in the past. Gutman's history of the falcon includes both the Old World and the New.

Both McKay and Orwell were fans of popular culture and would make use of the pulps, but each was educated in a highbrow artistic tradition, sometimes formal, sometimes informal. McKay found mentors like Walter Jekyll, Frank Harris, George Bernard Shaw, while Orwell grew up in a Victorian world of high culture shattered by the Great War. In "Why I Write," Orwell says in a poem that "two hundred years ago" I would have been a "happy vicar" watching "my walnuts grow":

> I wasn't born for an age like this;
> Was Smith? Was Jones? Were you? (Howe 142)

The Great War created a new age, a theme in *Home to Harlem*. Orwell would give up the thought of watching walnuts and write about people like Smith or Jones in *A Clergyman's Daughter* (1935) *The Road to Wigan Pier* (1936) and *Nineteen Eighty-Four* (Winston Smith). So too with McKay. If he had stayed in Jamaica, he would have continued to write *Songs of Jamaica* (1912) and *Constab Ballads* (1912), pastorals poems often with an edge but ones that did not embody the expansive garden-city connections that his travels and the new age would introduce him to.

Both authors were thrust into worlds that would radically change their lives, and they would confront new literature, both high and low, that would influence them. Although they embraced the modernists who replaced the voices of the past, those voices continued to belong to a shared literary tradition. The triumph of both writers was that they mined popular culture for what they could use in their attempt to restore or rethink the past in terms of some kind of "objective truth." Their great achievement would be that they would weave their experiences in the modern world into memorable works of art.

AFTERWORD/AFTERMATH

CLAUDE MCKAY AND RICHARD WRIGHT

As students of the Harlem Renaissance know, Richard Wright's "Blueprint for Negro Writing" in 1937 was a watershed moment. It signaled the break of a new generation of Black writers from the old. James Baldwin and Ralph Ellison would have their own quarrels with Wright, but they too rejected what Wright called "the so-called Harlem school of expression" (Lewis 203). Wright's critique was even more damning; the "so called writers" of the Harlem Renaissance were received by the white critical establishment as though they were "French poodles who do clever tricks" (195). Now anyone familiar with the rich and diverse body of Black writing in the 1920s and 1930s knows that this is (to quote Huck Finn) a "stretcher." Jean Toomer, Jessie Fauset, Nella Larsen, Langston Hughes, Zora Neale Hurston, Wallace Thurman, Walter White, Countee Cullen, W. E. B. Du Bois (the list goes on) were a diverse bunch. Moreover, Wright did not hesitate to borrow or rewrite some of their texts. "Long Black Song" in *Uncle Tom's Children* (1938) reprises Toomer's "Karintha" and "Blood Burning Moon" in *Cane* (1923), and the ending of *Lawd Today!* repeats in a new key the ending of "Mattie and Her Sweetman" in *Gingertown*. In his essay "*Lawd Today*: Wright's Tricky Apprenticeship," William Burrison notes "a kinship with McKay's earlier *Gingertown* stories (such as 'Brownskin Blues,' 'The Prince of Porto Rico,' 'Mattie and her Sweetman' and 'Truant'" (107–8).

And as for "French Poodles" spinning tricks for white critics, consider McKay's tough-minded observation to Walter White in 1925: "I am so happy about the aroused interest in the creative life of the Negro," but the writers themselves have "to do work that will hold ground beside the very highest white standard. Nothing less will help Negro art forward. A boom is a splendid thing but if the wares are not up to standard people turn aside from them after the novelty has worn off" (*Letters in Exile* 120). Earlier, he had this to say to White: "If we are going to do anything in literature and art we've got to stand good straight out criticism and not allow ourselves to be patronized as Negro artists in America" (*Letters in Exile* 104). Richard Wright could not have said it any better.

This raises the question of Wright's literary relationship with McKay. In "Blueprint for Negro Writing," Wright argued that today's "Negro writer" needed a new "perspective," one different from the previous generation of "bourgeois" Black artists: "A Negro writer must learn to view the life of a Negro living in New York's Harlem or Chicago's South Side with the consciousness that one-sixth of the earth's surface belongs to the working class. It means that a Negro writer must create in his readers' minds a relationship between a Negro woman hoeing cotton in the South and the men who loll in swivel chairs in Wall Street and take the fruits of her toil" (202). That was precisely Du Bois's theme in *The Quest of the Silver Fleece* (1913), as it would be a theme in *Home to Harlem*, not the situation of "a Negro woman hoeing cotton in the South" but the theme of an urban working-class African American who must scramble to find work. McKay told James Weldon Johnson that his was "a real proletarian novel" (*Letters in Exile* 246), meaning that the "work" that Jake, Zeddy, and Felice did was indirectly controlled and shaped either by Wall Street or white labor unions. As Zeddy says to Jake: "Ain't you a good carpenter? And ain't I a good blacksmith? But kain we get a good look-in on our trade heah in this white man's city?" (48).

If McKay is as angry as Wright, and is as focused on the working class as Wright, what is the difference between the two writers? If we look closely at *Lawd Today!* in terms of Wright's attempt to rewrite *Home to Harlem*, we not only see Wright's break with a past generation of writers, but his inescapable connection to that generation.

Richard Wright began writing *Lawd Today!* in 1932, finished it in 1937, but it would not be published until three years after his death (1963). In the same year he completed it, both Claude McKay and he were working for the Federal Writers Project. McKay had been asked to write the essay on Harlem, but the task was eventually taken over by Wright. It is not clear who wrote what in the essay or why McKay gave it up, but the last paragraph is intriguing because it could have been written by either man: "The question of what will ultimately happen to the Negro in New York is bound up with the question of what will happen to the Negro in America. It has been said that the Negro embodies the "romance of American life"; if that is true, the romance is one whose glamor is overlaid with shadows of tragic premonition" (https://sadmen.tumblr.com/post/16791529344/

richard-wright-forgotten-harlem). In "How Bigger Was Born," his essay on the origin and background of *Native Son*, Wright argued that "we have in the oppression of the Negro a shadow athwart our national life dense and heavy enough to satisfy even the gloomy broodings of a Hawthorne. And if Poe were alive, he would not have to invent horror; horror would invent him" (Wright, *Native Son* 540). In linking "romance" and "shadows," he also echoes McKay in *Home to Harlem* who combined "the romance of being black" with the blues, music that chased "out the shadow of the moment before" (*Home to Harlem* 154, 54). McKay would extend the "romance" of the Negro to the history of Haiti and Ethiopia in *Home to Harlem*, suggesting that their collective histories were as fabulous as that of the Negro in the United States, that their shadows too were interwoven with the romance of Black survival in dire conditions.

The protagonists of the two novels are Jacob Brown and Jake Jackson, respectively—in short, the two Jakes. Wright's novel is not set in Harlem but the South Side of Chicago during the Depression. Although we associate Wright with later post-Renaissance Black writers, *Lawd Today!* belongs to the 1920s, as the epigraph to each of its three sections suggests. Its penultimate scene, set in Rose's buffet flat, not only recalls a scene like Laura's buffet flat in *Home to Harlem* but its language is that of Harlem in the 1920s: "'Glory Be! if it ain't my four aggravating Papas,' said Rose," as she greets Jake and his three pals at the door: Bob, Slim, and Al (Wright, *Early Works* 194. All citations are to this edition). Despite Wright's use of modernist techniques (John Dos Passos's headlines, T. S. Eliot's "fragments shored . . . against my ruins"), *Lawd Today!* is both a critique of McKay's novel and a recycling of its themes and tropes.

We know from the historical record that McKay and Wright knew one another but did "not get along." McKay was "two decades older than Wright" and belonged to an African American literary generation that Wright thought was timorous and sycophantic, and McKay believed that the younger writer was arrogant and rude (Borchert 228). Also, in 1937, Alain Locke accused McKay of betraying every group he ever joined, concerned only with his own self-expression, unlike Wright whose Marxist perspective on Black life was incisive, communal, and relevant to the moment, the Depression (Cooper, *Rebel Sojourner* 319). Ironically, McKay had moved beyond his Communist past, seeing a malaise within it that Wright would only come to recognize later.

Critics of Wright's novel note that he sets his novel in a single day, as Joyce did with *Ulysses*, but the difference between Joyce's novel and Wright's is that the one day in *Ulysses* is unique: Bloom becomes Stephen's surrogate father, Molly's "yes" restores the Wandering Jew to home. In *Lawd Today!* one day is much like another—except of course for the novel's violent ending. At the end of *Home to Harlem*, Felice convinces Jake to leave Harlem for Chicago (too much violence in Harlem): "I hear it's a mahvelous place foh n----rs" (333). *Lawd Today!* is a response to that line.

Despite the differences between the two novels, there are moments in *Lawd Today!* where Wright had McKay in mind. McKay's Jake is "tall, brawny, and black," self-confident but not vain (*Home* 3), whereas Wright's Jake is fat, has "piggish eyes," and whose vanity extends to conked hair and ten suits (McKay's Jake has one until it wears out) (6, 27). One incident in *Home to Harlem* involves Jake's relationship with Congo Rose who doesn't want him to work: "hard work is no good for a sweet loving pappa" (*Home* 40). But for Jake "work" is the sign of his independence: "Never lived off no womens and never will. I always works" (40). Although McKay's Jake is a "boss carpenter," there is no description of him actually working; whereas Wright has Jake Jackson and his friends suffering in assembly line jobs in the post office that are mechanical and endlessly repetitious.

If we want a model for Wright's Jake, it is McKay's Zeddy who mistreats women, lives "sweet" and who "scabs" without compunction. McKay's Jake will not scab and refuses to join a union because he knows that the cushy jobs on the piers go to the Irish. Yet it is Jake's relationship to Congo Rose that is mirrored specifically in *Lawd Today!* Al tells of his relationship with a woman who wants Al not to work because "I don't want no tired mens sleeping with me in the bed at night" (*Early Works* 156). Moreover, he gives her "two ringing sounding slaps" to settle an argument and claims that she liked being beaten "black and blue" so she could forget her fatigue from working all day (156–57).

Al brags that he left her because he got "fedup" with her strange behavior, whereas McKay's Jake leaves Congo Rose because he was disgusted with himself for hitting her. When he discovers she's been cheating on him, he "gave her two savage slaps full in the face," but instead of being angry with him, she grovels at his feet and later tells her friends that knocking her silly proves that "he's a *ma-an* all right" (*Home* 116–17). The difference between Wright and McKay is that Al is indifferent to his girlfriend's hard life, whereas Jake feels genuine guilt over hitting a woman and is especially distressed and puzzled by Congo Rose's perversity in liking it. Although McKay makes no comment on Congo Rose's behavior, he sees it as part of a skewed pattern of male-female relationships that exists in a colonized Harlem.

Wright's view of America's racist past is much darker than McKay's—and that is saying a lot. The legacy of slavery is a terrible one. In *Black Boy*, Wright casts a cold eye on the Whig interpretation of history:

> Whenever I thought of the essential bleakness of Black life in America, I knew that Negroes had never been allowed to catch the full spirit of Western civilization, that they lived somehow in it but not of it. And when I brooded upon the cultural barrenness of black life, I wondered if clean, positive tenderness, love, honor, loyalty, and the capacity to remember were native with man. I asked myself if these human qualities were not fostered, won, struggled and suffered for, preserved in ritual from one generation to another. (*Black Boy* 37)

What he is describing is a terrain of cultural blight (265), a void where communal values no longer exist. In the paragraph before this one, Wright despairs of "how bare our traditions, how hollow our memories, how lacking we were in those intangible sentiments that bind man to man." He then makes an observation that has a direct relevance to *Home to Harlem*: "I used to brood upon the unconscious irony of those who felt that Negroes led so passional an existence!" (Wright 37). Although Wright is probably referring to those white authors who sentimentalize the race, he could be singling out *Home to Harlem*, especially a passage in which McKay describes Jake's enthusiastic response to being "home" after returning from Europe and the Great War: "Oh, to be in Harlem again after two years away. The deep-dyed color, the thickness, the closeness of it. The noises of Harlem. The sugared laughter. The honey-talk on its streets. And all night long, ragtime and 'blues' playing somewhere, . . . singing somewhere, dancing somewhere! Oh, the contagious fever of Harlem. Burning everywhere in dark-eyed Harlem. . . . Burning now in Jake's sweet blood. . . . " (15). Wright sees this as a fantasy without a foundation. What follows Wright's rejection of "so passional an existence" is a sentence that describes the male characters of *Lawd Today!*: "I saw that what had been taken for our emotional strength was our negative confusions, our flights, our fears, our frenzy under pressure" (37).

McKay also saw the "negative confusions" in some of his characters (Ray and Zeddy, e.g.), especially their "fears." He was also aware like Wright that the Great War was a watershed moment for literature. In "Blueprint for Negro Writing," Wright argues that the new Black writer must know modernists like "Eliot, Stein, Joyce, Proust, Hemingway and Anderson."

McKay had already read most of the people on that list. Where the two Black authors differ is in the access they had to literature, white or Black, old or new. Wright was banished from the white man's library. He had to lie to get access to books in Memphis. McKay had access to Walter Jekyll's library in Jamaica and had friends in Harlem who would provide him with books.

Perhaps the most compelling scene in *Black Boy* is the one where Wright forges a note ("Will you please let this n----r boy . . . have some books by H. L. Mencken") that he gives to a Memphis librarian. Although Mencken's powerful, satiric prose inspires him to write, it's the books Mencken recommended in *A Book of Prefaces* that opens his eyes to rebellious hearts closer to his own. One day, for instance, a white man, knowing nothing of Wright's reading, says, "You act like you've stolen something" (251). And he has. He has stolen fire from the gods.

McKay's reading experiences would involve two libraries: Walter Jekyll's, which gave him access to the white literary canon and more (the Romantic poets and the literary giants of nineteenth-century Europe), and his second library of self-discovery after the Great War. It's this last literary awakening that puts him in partnership with Wright. Both McKay and Wright admired writers who held civilization to account, not just for the Great War but for its industrial, mercenary past that sacrificed everything to the myth of progress, all the while erasing the truth of those whom it has crushed.

But they would differ in their view of the past. Through Ray, McKay would make an argument for a Pan-African past, especially the "romance" of Toussaint L'Ouverture, whose embrace of the "universal ideas" of the Enlightenment led Haiti to throw off the shackles of French imperialism (*Home* 132–33). That Ray's Haiti is now occupied by a new colonial power, the United States, does not negate his belief (and McKay's) that resistance exists as a possibility and is always necessary. Wright casts doubt that a working-class stiff like McKay's Jake would be inspired by Ray's story of Toussaint L'Ouverture and Haiti. The mental makeup of his Jake consists of fragments from newspapers, movie posters, circulars, and flyers in the mail. Although he is moved by the patriotic parade celebrating Africa arising from the ashes, the music means more to him than the message. And Wright lets us know that the message itself is as fantastical as the movie posters that enthrall Jake: the soldiers of the "mythical African republic" wore "medals of unfought wars and unwon victories," and the fatuous rhetoric of their organization mirrors that of the Swift's mock-heroic send-up of the six-inch Emperor of Lilliput: "whose Dominions extend five Thousand Blustrugs, (about twelve miles in Circumference) to the extremities of the Globe" (*Early Works* 107; *Essential Writings* 340).

Wright's "International Negro Uplift Association" is no less grandiose: a "noble, friendly, kindly, brotherly, helpful, decent, respectable, law abiding, progressive, humanitarian, charitable, educational, instructive, constructive, institutional, benevolent, religious, fraternal, expansive, growing, and rising society" (*Early Works* 108). Wright's South Side, Chicago is less than Swift's twelve miles, but inflated language knows no bounds.

In *Lawd Today*! the "heroic" past is filtered through one ubiquitous medium of mass culture, the radio. The novel's setting is Lincoln's Birthday, February 12, and throughout we hear eulogistic fragments from professors and pundits as to Lincoln's stature as the nation's savior. Slavery is never mentioned as the cause of the Civil War except as a "work" that must be finished, a nice juxtaposition to the "work" that Wright's Jake does.

Wright's characters (Jake, Bob, Slim, and Al) occasionally listen and comment, but Lincoln means no more to them than Hitler or Mussolini. In one radio segment, Lincoln is heard saying "LET US FINISH THE WORK WE ARE NOW IN" (*Early Works* 200), and in the next line Jake says, "Lets finish the bottle." What does have "finality" for Jake is despair: "the sense of uneasiness which had haunted him all day descended now with abrupt finality and became real" (120). This is Wright's comment on the Negro's passionate existence.

Americans like the idea of closure, especially when it concerns the nation's hidden cancer, and the radio program does just that: Lincoln and the Civil War solved the Negro Problem. With his death, Lincoln "belonged to the ages" (190); his memory, via the radio, closes a chapter on American life. Although we only hear fragments of the eulogy throughout the novel, its narrative of beginning, middle, and end is comparable to the movies that Jake wants to see (and that Wright brilliantly parodies). Wright's novel, especially revealed in the title of part Two, "Squirrel Cage," shows that nothing is finished, nothing has changed: African Americans continue to run in place.

Wright's two other epigraphs, for parts one and two, give us another view of the past. As a preface to part one ("Commonplace"), Wright quotes lines from Van Wyck Brooks's famous *America Coming-of-Age* (1915): "a vast Sargasso Sea—a prodigious welter of unconscious life, swept by ground swells of halfconscious emotion . . ." (3). The original context for the quotation has "America" as that sea, Brooks blaming the Puritan/Pioneer tradition for failing to create an organic community; whereas Wright, in placing it where he does, underlines America's failure to integrate African Americans into a meaningful community. African American half-life has its source in a botched promise (the 13th, 14th and 25th amendments) and a civilization defined by mass culture. The difference between Brooks and Wright is that Brooks believes that America is on the verge of a spiritual renewal. The "sap" is about to shoot through the tree; the invisible "social ideal" at the nation's founding will soon "act upon us as the sun acts upon a photographic plate" (Brooks, *Early Years* 149). In his even more famous essay, "On Creating a Usable Past," he goes further. Why accept a history defined by those who benefit from its definition? The conception of America differs from nation to nation, from England to France to Italy: "there are just as many histories of America as there are nations to possess them" (*Early Years* 224). And if that is the case, can we not "invent" or "discover" an America closer to the "social ideal" of the nation's founding? This would resonate with McKay but not with Wright. Wright saw that the "many histories of America" that Brooks urged did not include the bleak history of African Americans.

Wright's epigraph then is a rewriting of Brooks, an ironic comment on his optimism. Jake and his pals live in a maelstrom of floating objects that refuse to cohere into a spiritual whole: movie posters, snake oil salesmen (both secular and religious) and Black people like Doc Higgins and Rose who prey on their own. McKay also depicted a city made up of fragments, predators, and separate stories that read like a short story cycle, but some of the people in those stories resisted being fragments. Wright appropriated Brooks's insight into the source of America's spiritual sterility but rejected the "photographic plate" that responded to the light. How could one respond to a light that had never existed for African Americans? For McKay that "light" was an ideal from a faraway star, but it was always a possibility in the here and now because embedded in the stories people told of themselves or were told about them (e.g., Rosalind and Jerco).

Wright's epigraph from Waldo Frank's *Our America* (1919) in "Part Two: Squirrel Cage" would echo Brooks: "Now, when you study these long, rigid rows of desiccated men and women, you feel that you are in the presence of some form of life that has hardened but not grown, and over which the world has passed." Frank sees the deadening impact of Puritan tradition upon white America as a hardening of the arteries, but it's the phrase "over which the world has passed" that catches Wright's eye. The Lincoln broadcast suggests America has moved on, but Wright sees that the legacy of slavery has caused Black life to stand still. McKay counters the devastating effects of racism with storytelling and the image of the dance. Black life for him is always in motion.

In *Lawd Today!* Wright sees only Eliot's "immense panorama of futility and anarchy" in the African American past and present, subjects become the theme of "Part Three: 'Rats Alley.'" Wright uses both Eliot's phrase ("rats alley") and a quotation from *The Waste Land* as a title and an epigraph to his last section: " . . . But at my back in a cold blast I hear / The rattle of bones, and chuckle from ear to ear" (*Waste Land* 3: 185–85; *Early Works* 189). These lines are a perfect introduction to Rose's buffet flat, the "joint" on Calumet Avenue where Al and his pals lose their money and almost lose their bones. Rose's buffet flat is also Bella Cohen's brothel in Joyce's *Ulysses*, but there is no father-son reunion between Odysseus and Telemachus (Bloom and Stephen).

However, there is a boy/girl reunion in a cabaret in *Home to Harlem*. Despite his contempt for Hollywood, McKay frames his plot around boy meets girl, boy loses girl, boy finds girl. Jake meets Felice in a cabaret in the novel's second chapter ("Arrival") and has sex with her in her room. She's a prostitute, but not one out of Rose's stable in *Lawd Today!* Felice is a whore with a heart of gold (another pulp cliché), and, after a night of mutual delight, she returns Jake's $50, which Jake finds in his pocket the next day. He fails to note her address, however, and spends the rest of the novel trying to find her. By accident, he does in a cabaret at novel's end. The two then plan to leave for Chicago because a jealous Zeddy threatens to spread the word that Jake was a deserter. Zeddy and Jake make up, Felice disappears to Jake's dismay, then reappears with the "necklace" that her grandmother gave her and that she left in Zeddy's flat. The novel's last words are hers: "I'll never fohgit it again and it'll always give us good luck" (340). No wonder Wright would rewrite this final scene.

Wright's last words in *Lawd Today!* are the narrator's after his Jake returns home, brutally beats his wife, as she in turn slashes him with a "jagged" piece of glass, possibly killing him: "Outside an icy wind swept around the corner of the building, whining and moaning like an idiot in a deep dark pit" (219). Revising the lines from *Macbeth*, Wright's grim "tale" is not "told by an idiot," but about one who is so full of "sound and fury" that he can't imagine a life outside the "cage" in which he is placed: "*You sonofabitch!*," Jake thinks, referring to a white inspector who has power over him, "*It ain't always going to be this way!* His mind went abruptly blank. He could not keep on with that thought, because he did not know where that thought led. He did not know of any other way things could be, if not *this* way" (142). Jake's mind is circumscribed by fragments from mass culture that signify nothing, provide no spiritual nourishment. History for African America, as Wright sees it, is Van Brook's "welter of unconscious life" without the redemptive usable past, and Frank's "desiccated" human beings without a hopeful future, America as "a promise and a dream" (*Our*

America 9). Wright's ending is a comment on McKay's ending, its sentimental view of the past—the gift from of Felice's grandmother (the neckless) as a symbol of their (Jake and Felice's) hopeful future and the ending as a Hollywood scenario that has no meaning for African Americans living in an ongoing dystopia.

Wright's critique of McKay is not the last word on *Home to Harlem*. As McKay's Jake tells the Chef, "We may all be n----rs aw'right, but we ain't all the same," a remark that foreshadows James Baldwin, Ralph Ellison, and Toni Morrison who complained that Wright ignored resources within African American life (Baldwin—blues, storytelling, and the Black church; Ellison—oral tradition, myth, and multiple literary traditions; Morrison—the emotional and intellectual strength of Black women). Wright saw his characters as caught within the vortex of a debilitating past and hence reduced to a frightening sameness, existing in a Hobbesian state of nature without the possibility of escaping the squirrel cage. McKay saw the same "cages" (265), but they didn't trap everyone in the same way. Nevertheless, he could sound like Wright: Jake "used to wonder at the great body of people who worked in nice cages: bank clerks in steel-wire cages, others in wooden cages, salespeople behind counters, neat, dutiful, respectful all of them" (265). That race is not involved in Jake's take on the American trap tells us something of his difference from Wright, and his similarity to both Brooks and Frank. Felice tells Jake that "this heah is you' country, daddy" and what she says next reflects McKay's view of space in America and African Americans: "This heah country is good and big for us to get lost in. Do you know Chicago?" The difference between McKay and Wright is that space expands with McKay; it contracts with Wright.

McKay's novel is a diversity of contradictions and perspectives, which also includes Wright's: "wese too thick together in Harlem. Wese all just lumped together without a chanst to choose and so we nacherally hate one another" (285). Jake reiterates Billy's observation several lines later: "N----rs fixing to slice one another's throats. Always fighting. Got to fight if youse a man" (287). Also, McKay doesn't shy away from male/female violence, even using a racial epithet to describe it: "That gorilla type wriggling there with his hands so strangely hugging his mate, may strangle her tonight" (337). He could be describing Wright's Jake dancing with Blanche at Rose's buffet flat, or what he tries to do to Lil when he comes home.

Jake's being a "man" isn't McKay's last word on gender. Jake sneers at Lesbians (bulldykers are "all ugly womens"), but Ray defends them: "Harlem is too savage about some things" (129). Even the vain Miss Curdy adds to the gender confusion: "Men's got a whole lot of women in their nature,

I tell you," a thought verified by the manly Jake getting all mushy thinking about Felice in springtime. McKay's array of Harlem's multiple skin types is mirrored by multiple sexual orientations: Billy is gay; Ray, bisexual; Jake, straight (but not always). Jake sometimes retreats to his masculinity when he concludes "that a woman could always go farther than a man in coarseness, depravity, and sheer cupidity" (69). He has yet to see Zeddy in full—though Felice has, perhaps accounting for her generalization that "a hen-fight was more fun than a cock-fight. . . . The hens plucked feathers, but they never wring necks like the cocks" (310). Nor are hens, even when they are prostitutes, all of one type. It's Ray who says "I lump all those ladies together, without difference in race," but this time he stands corrected by Jake: "as for them sweet merchants, there's as much difference between them as you find in any other class of people" (202).

And Ray should know better. He's the one who tells the strange, surreal tale of Jerco and Rosalind, pimp and prostitute. Even the idea of "civilization" refuses to be pinned down. Ray says that Napoleon's betrayal of Toussaint's trust was a "civilized trick," but Jake makes a plea that now that the Chef has been punished, "I hope all we n----rs will pull together like civilization folks" (132, 187). There is more than one "civilization" in *Home to Harlem*. McKay's comedy extends to Jake and his prejudice against the Arabs on board ship coming home. He's being more than a little American despite his racial pride in being Black. McKay's point is that Harlem is a mixed bag no matter what cherries you pick out of it. It is not Alain Locke's "common consciousness," nor Wright's welter of "half-conscious" life. It is a swirling whirlpool of vitality and viciousness, sometimes Hobbes's state of nature that threatens McKay's natural man (as Ray warns Jake), and sometimes it's the water you want to swim in because it heightens your senses. But dull is the one thing it never is.

MULTIPLE WORLDS

Throughout McKay's life, there existed a tension between McKay the pagan or "vagabond" and McKay the "pilgrim," the seeker of communal life and a sacred place. Were the two sides reconciled in Jake as a Black Ulysses? 1928 not only saw the publication of *Home to Harlem* but Howard W. Odum's *Rainbow Round my Shoulder: The Blue Trail of Black Ulysses*. Like Bob Dylan's Odysseus, Odum's Ulysses is a "traveling man" who makes "a lot of stops," very much like Jake in *Home to Harlem*. There is no evidence that McKay knew Odum's text (part folklore, part poetry, part sociology) which was the first of a trilogy about left-wing Gordon, the Black Ulysses. Nonetheless, his "Negro wanderer" (Sanders 115) and low-life roustabout bears a striking resemblance to Jake. Although Gordon fights in the Great War and Jake deserts, both return from the war to the war at home like Homer's Odysseus. In naming Gordon a "Black Ulysses," Odum saw his character in epical terms (despite his violent, working-class life) which then raises the question for *Home to Harlem*. Did McKay see *Home to Harlem* as an epic and his Jake as an epic hero? Jake has his Calipso in Congo Rose and his Penelope in Felice. During McKay's novel, Jake finds then loses Felice and finds her again ("Happiness"), suggesting that "home" is neither a house, place, nor idea, but an elusive quest for some kind of permanent grail. If McKay's Jake is a "Black Ulysses," he exists somewhere between Joyce's Bloom and Odum's Left-Wing Gordon, or between high modernism and the pulps.

This perhaps explains Alain Locke's hostility toward McKay. You just could not pin him down. Locke called him a "spiritual truant," playing off the title of McKay's splendid short story in *Gingertown*, as did Melvin Tolson, the one complaining that McKay failed to join forces with the writers of the Harlem Renaissance, the other that McKay was not the committed Marxist that Richard Wright had become (Cooper 319–20). Gary Edward Holcomb has expanded our understanding of McKay by claiming that McKay wanted a radical transformation of society at all levels—sexual, political, and economic. His was to be an open city in which "queer," "Marxism" and "black" redefined the entire notion of the polis as home (Holcomb, *Claude McKay, Code Name Sasha*).

McKay is also Keats's chameleon poet: "What shocks the virtuous philosopher, delights the cameleon poet" (Perkins 1220). While the analogy is not as precise as I would like (McKay would never say, as does Keats, that the artist has no "identity"), McKay moves gracefully from Swift's savage indignation to vaudevillian comedy to celebrations of beauty as a "joy forever." He could be as brutally incisive as Richard Wright in his critique of white society from an economic and racialist perspective, and as carnivalesque as Ralph Ellison in his treatment of Harlem.

He attempted many different types of writing, ranging from autobiography, sociology, poetry and fiction, to even a novel as a film script. He was a spatial artist—hence his interest in film and visual artists like Goya, Grosz, Hogarth, and a writer like Hemingway whose influences were visual artists like Cezanne, Bruegel, and Bosch. He was an urban landscape painter in words, and like Langston Hughes was fascinated by "all cities." As a vagabond, he delighted in traveling from place to place, and as a pagan he could embrace multiple gods, responding to both the dynamo and the virgin. As a nomad, he understood on one level that society itself was only a polite fiction, that "home" as a precise dwelling space was an illusion. McKay was never a good Marxist, or a good anything if "good" meant embracing an ideology that enchained you. McKay agreed with Bita: "I believe I could live anywhere there's space for free movement." His artistry critiqued spaces that weren't free.

In his recent study, *The Parallax View* (2006), Slavoj Žižek uses Henry James to illustrate his point that "the parallax view" does not simply mean seeing the same thing from two different perspectives (Žižek 125–44). They reflect two different gestalts, or as Hugh Kenner observes in his book on James Joyce: "'Parallax'—seen from different spots, *Gestalts* alter" (Kenner 73). Žižek puts it this way: "Every field of 'reality' (every 'world') is always-already enframed, seen through an invisible frame. . . . We do not have two perspectives, we have a perspective and what eludes it, and the other perspective fills in this void of what we could not see from the first perspective" (17, 29). "The Harlem Dancer" is an infinitely rich poem because it illustrates "the parallax view." On the one hand, the dancer is McKay's double, although her artistry is spatial and his verbal. On the other hand, McKay's dancer fades into myth as do Porphyro and Madeline at the end of Keats's "The Eve of St. Agnes." In the poem's last line, McKay says that the dancer has removed herself from "that strange place" through her dance. The "strange place" is the finite world—its "gaze" and its sordid reality. For Keats, the perfect love of the lovers can only exist as myth outside of time, an ending that in itself is an example of the "parallax view." Earlier in the poem Porphyro had to convince Madeleine, through the physical act of love, that his reality in real time and space was as perfect as her dream of him. For McKay the dancer does not simply long for a different place. She is transformed by her dance and transplanted into another reality. Just as McKay's dancer has "grown lovelier for passing through a storm," Keats's lovers "are gone: aye, ages long ago/ These lovers fled away into the storm" (*CP* 172, l 8; Perkins 1179, lines 370–71). What they leave behind is the baron with his nightmares, Angela "the old," and the Beadsman who "slept among his ashes cold" (Perkins 1179, line 378). Similarly, what the dancer leaves behind is the world of mortality. Both the dancer and the lovers exist in an alternative universe, a different gestalt, just as Keats's urn in "Ode on a Grecian Urn" exists within two levels of reality. It exists in time as an object but outside of time as an expression of another reality, just as within the poem, as Kenneth Burke notes, Keats separates the "malignant bodily counterpart" from the "benign fever" of transcendence:

"all human passion far above" (Burke, *A Grammar of Motives* 455). So, too, does McKay's dancer dance in a Harlem street as a concrete presence but the dance itself is a transcendent moment. T. S. Eliot expresses it best in "Burnt Norton": "At the still point of the turning world. Neither flesh nor fleshless; / Neither from nor towards; at the still point, there the dance is."

And yet, for McKay, as for Colson Whitehead, the racial conflict in the United States was an expression of a Great War that had not ended. Dying "in an inglorious spot" (a phrase from his famous poem of 1919, "If We Must Die") was always a real possibility for African Americans. They lived, suffered, and died as though they were in the trenches of the Western Front. Hemingway had his Great War; McKay had his. McKay recognized a kinship that went beyond race. "Fighting back" foreshadowed Hemingway's grace under fire (*CP* 177, lines 2, 14).

And this points to another version of Žižek's "parallax view." Michael North has greatly expanded our view of 1922, the annus mirabilis that produced Joyce's *Ulysses* and Eliot's *Waste Land*, but we might refocus his *Reading 1922* (1999) to comment on those texts, also published in that year, that critique the American scene. Willa Cather's *One of Ours*, Waldo Frank's *City Block*, Lewis Mumford's *The Story of Utopias*, Harold Stearns's *Civilization in the United States*, Walter Lippmann's *Public Opinion*, Sinclair Lewis's *Babbitt*, and Ludwig Lewisohn's *Up Stream* all deal with the fallout from the Great War.

The theme in each is that the Great War is over, revealing both the fault lines within American society and, in some of these texts, the sources of its potential recovery. In *One of Ours*, Claude Wheeler finds renewal in the war. Although he dies over there, the source of his spiritual renewal lies over here—in America's agrarian heritage. In *City Block*, Frank uses the short story cycle as a vehicle to express a hidden connectedness within the city, as illustrated by a series of stories as triads that overcome the "block" as obstacle to become the block as a single soul, Jules Romains's *unanimisme*. In *The Story of Utopias*, Mumford argues that a usable past can inspire us to repair the ruins of civilization caused of the Great War. No such luck exists in *Civilization in the United States*, as thirty white Americans (only two women) take a hard, often cynical, look at America, yet no Black scholar appears in this text, no Du Bois to talk about American history. Lippmann is no less happy with American society. He sees America's propaganda during the war as destructive of an authentic collective voice, but he fails to talk about African American voices (oral traditions), those that would have altered his theory that Americans have given up their opinions to government manipulation. Sinclair Lewis satirizes America's consumerism as the result of America's emergence from the war as an economic powerhouse, and he also exposes the sinister side of postwar America. The Good Citizens League is a proto-Fascist group whose aim is to stifle dissent. Lewisohn locates his "American Chronicle" on America's hostility to both Jews and culture, and although he uses words like lynching and the KKK mentality to castigate his fellow citizens, racism against African Americans is not a theme in his satire on Mencken's Boobus Americanus.

In contrast to the above, McKay's poems in *Harlem Shadows*, also published in 1922, assume with Colson Whitehead's Amanda that the Great War has not ended, and "had always been about black and white. It always would be" (*Underground Railroad* 288). Ironically, Lothrop Stoddard in *Revolt Against Civilization: The Menace of the Under-Man*, published in 1922, would agree, but for him it's a different war. The colored hordes that threaten civilization predate the Great War. Unregulated immigration of people of color is only the latest manifestation of the "menace."

McKay has an answer for him in "Outcast," a poem in *Harlem Shadows*: "For I was born, far from my native clime, / Under the white man's menace, *out of time*" (my emphasis) (*CP*, lines 13–14, 174). Professor Stoddard of Harvard wants a white man's history. McKay argues that time, once disrupted by "the white man's menace," forces the Harlem Dancer to create a new time. Or perhaps "out of time" refers to America's materialistic civilization running "out of time," as in the last four lines of his poem "America" (with its echo of "Ozymandias"):

Darkly I gaze into the days ahead,
And see her might and granite wonders there,
Beneath the touch of Time's unerring hand,
Like priceless treasures sinking in the sand (*CP* 153, lines 11–14)

Time is the controlling theme of *Harlem Shadows*. The sequence of its poems functions as a short story cycle in which poems about the continuing war between Black and white alternate, and exist in tension with, poems of memory, mostly pastoral. In *The Great War and Modern Memory*, Paul Fussell proposes the thesis that "experiencing moments of war" inspires "moments of pastoral," and, he adds, "the classical tag *et in arcadia ego* " connects them both: "Even in Arcadia I, Death, hold sway" (Fussell 231, 245–60). He could be describing the structure for *Harlem Shadows*.

A pastoral poem like "Flame-Heart" is a poem of memory, but death is not far away: "I have forgotten much, but still remember / The poinsettia's red, blood-red in warm December" (*CP* 155, lines 9–10). Blood-red is the

Western Front's blood-red poppies (e.g., Isaac Rosenberg's "Break of Day in the Trenches") or McKay's "Birds of Prey" in which the lynchers "fasten in our bleeding flesh their claws" (*CP* 175, line 10), or his racial ambiguous love poem "Red Flower": "Your lips are like a southern lily red" (*CP* 184, line 1). But death is never the last word for McKay. Josh Gosciak has a nice insight about McKay's poinsettia. According to Walter Jekyll, its "great glory" is that it has two seasons, "six months green and six months red" (Gosciak 61). It dies and is reborn as either green or red.

It's appropriate that his most famous poem, "If We Must Die," is also about a resurrection and is placed at center of *Harlem Shadows*. On the one hand, it parodies the pastoral ("If we must die, let it not be like hogs," an echo of the Great War in which men did die like hogs in the trenches). On the other hand, he urges African Americans to be reborn as warriors: "If we must die, O let us nobly die, / So that our precious blood not be shed / In vain . . ." (*CP* 177, lines 1, 5–7). Coupled with "The Harlem Dancer," also placed near the volume's center, the two poems reflect two forms of resistance: the one aesthetic, the other militant. They are, however, only two sides of the many-sided McKay. James Weldon Johnson included both poems in *The Book of American Negro Poetry*, also published in 1922. Johnson's collection and McKay's volume of poems seem today to be wisdom crying out in the streets, demanding to be heard. Both are responses to the annus mirabilis of 1922.

As "The Harlem Dancer" illustrates, the strength of McKay's art lies in its "strangeness," the fact that there is more than one "spot" besides "an inglorious spot," even in *Harlem Shadows*. What he learned from Walter Jekyll's library was one "spot," and what he learned from the multiple worlds he traveled to was the existence of many others. *Harlem Shadows* ends with the word "quest" in the last line of the volume's last poem ("Through Agony"): after a night's rest, the poet will "wake with greater might, / Once more to venture on the eternal quest" (*CP* 196, line 14). This book has tried to trace the various quests that McKay pursued within his multifaceted art.

G. K. Chesterton's famous line, with its echo of Coleridge, applies to McKay: "The function of imagination is not to make strange things settled, so much as to make settled things strange, not so much as to make wonders facts as to make facts wonders" (*The Defendant* 60). As the "unchurched preacher" Baby Suggs told her followers in Morrison's *Beloved*, "the only grace they could have was the grace they could imagine. That if they could not see it, they would not have it" (88). Like Baby Suggs, McKay knew that if you could not imagine a world elsewhere, then you were condemned to live in a world that was "settled"—and a nightmare. McKay's greatness as an artist is that, like Baby Suggs and Bita Plant, he could imagine a place, a dance, a relationship, a community that existed both in time and outside of it.

WORKS CITED

Abrams, Jerold J. "From Sherlock Holmes to the Hard-Boiled Detective in Film Noir." *The Philosophy of Film Noir*, edited by Mark T. Conrad, UP of Kentucky, 2007, pp. 69–88.
Alighieri, Dante. *The Portable Dante*. Translated and edited by Mark Musa, Penguin, 2003.
Als, Hilton. "Ken Burns and Lynn Novick's 'Hemingway.'" *New Yorker*, April 12, 2021, pp. 71–73.
Anderson, Sherwood. *Collected Stories*. Edited by Charles Baxter, Library of America, 2012.
Auden, W. H. "The Guilty Vicarage," *Harper's*, vol. 196, 1948, pp. 406–12.
Augustine. *Concerning the City of God against the Pagans*. Translated by Henry Bettenson, Penguin, 1972.
Bachelard, Gaston. *The Poetics of Space*. Translated by Maria Jolas, Beacon Press, 1969.
Barbusse, Henri. *Under Fire*. Translated by Robin Buss, Penguin, 2003.
Barton, John. *A History of the Bible: The Book & Its Faiths*. Viking Press, 2019.
Benjamin, Walter. *Illuminations*. Edited by Hannah Arendt. Translated by Harry Zohn, Schocken Books, 1969.
Bernard, Emily. *Remember Me to Harlem: The Letters of Langston Hughes and Carl Van Vechten*. Vintage, 2002.
Bindman, David. *Hogarth*. Thames and Hudson, 1985.
Borchert, Scott. *Republic of Detours*. Farrar, Straus and Giroux, 2021.
Bordwell, David; Janet Staiger and Kristin Thompson. *The Classical Hollywood Cinema: Film Style & Mode of Production to 1960*. Columbia UP, 1985.
Bourne, Randolph. *The Radical Will: Selected Writings 1911–1918*. Edited by Olaf Hansen, U of California P, 1992.
Brown, Stephanie. "Marseille Exposed: Under Surveillance in Claude McKay's *Banjo* and *Romance in Marseille*." *Transhistoricizing Claude McKay's "Romance in Marseille,"* edited by Gary Edward Holcomb and William J. Maxwell. *English Language Notes*, vol. 59, no. 1, 2021, pp. 93–108.
Brownlow, Kevin. *The Parade's Gone By*. U of California P, 1968.
Bruccoli, Matthew J., editor. *Conversations with Ernest Hemingway*. UP of Mississippi, 1986.
Bruce, Dickson D., Jr. "W. E. B. Du Bois and the Idea of Double Consciousness." *The Souls of Black Folk*, edited by Henry Louis Gates Jr. and Terri Hume Oliver, Norton, 1999, pp. 236–44.
Burgess, Anthony. *Re Joyce*. Norton, 1968.
Burhans, Clinto S., Jr., "The Complex Unity of *In Our Time*." *Critical Essays on Ernest Hemingway's "In Our Time,"* edited by Michael Reynolds, G. K. Hall, 1983, pp. 88–102.

Burke, Kenneth. *A Grammar of Motives*. U of California P, 1969.
Burke, Kenneth. *The Philosophy of Literary Form: Studies in Symbolic Action*. Louisiana State UP, 1991.
Burke, Kenneth. "Definitions." *A Portrait of the Artist as a Young Man: Text, Criticism, and Notes*, edited by Chester B. Anderson, Viking, 1968, pp. 440–45.
Burke, Kenneth. *The Rhetoric of Religion: Studies in Logology*. Beacon, 1961.
Burnett, W. R. *Little Caesar*. The Dial Press, 1929.
Burrison, William. "*Lawd Today*: Wright's Tricky Apprenticeship." *Richard Wright: Critical Perspectives Past and Present*, edited by Henry Louis Gates Jr. and K. A. Appiah, Amistad Press, 1983.
Caldicott, C. E. J. *Marcel Pagnol*. G. K. Hall, 1977.
Calvino, Italo. *Invisible Cities*. Translated by William Weaver, Harcourt Brace Jovanovich, 1972.
Capozzola, Christopher. *Uncle Sam Wants You: World War I and the Making of the Modern American Citizen*. Oxford UP, 2008.
Chandler, Raymond. *The Simple Art of Murder*. Vintage, 1988.
Chaplin, Charlie, director. *Shoulder Arms*. Charles Chaplin Productions, 1918.
Chaplin, Sue. *The Gothic and the Rule of Law*. Macmillan, 2007.
Chesterton, G. K. "A Defense of China Shepherdesses," *The Defendant*. Dodd, Mead, 1902.
Cicero. *De Re Publica, De Legibus*. Translated by Clinton W. Keyes, Harvard UP, 1928.
Clarens, Carlos. *Crime Movies: From Griffith to the Godfather and Beyond*. Norton, 1980.
Cooper, Wayne F. *Claude McKay: Rebel Sojourner in the Harlem Renaissance*. Louisiana State UP, 1987.
Cowley, Malcolm. *The Portable Malcolm Cowley*. Edited by Donald W. Faulkner, Viking, 1990.
Cullen, Countee. *My Soul's High Song: The Collected Writings of Countee Cullen, Voice of the Harlem Renaissance*. Edited by Gerald Early, Doubleday, 1991.
Dos Passos, John. *Manhattan Transfer*. Houghton-Mifflin, 1953.
Dos Passos, John. *USA*. Library of America, 1996.
Dow, William. "*A Farewell to Arms* and Hemingway's Protest Stance." *The Hemingway Review*, vol. 15, no. 1, 1995, pp. 72–86.
Du Bois, W. E. B. *Dark Princess*. UP of Mississippi, 1995.
Du Bois, W. E. B. *Darkwater: Voices from Within the Veil*. Dover Publications, 1999.
Du Bois, W. E. B. *The Souls of Black Folk*. Penguin, 1989.
Eagleton, Terry. *Why Marx Was Right*. Yale UP, 2011.
Eliade, Mercea. *The Myth of the Eternal Return*. Translated by Willard R. Trask, Princeton UP, 2005.
Eliot, T. S. *Selected Prose of T. S. Eliot*. Harcourt, 1975.
Eliot, T. S. *The Waste Land*. Edited by Michael North, Norton, 2001.
Elliott, Robert C. *The Power of Satire: Magic, Ritual, Art*. Princeton UP, 1960.
Ellison, Ralph. *Collected Essays of Ralph Ellison*. Edited by John F. Callahan, Modern Library, 1995.
Ellman, Richard. *James Joyce*. Oxford UP, 1965.
Emre, Merve. "Getting to Yes: The Making of 'Ulysses.'" *New Yorker*, vol. 98, no. 1, 2022, pp. 68–73.
Fisher, Rudolph. *The Conjure Man Dies*. Michigan UP, 1992.

Fitzgerald, F. Scott. *The Great Gatsby*. Scribner, 1925.
Fox, Michael Allen. *Home: A Very Short Introduction*. Oxford UP, 2016.
Frank, Waldo. "Murder as Bad Art." *In the American Jungle*. Farrar & Rinehart, 1937.
Fussell, Paul. *Abroad: British Literary Traveling Between the Wars*. Oxford UP, 1982.
Fussell, Paul. *The Great War and Modern Memory*. Oxford UP, 1975.
Gaines, Jane. "*The Scar of Shame*: Skin Color and Caste in Black Silent Melodrama." *Cinema Journal*, vol. 26, no. 4, 1987, pp. 3–21.
Goddu, Teresa. *Gothic America: Narrative, History, and Nation*. Columbia UP, 1997.
Gosciak, Josh. *The Shadowed Country: Claude McKay and the Romance of the Victorians*. Rutgers UP, 2006.
Graham, Maryemma, and Amritjit Singh, editors. *Conversations with Ralph Ellison*. UP of Mississippi, 1995.
Groden, Michael, and Martin Kreiswirth, editors. *The Johns Hopkins Guide to Literary Theory and Criticism*. Johns Hopkins UP, 1994.
Hammett, Dashiell. *The Maltese Falcon*. Vintage, 1992.
Hawthorne, Nathaniel. *The Scarlet Letter and Other Writings*. Edited by Leland S. Person, Norton, 2005.
Heggland, Jon. "*Ulysses* and the Rhetoric of Cartography." *Twentieth Century Literature*, vol. 49, 2003, pp. 164–92.
Helbling, Mark. *The Harlem Renaissance: The One and the Many*. Greenwood Press, 1999.
Hemingway, Ernest. *The Complete Short Stories of Ernest Hemingway: The Finca Vigia Edition*. Scribner, 1987.
Hemingway, Ernest. *Death in the Afternoon*. Scribner, 1932.
Hemingway, Ernest. *A Farewell to Arms*. Scribner, 2014.
Hemingway, Ernest. *For Whom the Bell Tolls*. Scribner, 1940.
Hemingway, Ernest. *The Green Hills of Africa*. Simon & Schuster, 2016.
Hemingway, Ernest. *In Our Time*. Scribner, 2003.
Hemingway, Ernest. *Islands in the Stream*. Bantam, 1972.
Hemingway, Ernest. *The Letters of Ernest Hemingway 1926–1929*. Edited by Rena Sanderson, Sandra Spanier, and Robert W. Trogdon, Cambridge UP, 2015, 3 vols.
Hemingway, Ernest. *The Sun Also Rises*. Scribner, 2003.
Hobbs, David B. "Lyric Commodification in McKay's Morocco." *Transhistoricizing Claude McKay's "Romance in Marseille,"* edited by Gary Edward Holcomb and William J. Maxwell. *English Language Notes*, vol. 59, no., 1, 2021, pp. 181–200.
Hochschild, Adam. *American Midnight: The Great War, a Violent Peace, and Democracy's Forgotten Crisis*. Mariner Books, 2022.
Hodgart, Matthew. *Satire*. McGraw-Hill, 1969.
Holcomb, Gary Edward. *Claude McKay, Code Name Sasha: Queer Black Marxism and the Harlem Renaissance*. UP of Florida, 2007.
Holcomb, Gary Edward. "Hemingway and McKay, Race and Nation." *Hemingway and the Black Renaissance*, edited by Gary Holcomb and Charles Scruggs, Ohio State UP, 2012.
Horkheimer, Max and Theodor W. Adorno. *Dialectic of Enlightenment: Philosophical Fragments*. Translated by Edmund Jephcott, Stanford UP, 2002.
Horner, Avril, and Sue Zlosnik. *Gothic and the Comic Turn*. Palgrave, 2005.

Hughes, Langston. *The Big Sea*. Hill and Wang, 1963.

Hughes, Langston. *The Collected Poems of Langston Hughes*. Edited by Arnold Rampersad, Knopf, 1994.

Hughes, Langston. *The Collected Works of Langston Hughes*, vol. 9. Edited by Christopher De Santis, U of Missouri P, 2002.

Hughes, Langston. "The Negro Artist and the Racial Mountain." *The Portable Harlem Renaissance Reader*, edited by David Levering Lewis, Penguin Classics, 1994, pp. 91–95.

Hughes, Langston. *Not Without Laughter*. Collier Books, 1969.

Hughes, Langston. *Selected Letters of Langston Hughes*. Edited by Arnold Rampersad and David Roessel, Knopf, 2015.

Hughes, Langston. *The Ways of White Folk*. Vintage, 1990.

Hurston, Zora Neale. *Tell My Horse*. 1938. Turtle Island, 1981.

James, Winston. *A Fierce Hatred of Injustice: Claude McKay's Jamaica and his Poetry of Rebellion*. Verso, 2000.

Jameson, Fredric. "On Raymond Chandler." *The Southern Review*, vol. 6, pp. 624–50.

Joyce, James. *Dubliners*. Penguin, 1992.

Joyce, James. *A Portrait of the Artist as a Young Man*. Penguin, 1992.

Joyce, James. *Ulysses*. Penguin, 1992.

James Weldon Johnson Collection, Claude McKay Archives, Beinecke Library, Yale University.

Johnson, James Weldon. *Along This Way: The Autobiography of James Weldon Johnson*. Viking, 1968.

Johnson, James Weldon. *Black Manhattan*. Atheneum, 1972.

Johnson, James Weldon. *God's Trombones: Seven Negro Sermons in Verse*. Viking, 1969.

Keats, John. "On First Looking into Chapman's Homer," *English Romantic Writers*, edited by David Perkins, Harcourt, Brace & World, 1967, p. 1126.

Kennedy, David M. *Over Here: World War I and American Society*. Oxford UP, 1980.

Kenner, Hugh. *The Pound Era*. U of California P, 1971.

Kenner, Hugh. *Ulysses*. Johns Hopkins UP, 1987.

Kermode, Frank. *The Romantic Image*. Routledge & Kegan Paul, 2002.

Knust, Herbert. "George Grosz: Literature and Caricature," *Comparative Literary Studies*, vol. 12, no. 3, 1975, pp. 218–47.

Korda, Alexander, director. *Marius*. Les Films Paramount, 1931.

Lawrence, D. H. *Studies in Classic American Literature*. Doubleday, 1951.

Lawrence, D. H. *Lady Chatterley's Lover*. Signet, 2011.

Le Guin, Ursula K. *The Left Hand of Darkness*. Ace, 2019.

LeRoy, Mervyn, director. *Little Caesar*. Warner Bros., 1931.

Lewis, David Levering, editor. *The Portable Harlem Renaissance Reader*. Penguin, 1994.

Litz, A. Walton. *The Art of James Joyce: Method and Design in Ulysses and Finnegans Wake*. Oxford UP, 1964.

Locke, Alan, editor. *The New Negro*. Atheneum, 1986.

Luscher, Robert M. "The Short Story Sequence: An Open Book." *Short Story Theory at a Crossroads*, edited by Susan Lolafer and Jo Ellyn Clarey, Louisiana State UP, 1989, pp. 148–67.

Lynn, Karen. *That Half-Barbaric Twang: The Banjo in American Popular Culture*. U of Illinois P, 1994.
Maxwell, William J. "Banjo Meets the Dark Princess: Claude McKay, W. E. B. Du Bois, and the Transnational Novel of the Harlem Renaissance." *The Harlem Renaissance*, edited by George Hutchinson, Cambridge UP, 2007, pp. 170–83.
Maxwell, William J. *New Negro, Old Left: African-American Writing and Communism Between the Wars*. Columbia UP, 1999.
McKay, Claude. *Amiable with Big Teeth*. Penguin, 2017.
McKay, Claude. *Banana Bottom*. Harcourt, 1961.
McKay, Claude. *Banjo: A Story Without a Plot*. Harcourt, Brace, Jovanovich, 1957.
McKay, Claude. *Complete Poems: Claude McKay*. Edited by William J. Maxwell, U of Illinois P, 2008
McKay, Claude. *Harlem: Negro Metropolis*. Harcourt Brace Jovanovich, 1968.
McKay, Claude. *Home to Harlem*. Northeastern UP, 1987.
McKay, Claude. *Gingertown*. Harper, 1932.
McKay, Claude. *Letters in Exile: Transnational Journeys of a Harlem Renaissance Writer: Claude McKay*. Edited by Brooks E. Hefner and Gary Edward Holcomb, Yale UP, 2025.
McKay, Claude. *A Long Way from Home: An Autobiography*. Harcourt, Brace & World, 1970.
McKay, Claude. *My Green Hills of Jamaica*. Heinemann Educational Books, 1979.
McKay, Claude. *Romance in Marseille*. Penguin, 2020.
McNiece, Gerald. *The Knowledge that Endures: Coleridge, German Philosophy and the Logic of Romantic Thought*. Macmillan, 1992.
Melville, Herman. "Hawthorne and His Mosses." *Nathaniel Hawthorne's Tales*, edited by James McIntosh, Norton, 2013, pp. 370–84.
Mencken, H. L. H. L. Mencken Papers, New York Public Library.
Miller, Arthur. *The Misfits*. Viking Press, 1961.
Morrison, Toni. *Beloved*. Knopf, 1987.
Morrison, Toni. *Playing in the Dark: Whiteness and the Literary Imagination*. Harvard UP, 1992, pp. 69–86.
Murray, Albert. *The Hero and the Blues*. Random House, 1995.
Naremore, James. *More Than Night: Film Noir in Its Contexts*. U of California P, 1998.
Newman, Eric H. "Ephemeral Utopias: Queer Cruising, Literary Form, and Diasporic Imagination in Claude McKay's *Home to Harlem* and *Banjo*." *Callaloo*, vol. 38, no. 1, 2015, pp. 167–85.
Nietzsche, Friedrich. *The Birth of Tragedy*. Translated by Shaun Whiteside, Oxford UP, 1993.
Orwell, George. *The Collected Essays, Journalism and Letters of George Orwell*. Edited by Sonia Orwell and Ian Angus, Harcourt, Brace & World, 1968. 4 vols.
Orwell, George. *Nineteen Eighty-Four: Texts, Sources, Criticism*. Edited by Irving Howe, Harcourt, Brace, & World, 1963.
Pascal, Blaise. *Pensees*. Translated by A. L. Krailsheimer, Baltimore: Penguin, 1966.
Patterson, Orlando. *Slavery and Social Death: A Comparative Study*. Harvard UP, 1982.
Paulson, Ronald. *Hogarth: His Life, Art, and Times*. Yale UP, 1974.
Penzler, Otto, editor. *The Black Lizard Big Book of Black Mask Stories*. Vintage, 2010.
Perkins, David, editor. *English Romantic Writers*. Harcourt, Brace & World, 1967.

Pinter, Harold. *No Man's Land*. Grove Press, 1975.
Pope, Alexander. *Poetry and Prose of Alexander Pope*. Edited by Aubrey Williams, Houghton Mifflin, 1969.
Poulet, Georges. *The Metamorphoses of the Circle*. Translated by Carley Dawson and Elliot Coleman, Johns Hopkins UP, 1966.
Pound, Ezra. "Briefer Mention." *Dial*, vol. 70, 1921, p. 110.
Quintana, Ricardo. *Swift: An Introduction*. Oxford UP, 1962.
Rabinowitz, Paula. *American Pulp: How Paperbacks Brought Modernism to Main Street*. Princeton UP, 2014.
Rampersad, Arnold. *The Life of Langston Hughes*. Oxford UP, 1986, 1988. 2 vols.
Reynolds, Michael. *Hemingway: The Paris Years*. Norton, 1999.
Reynolds, Michael. *The Young Hemingway*. Norton, 1986.
Rogin, Michael. "Blackface, White Noise: The Jewish Jazz Singer Finds His Voice." *Critical Inquiry*, vol. 18, no. 3, 1992, pp. 417–53.
Ryan, Laura. "The 'Late' Modernism of Claude McKay's *Romance in Marseille*." *The Modernist Review*, 3 July 2020, https://modernistreviewcouk.wordpress.com/2020/07/03/the-late-modernism-of-claude-mckays-romance-in-marseille.
Sanders, Lynn Moss. "'Black Ulysses Singing': Odum's Folkloristic Trilogy." *Southern Literary Journal*, vol. 22, no. 1, 1989, pp. 107–16.
Sante, Luc. "The Gentrification of Crime," *New York Review of Books*, March 28, 1985, pp. 18–20.
Sayers, Dorothy L. *Further Papers on Dante*. Methuen, 1973.
Schaffer, Ronald. *America in the Great War: The Rise of the War Welfare State*. Oxford UP, 1991.
Schatz, Thomas. *The Genius of the System: Hollywood Filmmaking in the Studio Era*. Henry Holt and Company, 1989.
Scruggs, Charles. "George Orwell and Jonathan Swift: A Literary Relationship." *South Atlantic Quarterly*, vol. 76, no. 2, 1977, pp. 177–89.
Sehgal, Parul. "Do we need to hear another story?" *The New Yorker*. July 10 &17, 2023, pp. 68–72.
Shelley, Mary. *Frankenstein*. Edited by J. Paul Hunter, Norton, 1996.
Smith, Jennifer J. *The American Short Story Cycle*. Edinburgh UP, 2018.
Soitos, Stephen F. *The Blues Detective: A Study of African American Detective Fiction*. UP of Massachusetts, 1996.
Spahr, Juliana. "Hearing the Pandemic in Claude McKay's 'If We Must Die,'" *PMLA* vol. 136, no. 2, 2021, pp. 254–57.
Swift, Jonathan. *The Complete Poems*. Edited by Pat Rogers, Penguin Books, 1983.
Swift, Jonathan. *The Essential Writings of Jonathan Swift*. Edited by Claude Rawson and Ian Higgins, Norton, 2010.
Swift, Jonathan. *A Tale of a Tub*. Oxford UP, 1958
Tanner, Tony. *Adultery in the Novel: Contract and Transgression*. Johns Hopkins UP, 1981.
Thomson, James. *The City of Dreadful Night*. E-book, Project Gutenberg, 1998.
Thurman, Wallace. *The Collected Writings of Wallace Thurman, A Harlem Renaissance Reader*. Edited by Amritjit Singh and Daniel M. Scott, Rutgers UP, 2003.

Toomer, Jean. *Cane*. Edited by Rudolph P. Byrd and Henry Louis Gates Jr., Norton, 2011.
Trombold, John. "Harlem Transfer: Claude McKay and John Dos Passos." *Juxtapositions: The Harlem Renaissance and The Lost Generation*, edited by Lesley Marx and Los Nas, U of Cape Town P, 2000, pp. 4–20.
Tuggle, Lindsay. "'A love so fugitive and so complete': Recovering the Queer Subtext of Claude McKay's *Harlem Shadows*." *The Space Between*, vol. 4, 2008, pp. 63–81.
Van Vechten, Carl. *Nigger Heaven*. Knopf, 1926.
Vernet, Marc. "The Filmic Transaction: On the Openings of Film Noirs." *Film Noir Reader 2*, edited by Alain Silver and James Ursini, Limelight Editions, 2003, pp. 57–72.
von Sternberg, Josef, director. *The Docks of New York*. Paramount, 1928.
von Sternberg, Josef, director. *Morocco*. Paramount, 1930.
von Sternberg, Josef, director. *Underworld*. Paramount, 1927.
Walsh, Raoul, director. *The Roaring Twenties*. Warner Bros., 1939.
Watts, Emily. *Ernest Hemingway and the Arts*. U of Illinois P, 1971.
Whalen, Mark. *The Great War and the Culture of the New Negro*. UP of Florida, 2008.
Whitehead, Colson. *Harlem Shuffle*. Doubleday, 2021.
Whitehead, Colson. *The Underground Railroad*. Doubleday, 2016.
Whitehead, Colson, and Barry Jenkins. "Colson Whitehead and Barry Jenkins on Making *The Underground Railroad* (Rebroadcast)." Interview by Jenn White, *1A*, January 17, 2022, https://the1a.org/segments/colson-whitehead-and-barry-jenkins-on-making-the-underground-railroad-rebroadcast/.
Wicksteed, Phillip H. "Hell." *Discussions of the Divine Comedy*, edited by Irma Brandeis, D. C. Heath, 1961, pp. 63–68.
Williams, Linda. *Hard Core: Power, Pleasure, and the Frenzy of the Visible*. U of California P, 1989.
Williams, Linda. *Playing the Race Card: Melodramas of Black and White from Uncle Tom to O.J. Simpson*. Princeton UP, 2001.
Wilson, Peter. *Crab Antics: The Social Anthropology of English-Speaking Negro Societies of the Caribbean*. Yale UP, 1973.
Yeats, W. B. *The Collected Poems of W. B. Yeats*. Macmillan, 1959.
Žižek, Slavoj. *The Parallax View*. MIT Press, 2006.

INDEX

Abrams, Jerold J., 106
Adams, Henry, 75, 79
Africa: *Green Hills of Africa* (Hemingway), 12; Morocco, 20–22, 125; Pan-Africanism, 174; presence in Jamaica, 142–43; Western world and, 124–25
African Americans: Black art, 7–8, 86, 87, 169–70; Black culture, 53, 75, 79–80, 81, 82–83, 173, 178; Black life, 6–7, 86–87, 116, 126, 171, 173, 176; Black writers, 26, 169–70, 173–74, 180; citizenship of, 60; as clowns, 75–76; Du Bois on, 127–28; Hemingway and, 66; Hollywood and, 153; Locke on, 31–32; in Marseilles, 101–2; in the United States, 57; white people and, 11, 27–28; working-class, 170; Wright on, 175. *See also* racism
African culture, 145, 154. *See also* Africa
ambiguity, 54, 95–96, 124, 131, 157
American Protective League (APL), 150
Amiable with Big Teeth (McKay): ending of, 153–54, 165; *Gulliver's Travels* (Swift) and, 159, 160; *Harlem Glory* and, 154–55, 163–64; Hogarth in, 47–48; plot of, 155–57; setting of, 149, 160
Anderson, Sherwood, 84, 107–8, 109–10, 111
Andreyev, Leonid, 75–76
anger, 25, 26, 30–31
animal imagery: in *Amiable with Big Teeth*, 165; in *Animal Farm* (Orwell), 4, 165; in *Gingertown*, 113–14; in *Home to Harlem*, 62–63, 178; in *Romance in Marseille*, 95–96, 97, 99, 101, 106

Apollo and Dionysus, 70–72, 76, 82, 84, 101, 145, 146
Arendt, Hannah, 57
Arlen, Michael, 63–64
art: anger and, 25; Apollonian/Dionysian terms, 80–81; "art of life," 11, 53, 127; Black art, 7–8, 86, 87, 169–70; cinema as, 88–89; desire and, 71–73; McKay on, 6; misery and, 78; money and, 81–82; originality in, 3, 147–48; the self and, 42
artifice, 70–72, 83, 103, 146
artist, the: as an outsider, 11, 12–13, 32–33, 81; Apollo and Dionysus, 70–71; the clown as, 78; conceptions of, 70; courage and, 7; Dionysus and Apollo, 43; race and, 87
Augustine of Hippo, 28

Bakhtin, M. M., 142
Baldwin, James, 75, 143, 169
Banana Bottom (McKay): art in, 3, 11, 12; circles in, 138–41; dance in, 14, 145–46; *Dark Princess* (Du Bois) and, 132, 133; home in, 22, 133–34; Jamaican society in, 128, 136–38; "The Little Black Boy" (Blake) in, 144–45; morality in, 141–44; self-knowledge in, 133–34, 140–41, 144, 147–48; setting of, 9–10
banjo (instrument), 74–75
Banjo (McKay): art in, 78, 88; the artist in, 9, 11, 43, 70, 73–74, 81, 87; banjo (instrument), 74–75; desire in, 73–75; fluidity

in, 79–80; storytelling in, 82–83; the
United States in, 101–2
Baraka, Amiri, 46
Barbusse, Henri, 58–60
beauty, 13, 20, 38, 67
Benjamin, Walter, 33
Berlin, Germany, 20, 91
Bible, 15, 16, 20, 23, 25, 28, 65, 143–44
Bindman, David, 48
Black Americans. *See* African Americans
blackface, 76, 113
Black people. *See* African Americans
Blake, William, 25, 144–45, 146
"Blueprint for Negro Writing" (Wright), 169, 170, 173–74
blues tradition, 52, 62, 67, 75, 113–14. *See also* music
Bourne, Randolph, 151–52
Brecht, Bertolt, 153
Brooks, Van Wyck, 85, 175–76
Brown, Stephanie, 88
Budgen, Frank, 9
bullfighting, 60, 64, 65
Burgess, Anthony, 73
Burke, Kenneth, 13, 36, 46, 52, 73, 181–82
Burleson, Albert, 150
Burrison, William, 169

Cadiz, Spain, 20
Cain, James M., 159
Calvino, Italo, 68
capitalism, 31, 45–46, 91–92, 105, 110–11, 170
Capozzola, Christopher, 150
Caribbean culture, 118. *See also* Jamaica
cathedrals, 15, 21, 22–23, 101, 164. *See also* Christianity; churches
Cather, Willa, 84, 182
Catholic Church, 12, 162
censorship, 96–97, 150
Chandler, Raymond, 105, 149, 159, 167
Chaplin, Charlie, 66, 78–79, 88–89, 91, 92–93, 124
Chase, James Hadley, 166–67
Chefchaouen. *See* Xauen, Morocco
Chesterton, G. K., 184–85

Christianity: Apostle Paul, 30–31; in *Banana Bottom*, 134–36; the Bible, 15, 16, 20, 23, 25, 65, 143–44; Cullen and, 26; the law and, 30; McKay and, 12, 28
churches, 15, 134–35. *See also* cathedrals; Christianity
cinema: as an art form, 88; Black cinema, 89; Chaplin, 66, 78–79, 88–89, 91, 92–93, 124; cinematic elements, 55, 93–96, 98, 108; film noir, 93–94, 95, 99–101, 103, 104, 106; gangster movies, 151, 153, 154, 157–58; Hays Code, 151, 158; Hollywood, 99, 125, 151, 153, 177; McKay's interest in, 88–89; pornography, 78–79
circles, 137–38, 139–41, 142, 148
cities: artifice in, 39–40; the artist and, 24; city poems, 34, 44; garden-cities, 13–16, 42–43, 135, 145; gardens and, 116; the law and, 30–31; place and, 38; the self and, 20; souls of, 21–22, 31, 42; villages and, 55, 107–8, 119–20, 122–24; white cities, 27–28
city poems, 34, 44
civilization, 61, 139–40, 179
Claude McKay, Code Name Sasha (Holcomb), 4–5
Claude McKay: The Making of a Black Bolshevik (James), 4
"clear thinking," 140–41, 142, 144, 145
clothing, 49, 111–12
clowns, 75–79
Cohn, Robert, 64
Coleridge, Samuel Taylor, 22, 38–39, 40, 41–42, 44, 100, 142, 144
colonization, 118, 134–35
comedy, 54, 93, 155, 157–58, 161
commerce, 74, 79–80
Committee for Public Information, 150
conjunction, 11, 12, 79–80, 83–84, 87
Cooper, Wayne F., 9, 12, 128, 164
Cowley, Malcolm, 67
Crane, Hart, 33
Creel, George, 150
crime novels, 45, 157, 159

"cruising," 47
Cullen, Countee, 26

dance: African Americans and, 32–33; in *Banana Bottom*, 134, 145–46; in *Banjo*, 74; in *Gingertown*, 109–13, 121; in *Home to Harlem*, 62, 68; reality and, 181; religion and, 43; union in, 13–14. *See also* "Harlem Dancer, The" (McKay); music
Dante Alighieri, 128–32
darkness, 67, 103–6, 132
Dark Princess (Du Bois), 127–33
death, 64, 74, 77, 182, 183–84
desire, 71–73, 79, 82–83, 103, 139
detective stories, 100, 106, 160
Dionysus and Apollo, 70–72, 76, 82, 84, 101, 145, 146
Divine Comedy (Dante), 128–32
Dos Passos, John, 7
downfalls, 49–51, 62–63, 158
drawings, 60, 65–66, 91. See also *Harlot's Progress, A* (Hogarth)
dreams, 71, 92, 125, 127–28
Dublin, Ireland, 9, 80
Du Bois, W. E. B.: on art, 11, 86; "The Damnation of Women," 132; *Dark Princess*, 127–33; *Dark Water*, 132; "double consciousness," 85; on *Home to Harlem*, 6, 127; *The Philadelphia Negro*, 128; *The Quest of the Silver Fleece*, 134, 170; *The Souls of Black Folk*, 128, 133
Dyer, Geoff, 51

Eagleton, Terry, 61
Eastman, Max, 12, 69–70, 150
Eliot, T. S., 7, 41–42, 43, 128, 130, 133–34, 176–78, 182
Elliot, Robert C., 154
Ellison, Ralph, 52, 169
Ellman, Richard, 70
Emerson, Ralph Waldo, 85
England, 20, 48, 126, 133, 135–36, 147, 148, 164
engravings. See *Harlot's Progress, A* (Hogarth)
Ethiopia, 149, 155–56

Farewell to Arms, A (Hemingway), 56, 66, 67, 111
Father Divine, 102, 161–64
Federal Bureau of Investigation (FBI), 150–51
Federal Writers Project, 170
Fez, Morocco, 20, 21–22
Fiedler, Leslie, 55
"figuring," 139, 143, 144
film noir, 93–94, 95, 99–101, 103, 104, 106. *See also* cinema
Fitzgerald, F. Scott, 46, 85
fluidity, 79–80, 83–84, 142, 155–56
fountains, 20, 21, 40, 42, 124–26
fragments, 44, 102, 171, 175, 176
France, 23–24, 27, 69, 89, 90, 101–2, 123–24
Frank, Waldo, 64, 84–85, 176, 182
"Frost at Midnight" (Coleridge), 38–39
Fussell, Paul, 60, 183

Gaines, Jane, 89
gangster movies, 151, 153, 154, 157–58. *See also* cinema
gangsters, 149, 151, 153–58, 166–67
garden-cities, 13–16, 42–43, 135, 145. *See also* cities
gardens, 13–15, 39–41, 116, 134–35, 142, 146
gazes, 40–41, 109–10
gender: masculinity, 61–62, 112, 120–22, 178–79; women, 62, 83, 120–21, 122–23, 137–38, 146–47, 179
Gingertown (McKay): "The Agricultural Show," 11, 116–20, 123; "Brownskin Blues," 110–11, 119; "Crazy Mary," 120–21; "The Harlem Dancer" in, 108; Harlem/New York stories in, 119; "Highball," 113–14, 119; "Little Sheik," 124–26; "Mattie and Her Sweetman," 112; "Moorish Limerick," 124–25, 126; "Near White," 112–13, 119; "Nigger Lover," 123–24; "The Prince of Porto Rico," 6–7, 111–12, 119; setting and structure of, 107–8, 110; "The Strange Burial of Sue," 121, 122–23; title of, 107, 119; triptych in, 121, 123; "Truant,"

11, 114–16, 119; "When I Pounded the Pavement," 121–22, 164
Goddu, Teresa, 55
Gosciak, Josh, 8, 13–14, 184
Gothic fiction, 50, 55, 91–92, 103–4
Goya, Francisco, 35, 47–48, 66, 79, 91, 93
grace, 16, 28, 103, 160
Great War (World War I): "Backs to the Wall," 8–9; capitalism and, 91–92; cinema about, 92–93; grotesquerie of, 104; Harlem and, 45, 51, 53, 149–50, 183; images from, 91; impact of, 62–63, 67, 152, 168; literature and, 7, 43–44, 56, 58–60, 64, 107, 166, 173–74, 182–83
greed, 94, 97, 104–5, 152, 154–55
Grosz, George, 66, 91
grotesqueries, 35, 43, 50, 58, 91–93, 104, 108, 111
"group life," 31–32, 54, 102
Gulliver's Travels (Swift), 25, 35, 152, 158–59, 160, 165

Haig, Douglas, 8–9
Haiti, 46, 174
Hammett, Dashiell, 104–5, 152, 155, 159, 166
happiness, 52, 67, 141, 180
Harlem: Father Divine and, 161–64; the Federal Writers Project, 170; *Harlem: Negro Metropolis*, 58, 102, 161; history of, 45–46; as home, 29, 51–52, 56–57, 58, 63, 173; McKay's perspective of, 54–55; poems about, 31–33; social life of, 159–60. *See also Amiable with Big Teeth* (McKay); *Harlem Glory* (McKay); *Home to Harlem* (McKay); New York City
"Harlem Dancer, The" (McKay), 13, 16, 32, 40–41, 83, 108–10, 181–82, 184
Harlem Glory (McKay), 11–12, 154–55, 160–64
Harlem Renaissance, 26, 84–86, 169–70, 180
Harlem Shadows (McKay): "Courage," 8; "The Harlem Dancer," 13, 16, 32, 40–41, 83, 108–10, 181–82, 184; "If We Must Die," 8–9, 26, 106, 149–50, 184; "Outcast," 183; preface to, 5–6; quests in, 184

Harlot's Progress, A (Hogarth), 48, 49, 50
Harris, Frank, 41
hatred, 4, 25–27
Hawthorne, Nathaniel, 41, 103, 171
Hays Code, 151, 158
Helbling, Mark, 141
Hemingway, Ernest: "A Clean, Well-Lighted Place," 56; *Death in the Afternoon*, 54–55, 57, 60, 64; *A Farewell to Arms*, 56, 66, 67, 111; *For Whom the Bell Tolls*, 66; *Green Hills of Africa*, 12; iceberg thesis, 54–55; *In Our Time*, 6, 51, 53, 55, 59, 60, 61, 107; "The Killers," 6, 10, 57–58, 62–63, 112; on *Le Feu* (Barbusse), 58–59; McKay and, 5–6, 10, 52–53, 54, 66, 68, 109, 111, 182; "The Porter," 66–67; racism of, 66–67; sense of place, 55–60; "Soldier's Home," 56; *The Sun Also Rises*, 52, 60, 62–66; "The Three-Day Blow," 50–51; *To Have and Have Not*, 67
Henry V (Shakespeare), 8
He Who Gets Slapped (film by Sjostrom), 76–78
He Who Gets Slapped (play by Andreyev), 75–76
high and low, 28, 53, 105, 128, 134, 146
Himes, Chester, 54
Hobb, David B., 88
Hochschild, Ian, 45, 150
Hodgart, Matthew, 35
Hogarth, William, 44, 47–48, 49, 50, 52
Holcomb, Gary Edward, 4–5, 54, 89, 101, 180
Hollywood, 99, 125, 151, 153, 177. *See also* cinema
home, 29, 39–40, 46–47, 51, 53, 83–84, 135–36, 145, 180–81
homelessness, 46, 55, 58, 59. *See also* outcasts
Home to Harlem (McKay): art in, 11, 53; Barbusse and, 58–59; cinema in, 89; Du Bois on, 127; ending of, 177; the Great War and, 7; Harlem in, 45–46, 54–55, 60, 67–68; Hemingway and, 6, 51–52, 63, 159; home in, 46–47, 56–57, 63, 68,

179–80; Joyce and, 69–70; *Lawd Today!* (Wright) and, 170–74; obscenity in, 165; setting of, 9; structure of, 61–63, 159–60; Thurman on, 26–27; Van Vechten and, 53–54
Horner, Avil, 54
Hughes, Langston: on film, 89; Harlem and, 45; "Harlem Dance Hall," 13–14; on *Home to Harlem*, 47; McKay and, 6–8, 90, 153; "The Negro Artist and the Racial Mountain," 8; outcasts and, 25; Schuyler and, 86–87; on Twain, 85

iceberg thesis, 54–55, 57, 60
identity, 4, 11, 62, 87, 93–94, 180–81
imagination, 22, 142, 144, 184–85
impotence, 42, 44, 62, 63
Ingram, Rex, 88
injustice, 4, 8–9, 25, 67, 124, 144–45
In Our Time (Hemingway), 6, 51, 53, 55, 59, 60, 61, 107
intelligence, 141–42
intuitive mind, 141–42
Ireland, 9, 72, 80. *See also* Joyce, James
irony, 34–37, 38–41, 44, 46, 72–73, 116–17, 157–58

Jackman, Harold, 12–13, 43, 69
Jamaica, 14–15, 107, 116–18, 128, 134–37, 142. *See also* African culture
James, Henry, 181
James, Winston, 4, 25
Jameson, Fredric, 159
Jekyll, Walter, 3, 11, 14, 19, 48, 174, 184
Johnson, James Weldon, 12, 54, 68, 85, 122, 166, 170, 184
Joyce, James: *Dubliners*, 9, 70, 71–72; Eliot and, 43; McKay and, 9, 69–70; as a modernist, 10; Nietzsche and, 70; *A Portrait of the Artist as a Young Man*, 9, 70, 71–73, 81; *Ulysses*, 9, 43, 69–70, 73, 79–80, 81, 83, 171–72

Keats, John, 16–17, 36, 74, 181–82
Kenner, Hugh, 181

Kermode, Frank, 109
"Killers, The" (Hemingway), 6, 10, 57–58, 62–63, 112

language, 59, 123, 164–65
Larsen, Nella, 85
law, 30–31, 101, 105–6, 121, 122–23, 139, 157
Lawd Today! (Wright), 170–72, 175–78
Lawrence, D. H., 7, 9–10, 36, 57, 103, 166
Le Guin, Ursula K., 80–81
Lenin, Vladimir, 22–23
Leningrad, Russia, 22–23
Lewis, Sinclair, 182–83
Lewisohn, Ludwig, 182–83
light, 20, 23–24, 28, 67–68, 132, 176
Lincoln, Abraham, 175, 176
Linn, Karen, 75
Lippmann, Walter, 182
literary art, 5–7, 13, 26, 43, 159, 174. *See also* modernism; pastoral literature; pulp fiction; Romantics; writing
"Little Black Boy, The" (Blake), 144–45
Locke, Alain, 30, 31–32, 54, 85, 86, 171, 179, 180
London, England, 20, 48, 49. *See also* England
Long Way from Home, A (McKay), 13, 15, 22–23, 27–28, 31, 41, 78–79, 88–89, 91
loss, 53, 67, 71–72, 123–24
L'Ouverture, Toussaint, 174
low and high, 28, 53, 105, 128, 134, 146

Maltese Falcon, The (Hammett), 104–5, 155, 167
Marrakesh, Morocco, 20, 21. *See also* Morocco
marriage, 10, 83–84, 97, 139, 147
Marseille, France (also Marseilles), 69, 89, 90, 101–2, 123–24. *See also* France; *Romance in Marseille* (McKay)
Marxism, 61, 74, 99, 164, 171, 181
masculinity, 61–62, 112, 178–79
mass culture, 78, 152–53, 175–76, 177. *See also* cinema
mathematical mind, 141–42

Maxwell, William J., 5, 25, 30, 33, 41, 53, 89, 101, 127

McKay, Claude: anger of, 8–9, 26–27; on cities, 19–20, 24–25; critics of, 33; diversity of work, 6–8, 14, 180–81, 184; FBI and, 150–51; health of, 42–43; identity of, 4, 11, 87, 180–81; influences of, 3, 5–8, 11, 16–17, 167, 174; on Jamaican society, 128; personal life of, 12–15, 121–22; political views of, 4, 61, 164; on romance, 54; sexuality of, 5–6, 7, 10, 11; spirituality of, 12, 15, 28, 30–31, 180–81; texts on, 4–5

McKay, Claude, works by: "The Agricultural Show," 11, 116–20, 123; "America," 126; "Baptism," 28; "Birds of Prey," 183–84; "Black Belt Slummers," 32–33; "Brownskin Blues," 110–11, 119; "A Capitalist at Dinner," 91–92; "Cities," 19; "City of Light," 23–24; "The City's Love," 28–29; "Color Scheme," 9, 54; *Complete Poems* (ed. Maxwell), 5; *Constab Ballads*, 121; "Courage," 7–8; "Crazy Mary," 120–21; "Crossing Brooklyn Ferry," 27; "Cycle" poems, 153, 154; "Dawn in New York," 33–34; "The Desolate City," 40, 41–44; "Flame-Heart," 183–84; "Harlem," 32; "The Harlem Dancer," 13, 16, 32, 40–41, 83, 108–10, 181–82, 184; *Harlem Glory*, 11–12, 154–55, 160–64; *Harlem: Negro Metropolis*, 58, 102, 161; "Highball," 113–14, 119; "Home Thoughts," 40; "If We Must Die," 8–9, 26, 106, 149–50, 184; "I Pound the Pavement," 157; "Lenox Avenue," 32; "Little Sheik," 124–26; *A Long Way from Home*, 13, 15, 22–23, 27–28, 31, 41, 78–79, 88–89, 91; "Mattie and Her Sweetman," 112; "Moorish Limerick," 124–25, 126; "Moscow," 23; *My Green Hills of Jamaica*, 12, 14–15; "Near White," 112–13, 119; *The Negroes in America*, 52–53; "New York," 31; "Nigger Lover," 123–24; "On the Road," 34; "Outcast," 183; "Petrograd: May Day, 1923," 19; "The Prince of Porto Rico," 6–7, 111–12, 119; "Russian Cathedral," 22–23; "The Strange Burial of Sue," 121, 122–23; "Subway Wind," 40; "Tetuan," 21; "The Tired Worker," 34; "The Tropics in New York," 39–40; "Truant," 11, 114–16, 119; "When I Pounded the Pavement," 121–22, 164; "The White City," 24, 27, 28, 31; "The White House," 29–31, 79; "Winter in the Country," 38–39. See also *Amiable with Big Teeth* (McKay); *Banana Bottom* (McKay); *Banjo* (McKay); *Gingertown* (McKay); *Harlem Shadows* (McKay); *Home to Harlem* (McKay); *Romance in Marseille* (McKay)

McNiece, Gerald, 36

melodrama, 89, 98–99, 100–101

Melville, Herman, 103

memory, 33, 36, 37, 38, 123–24

Mencken, H. L., 85

Micheaux, Oscar, 89, 153

Miller, Arthur, 90

Milton, John, 8, 25–26

"mintoe," 14, 144, 146. See also *Banana Bottom* (McKay)

misdirection, 94, 155

modernism: "The Harlem Dancer," 108–9; high and low, 28, 53, 105, 128, 134, 146; modernist authors, 10, 70, 78, 152, 166, 167, 171; popular culture and, 152–53; romantics and, 109; short story cycle, 107

money, 74, 81–82, 94–95, 97, 99–100, 105, 124, 161. See also capitalism

morality, 62–63, 71–72, 101, 141–42

Morocco, 20, 21–22, 125. See also Africa

Morrison, Toni, 5, 84, 184

Moscow, Russia, 22–23

movement, 19, 46–47, 133, 181. See also space

movies. See cinema

multiple perspectives, 60, 94–95, 161, 178–79, 181

Mumford, Lewis, 182

Murray, Albert, 52
music, 43, 74, 75, 113–14. *See also* blues tradition; dance

Naremore, James, 106
Newman, Eric H., 47, 54
New York City: architecture of, 31; in *Gingertown*, 114–15, 119; history of, 45–46; McKay and, 15–16, 24–25, 27–29, 33–34; in *Romance in Marseille*, 105; Romantic irony and, 40. *See also* Harlem
Nietzsche, Friedrich, 70, 80–81
Nigger Heaven (Van Vechten), 53–54, 86
no-man's land, 47, 56, 112. *See also* place
North, Michael, 39, 116–17, 182

obscenity, 35, 165
Odum, Howard W., 179–80
Orwell, George, 3–4, 164–68
outcasts, 16, 25, 32, 81, 102, 128, 183. *See also* homelessness
outsiders, 12, 81, 88
Ovington, Mary White, 7

paganism, 12, 15, 20, 23–24, 26, 28, 30, 31, 141
Pagnol, Marcel, 89–90, 124
Pan-Africanism, 174. *See also* Africa
parallax view, 181–82
Parallax View, The (Žižek), 181
Paris, France, 23–24, 27. *See also* France
Pascal, Blaise, 140–42, 144, 147
passing, 85, 112–13, 131. *See also* skin color
pastoral literature, 13–14, 33–34, 40, 116, 118, 119–20, 183–84
perspectives, 60, 94–95, 161, 178–79, 181
Petrograd, Russia, 22–23
picaresque novels, 7, 18, 54, 159–60
pig metaphors, 4, 95–96, 97, 99, 106, 113
pimps, 46, 58, 99
place: no-man's land, 56; nonplace, 58; Romantic conception of, 36; sense of, 10, 16, 55–60; in the short story cycle, 107; spirit of, 108; strange places, 16–17,
37–39, 40–41, 109–10. *See also* space; urban place
poinsettia, 183–84
police, 25, 121–22
police state, 149–52
politicians, 129–30, 153, 165, 167
Pope, Alexander, 19, 35, 153
popular culture, 78, 79, 104, 119
Popular Front, 149, 156–57
pornography, 78–79. *See also* cinema
Poulet, Georges, 140
Pound, Ezra, 55, 86
poverty, 82, 164
power, 152, 155–59, 165–66, 167
proletarianism, 68, 130, 166, 170
prostitution, 25, 40–41, 46, 48, 99–100, 104, 123–24, 177
Prudhomme, René-François Armand "Sully," 67–68
pulp fiction, 104–6, 152–54, 159, 165–67

queer culture, 5–6, 47, 54, 71, 82–84. *See also* sexuality

Rabinowitz, Paula, 152–53
racism: art and, 52, 87; in cities, 24, 43; economy and, 61–62; films about, 76–78; Hemingway and, 61, 66, 67; in *He Who Gets Slapped* (film by Sjostrom), 77–78; war and, 51, 182, 183; white authors and, 84; Wright on, 173. *See also* African Americans; whiteness
radio, 175
rape, 137, 142, 143, 146–47
reality, 36, 54, 71, 103, 127–28, 181–82
re-creation, 3, 33, 58, 142, 144, 147–48
red, 23, 28, 111, 183–84
Red Scare, 150
religion. *See* Christianity; paganism
reputation, 118, 137–38
resistance, 70–71, 109, 174, 184
respectability, 118, 137–38, 146
romance: of America, 101, 170; Black survival and, 171; darkness and, 105–6; *Dark Princess* (Du Bois) as, 130–31; in

"The Harlem Dancer," 108–9; as literary genre, 102–4; of Marseille, 101–2; *Romance in Marseille* as, 100, 130–31; romantic skeleton, 54–55, 60, 159–60

Romance in Marseille (McKay): cinematic elements in, 88, 90–91, 93–96, 98; film noir and, 95, 106; home in, 58; Marseille in, 101–2; obscenity in, 35; Pagnol's plays and, 89–90; plot of, 96–101; pulp fiction and, 104–5; title of, 89–90

Romantic irony, 34, 36, 37, 38–41, 44. *See also* irony

Romantics, 6, 22, 25, 33, 36–37, 42, 44, 109

Russian Revolution, 22–23, 154

Ryan, Laura, 100

Sante, Luc, 157

Satan, 25–26

satire: in *Amiable with Big Teeth*, 157; in city poems, 33–34, 44; grotesque and, 91–93; in *Harlem Glory*, 160–61, 163; Horatian satire, 35, 154, 159; of human nature, 117–19; Orwell and, 3–4; Swift's use of, 162

savage indignation, 18, 34–35, 44, 67, 160, 180. *See also* Swift, Jonathan

Sayers, Dorothy, 132

Schomburg, Arturo (Arthur), 9, 81

Schopenhauer, Arthur, 65, 70–71

Schorer, Mark, 10

Schuyler, George, 85, 86–87

"security state," 149–52

Sedition Act, 150

self, 20, 42, 44, 59, 97, 114, 148, 163

self-expression, 13, 81–82, 171

self-knowledge, 40–41, 133–34, 140–41, 142, 147–48

Seven Arts, The (journal), 5

sexuality: desire and, 73, 137–38; fluid sexuality, 83–84; of McKay, 7, 10; metaphors for, 42; music and, 74; nymphomania, 143; potency, 42, 44, 62, 63, 163; queer culture, 5–6, 47, 54, 62, 71, 82–84; sexual innuendo, 110; sexually transmitted diseases, 48, 49–50

sexual violence, 61–62, 137, 142, 143, 146–47

Shakespeare, William, 8

Shaw, George Bernard, 15

Shelley, Mary, 25

Shelley, Percy Bysshe, 16–17, 25

short story cycle, 55, 70, 107, 121, 176, 183

Shoulder Arms (Chaplin), 66, 88–89, 91, 92–93

Sjostrom, Victor, 76–78

sketches, 60, 65–66, 91. *See also Harlot's Progress, A* (Hogarth)

skin color, 85, 110–11, 112–13, 117, 131, 137

slapping, 75–76, 77, 172

slapstick comedy, 54, 93, 158, 161

slavery, 45–46, 84, 105, 132, 175, 176

Smith, Jennifer J., 107

social life, 10, 55, 58, 100, 111–12, 159

sonnets, 8–9, 16, 26–27, 108–9

Soviet Russia, 155–56, 164, 165

space, 46–47, 58–59, 133, 178. *See also* cities; place

Spain, 20, 21, 64

Spingarn, Joel, 5, 6

spiritual centers, 12, 15, 16, 19. *See also* cathedrals; churches

Stalin, Joseph, 4, 23

Stearns, Harold, 182

Stein, Gertrude, 159

Stoddard, Lothrop, 183

storytelling, 82–83, 142

St. Petersburg, Russia, 22–23

strange places, 16–17, 38–39, 40–41, 109–10. *See also* place

Sun Also Rises, The (Hemingway), 52, 60, 62, 63, 64, 65, 66

Sunny Ville, Jamaica, 14–15, 16

surveillance state, 149–52

Swift, Jonathan: "Description of a City Shower," 34; "A Description of the Morning," 33–34; *Gulliver's Travels*, 25, 35, 152, 158–59, 160, 165; influence of, 25, 33–35, 44, 91–92; Orwell and, 165; satire of, 154; *A Tale of a Tub*, 162

Tale of a Tub, A (Swift), 162

Tangier, Morocco (also Tanger), 20, 21, 125

Thomson, James, 41
Thurman, Wallace, 26
time, 36–41, 55, 183
Tolson, Melvin, 180
Toomer, Jean, 84–85
totalitarianism, 165–66, 167
towers, 21, 24, 27–28, 114. *See also* cathedrals; cities
transcendence, 40, 97, 181–82
Trombold, John, 7
Tuggle, Lindsay, 5–6, 7
Twain, Mark, 85

Ulysses (Joyce), 9, 43, 69–70, 73, 79–80, 81, 83, 171–72
unhoused. *See* homelessness
United States: African Americans in, 76, 86–87, 102, 178; American soul, 10; conceptions of, 176; imperialism of, 46, 125–26; reality of, 54; "security state" of, 149–52; social life of, 159; violence and, 51. *See also* Harlem; New York City
urban place, 9, 20–21, 33, 38, 39–41, 119. *See also* place
urban poetry. *See* cities

vaginas, 138–39, 141
Van Vechten, Carl, 53–54, 84, 86
vaudeville, 32, 114
villages, 55, 107–8, 120, 122–24. *See also* cities
visual elements, 55, 88, 91, 93–96, 98, 108, 130
von Sternberg, Josef, 104, 153

"wanton," 27–28
war, 45, 65–66, 182, 183–84. *See also* Great War
Waste Land, The (Eliot), 42–44
Wells, H. G., 60
Whalen, Mark, 46
White, Walter, 169–70
white cities, 27–28. *See also* cities
"White City, The" (McKay), 24, 27, 28, 31
Whitehead, Colson, 51, 183

"White House, The" (McKay), 29–31, 79
whiteness: African Americans and, 11, 27–28, 126, 183; in America, 176; art and, 86–87; the banjo and, 75; choice and, 84; death and, 77; the Harlem Renaissance and, 84–86; *He Who Gets Slapped* (film by Sjostrom), 76–77; "The Little Black Boy" (Blake), 144–45; white authors, 5, 11, 33, 84; white popular culture, 78; white power structure, 46–47, 62; white supremacy, 101; white values, 118; white women, 125. *See also* racism
Wicksteed, Phillip H., 132
Williams, Linda, 79, 100
Wilson, August, 75, 84
Wilson, Peter, 118
Wilson, Woodrow, 149, 157
women, 62, 83, 120–21, 122–23, 137–38, 146–47, 179
Wordsworth, William, 28, 32, 33–34, 37–38, 40; "Lines Composed a Few Miles Above Tintern Abbey," 37–38
working class, 68, 170
World War I. *See* Great War
Wright, Richard, 54, 112, 169–74, 175–79
writing: Black writers, 26, 169–70, 173–74, 180; Eliot on, 42; the Great War and, 64, 182–83; Hemingway on, 52, 64; Orwell on, 3–4; re-creations, 3, 33, 58, 142, 144, 147–48; rewriting texts, 25, 28, 34, 48, 169, 176

Xauen, Morocco, 20, 22. *See also* Morocco

Yeats, W. B., 109, 166

Žižek, Slavoj, 31, 181, 182
Zlosnik, Sue, 54

ABOUT THE AUTHOR

Photo courtesy of the University of Arizona

Charles Scruggs is an emeritus professor of American literature at the University of Arizona. He is the author of four books and published articles on Charles Chesnutt, Jean Toomer, Jessie Fauset, Richard Wright, Ralph Ellison, James Baldwin, Ernest Hemingway, John Fowles, Raymond Chandler, Alexander Pope, Jonathan Swift, and American film noir.

www.ingramcontent.com/pod-product-compliance
Lightning Source LLC
Chambersburg PA
CBHW022019220426
43663CB00007B/1145